Insurrection

Insurrection

HENRY VIII, THOMAS CROMWELL AND THE PILGRIMAGE OF GRACE

SUSAN LOUGHLIN

First published 2016

The History Press
The Mill, Brimscombe Port
Stroud, Gloucestershire, GL5 2QG
www.thehistorypress.co.uk

British Library Cataloguing in Publication Data.
A catalogue record for this book is available from the British Library.

ISBN 978 0 7509 6733 4

Typeset in 11/14.5pt Bembo by The History Press
Printed in Malta by Melita Press

Contents

Introduction

Of all the enigmas in the English Reformation, the motivations and intentions of King Henry VIII remain some of the most difficult to elucidate.[1]

Lucy Wooding's view echoed that of Felicity Heal, who stated that making sense of Henrician religious policy was a 'trying business'.[2] As is widely known, the king's break with Rome was caused by the refusal of the papacy to sanction his divorce from his queen, Katherine of Aragon. There appears to be a pervasive view that Henry's Anglican Church was merely an organisation which represented Catholicism without the pope. This is incorrect: the king, aided by his deputy in ecclesiastical matters, Thomas Cromwell (until his fall in 1540), simply chopped and changed doctrine according to expediency, whim or whatever suited him. Henry's later innovations will not be discussed here but Heal's assessment that Henry's own erratic and eclectic understanding of his role as Supreme Head was 'underpinned not by a coherent theology but by little more than a "ragbag of emotional preferences"'[3] is an accurate appraisal.

It is, perhaps, for these reasons that the study of the English Reformation remains an appealing and fascinating task. As Susan Wabuda has stated, the challenges for understanding what the Reformation presents are among the most rewarding in all fields of scholarship.[4] Writing in the same year, Alec Ryrie gave as his *raison d'être* for a study of *The Gospel and Henry VIII*, that the 'golden age of the local study of the English Reformation' was drawing to a close. Ryrie therefore justified his attempt at a national overview as 'traipsing once again through the crowded field of Tudor high politics … despite the fact that it might appear to be pointlessly repetitive'.[5]

The Reformation in England is indeed a fascinating subject to explore and this book focuses on one particular event, the Pilgrimage of Grace in 1536.[6] The Pilgrimage was a huge insurrection in which an estimated 30,000 men participated and has been described as the largest uprising against a Tudor monarch[7] – some historians have argued that it had the potential to threaten Henry VIII's throne.[8]

Although the Pilgrimage was confined to the North of England, its ramifications extended further and, whilst this is by no means an attempt at a national overview, the North cannot be viewed in total isolation, somehow divorced from the rest of England or, indeed, Christendom. In the same way as Dr Ryrie, I have had, once again, to traipse through a crowded field but would hope that the approach taken here will yield other topics for discussion. As Richard Hoyle has stated, the discovery of a new body of material on the Pilgrimage is 'a rare occurrence'.[9] Thus, this book explores different dimensions of the religious innovations in the North, using the Pilgrimage as its centrepiece, and concentrates on particular individuals and the parts they played in the movement.

It is necessary, at the outset, to provide a brief historiographical overview of the English Reformation, as well as a historiography specific to the Pilgrimage of Grace. The English Reformation has been the subject of much study and its common or dominant paradigm (until relatively recently) was dictated by the Whig interpretation of history – the inevitable march of progress. The Reformation was regarded as necessary in the process of state-building, forging a national identity and freeing the people from the foreign tyranny and superstition of the papacy. Since the 1970s, scholars have used the term 'confessionalisation' to describe how the Reformation became interlinked with the process of state-building. The contention is that monarchs (both Catholic and Protestant) rigorously promoted a single confession, or type of Christianity, within their territories in the sixteenth and seventeenth centuries. They repressed alternatives as a means of exercising and increasing control over their subjects.[10]

The first phase of that reformation in England, the Henrician Reformation, had been viewed as relatively easy and fast by many historians in the 1950s and 1960s, including G.R. Elton and A.G. Dickens. This rapid reformation theory influenced many scholars, including Claire Cross.[11] Where Elton and Dickens diverged was on their emphasis – Elton concentrated on a reformation imposed from the centre, whilst Dickens and Cross emphasised the religious, as opposed to the political, roots of the conversion.[12] However, both schools were underpinned by an acceptance of the Whiggish position and shared the belief that the populace acquiesced readily as there was an underbelly favourable to reform.

Christopher Haigh succinctly summarised the main strands of the historiography of the English Reformation in 1987 and placed four main approaches within a matrix structure. These four approaches were, broadly: a rapid reformation from above; a rapid reformation from below; a slow conversion from above (in the localities); and a slow reformation from below. The Whig interpretations of Elton and Dickens were analysed and largely refuted by Haigh. Elton was identified as being the foremost exponent of the idea of a rapid reformation, imposed and enforced from the centre, as a result of deliberate government action – the 'Protestant advance was entirely the result of official coercion'.

The Whig consensus paradigm began to be challenged by what became known as the 'revisionist' school. The revisionist historians questioned what was really happening to people's religious beliefs throughout the Tudor period. Christopher Haigh, alongside Eamon Duffy, is one of the foremost scholars of this genre. Haigh questioned the idea of a widespread anti-clericalism as a springboard for the Reformation. He also challenged the 'Whig' interpretation of the Reformation as 'an inexorable process, a necessary sequence unfolding easily to a pre-determined conclusion' and argued that there 'was nothing inevitable about the final Protestant victory'.[13]

One of the aims here is to avoid labels which, inevitably, will become redundant with the passage of time – hence it does not claim to be a revisionist account in itself. Eamon Duffy has explained the origins of the term and stated that the historians commonly described as revisionists 'shared no single agenda'. Although my paradigm model differs from historians such as Dickens and Elton, it seeks to harness the work of the revisionists in an attempt to identify the methods through which Henrician religious policy was enforced. However, at the outset, it should be acknowledged that I share the view that the Reformation had 'not been achieved on a tidal wave of popular enthusiasm, but had to be worked for, by force, persuasion and slow institutional transformation'.[14] The evidence presented here would appear to support the 'slow reformation from above' position.[15] The Pilgrimage of Grace appears to be a good example to support this contention, but will the evidence and indeed the events of the aftermath bear this out?

It is my belief that the Henrician phase of the English Reformation should properly be referred to as an experiment. A reformation presupposes that there was a need or desire for reform and the evidence of a genuine, widespread theological conviction would need to be present. The label 'Henrician religious experiment' or the description 'Henrician religious policy' appear to be more fitting. Indeed, as Peter Marshall has stated, it is highly probable that Henry VIII used his Royal Supremacy to create a hybrid theology in which no one but the king actually believed.[16]

The influence of religiosity on the uprisings in the North of England in 1536 is of fundamental importance and an awareness of theological debate and controversy is pivotal to an understanding of the nature of the opposition. Lutheran ideas are clearly reflected in the Ten Articles and the subsequent First Henrician Injunctions issued in August 1536. Luther's influence is evident: only three of the traditional seven sacraments were mentioned and there was a reduction in the number of holy days. Images, relics and miracles were condemned as superstitious and hypocritical.[17] These developments will be discussed more fully in the following chapter.

Bush and Bownes summarised the situation when they stated that the religious revolution that the changes represented was not a response to the wishes of the people or most of the clergy: 'Essentially, it was an act of state resulting from the control a small number of Protestants exercised over the government.'[18] It is the real experience of innovation and how it impacted upon the laity which is crucial in understanding dissent. It can surely be no coincidence that the Northern Rebellions broke out within eight weeks of the dissemination of the First Injunctions.[19] The injunctions fostered the sense of grievance at the time. The dissolution of the monasteries, more especially the suppression of the lesser houses, further represented an attack on the old order and threatened the sense of security of many of the laity.

It is appropriate, at this juncture, to consider the historiographical analysis specific to the Pilgrimage of Grace. The Pilgrimage of Grace was very much a large-scale insurrection and it is referred to as such in numerous sources from the period,[20] but its significance has been underplayed in the

Whig tradition. Elton and Dickens argued that socio-economic factors and not religion were the prime motivation in the rebellion. Elton also criticised the notion that it was large-scale.[21] There are numerous references in the contemporary sources to the extent of the rising, with estimates of between 20,000 and 50,000 rebels[22] – indeed the king himself referred to a 'great rebellion in Yorkshire'[23] – yet Elton refused to acknowledge the sheer magnitude of the rising. However, he stated elsewhere that virtually all of England north of the Trent was in rebel hands.[24]

His view can be challenged by many, including Michael Bush, who discussed the huge force consisting of nine separate hosts which 'dwarfed' the army royal. Bush is also of the opinion that the Pilgrimage was a 'great' rebellion because all three orders of the realm were involved.[25] This is echoed by Richard Hoyle, who states that the Crown had lost control of virtually all of the North of England and Shagan, who estimates 'perhaps 50,000 men at arms' and speculates that if this force had marched on London no royal force could 'possibly have stopped them'.[26]

Although the motivation of the participants in the rebellions has been the subject of debate among historians, there is an abundance of evidence to support the contention that the Pilgrimage of Grace was primarily motivated by religious issues and concerns. Elton appeared to disregard such evidence when he stated that it was 'not really possible to agree' that the risings were a 'religious movement'. He reiterated the point when he argued that the 'religious purposes of the Pilgrimage of Grace had shallow roots'. Dickens stated that he concurred with Rachel Reid that the Pilgrimage had a 'predominantly secular and economic causation'.[27] This view has been ably challenged by other scholars, notably Christopher Haigh, C.S.L. Davies, J.J. Scarisbrick, Peter Marshall, Scott Harrison and Ethan Shagan.

Dickens maintained that 'however the Pilgrimage may be regarded, it was not a war, not even a potential war between Protestants and Catholics'. This view can be sharply contrasted with that of Hoyle who stated that the insurrection 'was England's war of religion', whilst Marshall described the Pilgrimage as 'the most dangerous expression of internal disaffection' and stated that it was undoubtedly a reaction against interference with local religious culture. According to Shagan, it is 'indisputable that the Pilgrimage of Grace was a revolt against the Reformation', whilst Scarisbrick succinctly summed it up in his famous conclusion that the Pilgrimage 'must stand as a large-scale, spontaneous, authentic indictment of all that Henry most obviously stood for'.[28] The wide body of evidence to support the conclusion that the Pilgrimage was primarily motivated by religion will be discussed below.

Bush, Harrison and Hoyle are all of the view that the rebellion was a popular revolt and led by the commons,[29] whilst Elton was adamant that the rising could be attributed to a conspiracy. He maintained that the insurrection was 'not the spontaneous work of the commons but owed far more to the activities of alienated members of the ruling sort'.[30] Without much hard evidence to make such a claim, Elton argued that the Pilgrimage was the brainchild of a disappointed Aragonese–Marian faction, aided and abetted by London lawyers.[31] Elton's arguments appear contradictory: on the one hand, he stated that the outbreak of the Pilgrimage was 'sudden'[32] but he then asserted that 'no sizeable movement' could have been organised without inducement, management and influence.[33] In this statement, he actually concedes that the Pilgrimage was a sizeable movement.

The conspiracy theory is also a theme for Dickens, who stated that Lord Thomas Darcy was 'a frequenter of the back-room of Chapuys' and had urged Charles V to invade England in 1534.[34] Davies refuted any idea of a conspiracy and cited the examples of the Duke of Norfolk and the Earl of Northumberland as those who had potential sympathy with the rebels' cause and yet did not become involved. Indeed, 'Norfolk took an expedient and calculating decision' to lead the army royal when he potentially could have raised East Anglia.[35]

Andy Wood has stressed the idea of a society of orders but maintained that 'early modern historians remain oddly resistant to the category of class'.[36] Order and deference were undoubted features of the society within which the Pilgrimage occurred. Whether or not we accept the usage of the term 'class' in relation to the early modern period, it is essential to highlight the fact that the Pilgrimage embodied the co-operation of the different societal orders in an attempt to alter Crown policy. Arguing from a social history perspective, Wood had this to say of the Pilgrimage: 'The sudden intrusion of rebellious plebeians into conventional histories of government, court faction and administration, ruptures the assumption that politics stemmed only from the central state and the "political nation" of the gentry and nobility.'

Wood made the point that historians have often attempted to distinguish between 'religious' and 'secular' motivations in the Pilgrimage and

sees this as flawed. Secular issues, he stated, are seen as relating to economic and social concerns 'as though religion existed in a separate realm
from the "material world"'.[37] This is exactly the case: why indeed do the
two have to be regarded as mutually exclusive? It is a view also shared by
Anthony Fletcher and Diarmaid MacCulloch. Acknowledging that their
study, *Tudor Rebellions*, attempts to sift the economic from the religious
motivations, they state that the exercise is 'essentially artificial in terms
of contemporary understandings of economy, society and religion'. They
state, rightly, that economic and social grievances were seen as moral or
religious grievances, as economic and social misbehaviour was an offence
against God.[38]

The Henrician Reformation must have had the impact of an epistemological seismic shock on the king's subjects; securely held and cherished world
views were shattered and insecurity and fear had the potential to spread like
a virus in such circumstances. As Haigh has stated, the 'Reformation shift
from a ritualistic to a bibliocentric presentation of religion was a disaster in
the countryside',[39] and the events of the autumn and winter of 1536 in the
North of England bear this contention out. One thing we can speculate
about is the nature of the sudden and shocking withdrawal of one set of
practices and their replacement (or lack thereof) with another – this would
be bound to lead to a rupture in societal hegemony and cohesion.

In a society of orders where structure and strata were paramount, the
opportunity for individual agency was, of course, extremely restricted in
the sixteenth century. That as many as 30,000 individuals sought to take
action and exercise agency led to the spontaneous outburst that was the
Pilgrimage of Grace. In such a static society of orders, any departure from
the status quo was bound to be viewed with suspicion and hostility. Michael
Bush has placed great emphasis on the idea of the body politic[40] and this
contemporary perception of a Christian community will be examined in
conjunction with theological analysis.

This book is, therefore, not primarily a narrative account of the Pilgrimage
as, by common consensus, the Dodds' account remains the standard in this
respect.[41] Nor does it concentrate on the minutiae of military detail and
day-to-day accounts of manoeuvres – Bush has provided an in-depth study
in his *The Pilgrimage of Grace: A Study of the Rebel Armies of October 1536*
(1996). This book explores the methods used to secure compliance with

the Henrician religious innovations of the 1530s, particularly in the North. Broadly speaking, these can be identified as the promulgation of the Royal Supremacy, rhetoric, retribution and reward.

The primary sources, notably the State Papers, have been thoroughly read and scrutinised for evidence of both regime and anti-regime rhetoric and propaganda. The same method was adopted in relation to evidence for reward and patronage, as well as reports of sedition, disloyalty and retribution. Interrogations and depositions of the rebel Pilgrims have been examined to illuminate the areas of concern for the Crown and the views of the disaffected. Many of these papers have survived, as they were retained by the Lord Privy Seal, Thomas Cromwell.

As is obviously the case at this stage, the domestic State Papers have been well mined. However, the Spanish State Papers have provided useful alternative documents and other original manuscripts at the National Archives, Kew and the British Library have been examined, where appropriate. These include the Inquisitions Post Mortem. Copies of wills and inventories have also been obtained from the Archbishop's Register in York and the collections of the Surtees Society. Contemporary chronicles, such as those of Edward Hall and Robert Parkyn, have also been analysed, as they provide differing accounts of the religious innovations.

The regime's rhetoric and propaganda will be discussed from the period 1536 onwards, in the aftermath of the high-profile executions of Sir Thomas More and Bishop John Fisher and the survey of the monasteries, the *Valor Ecclesiasticus* of the previous year. Such rhetoric sought to promote the Royal Supremacy and reiterate the duty of obedience that subjects owed to the sovereign. The Royal Supremacy was indeed a ground-breaking innovation and imposed on Henry's subject a dual requirement of political and religious loyalty. Indeed the years surrounding the Pilgrimage have sometimes been described as the 'Henrician tyranny'.[42]

What can the Pilgrimage of Grace reveal to us about the themes of religiosity, reward and rhetoric? The *Pilgrims' Ballad* and the Pontefract Articles are two examples of hostility to the Crown's religious innovations during this period. The Pilgrimage in the North will form a central part of the book, but will be placed in a wider English context; examples of dissent, propaganda, reward and retribution existed in all parts of the realm. Was the North of England so very different from the rest of the realm?

Before turning attention specifically to the Pilgrimage of Grace, it is necessary to provide a brief description and summary of the North of England and seek to highlight the state of affairs there on the eve of the Pilgrimage. Writing in 1921, Rachel Reid addressed what she called the 'problem of the North'. In Reid's view, the country north of the Trent was mainly mountain, forest, high pasture and moorland waste – an area constantly menaced by Scottish raiders. It was, she argued, the 'home of feudalism' and a centre of resistance to royal authority. She even went so far as to label it 'the natural refuge of lost causes'.[43] Perhaps Reid was influenced by the fact that the North, and in particular the north-east, had been the power base of Richard, Duke of Gloucester, later, Richard III. According to A.J. Pollard, Richard had achieved unquestioned supremacy over the region – he reunited north-eastern society and created a following of 'awesome' proportions personally committed to him.[44] As W.G. Zeeveld has pointed out, the 'presence of an armed force in the northern counties led by disgruntled Yorkists with the avowed purpose of changing basic policy by coercion was a potent reminder that the wounds of civil war were still green'.[45]

Professor Steven Ellis has described the far north as a region of compact lordships. Its patterns of landholding and its political, social and governmental structures were unmistakably English. However, the region exhibited marked differences from those in lowland England. According to Ellis, the overriding concern of this marcher society was security and defence rather than peace and effective government.[46] Pollard, however, has concluded that 'by no stretch of the imagination … was north-eastern England a remote, poor and backward corner of the land'.[47]

It is also worth highlighting the insecurity many in the region (and indeed the whole realm) must have felt in the period prior to the outbreak of the northern risings. Not only was religious belief and practice being altered by the king, there was no indication of who his heir might be. Henry, by this time, had been married three times and his only issue were Mary and Elizabeth, both of whom had been declared illegitimate. Even his acknowledged illegitimate son, Henry Fitzroy, Duke of Richmond, had recently died.[48] There was a real concern in the North that the Crown might pass to Scotland, by way of Henry's sister, Margaret, who was queen there. The Scots were, after all, the perennial enemies of the English and the people in the North were acutely aware of the raids and ongoing enmity.

Whatever the situation with regard to the topography and landholding in the North, what can be said as to the predominant characteristics of its society and people? Richard Rex has described the North as the most religiously conservative region of the country. R.B. Merriman has also maintained that devotion and loyalty to the 'old faith' was far stronger in the North. Merriman was also of the opinion that 'Cromwell's spy system operated less perfectly there'.[49] It will be revealed that the North, though undoubtedly conservative, was by no means alone in opposing the changes Henry sought to make in religious policy and practice.

1

Background: Government and Religion in 1536

When looking back at the year 1536, Thomas Cromwell must have questioned the merits of astrology. In January, one astrologer, John Robyns, advised him that 'nothing noteworthy is to be expected'.[1] Robyns clearly did not predict the imminent death of Katherine of Aragon, the fall of Anne Boleyn or the outbreak of an insurrection so large that it had the potential to threaten Henry VIII's grasp on the throne – the largest popular revolt in English history.[2] The Pilgrimage of Grace was indeed a massive rebellion against the policies of the Crown and those closely identified with Thomas Cromwell. The underlying causes of the insurrection and the motivation of the participants has been the subject of much debate and controversy among historians and a consensus has not been achieved.

At the start of the New Year 1536, it is probable that Henry VIII thought that the worst of his tribulations in matters of religion had passed. Rome had been repudiated and Parliament had acquiesced in the king's desire to be recognised as the Supreme Head of the Church within his own realm. His treatment of Katherine of Aragon may have aroused condemnation and censure but Henry had escaped any meaningful retribution by her nephew, the Holy Roman Emperor, Charles V. Anne Boleyn had borne him (another) daughter and was pregnant again, undoubtedly desperate for the chance to present Henry with his longed-for son and heir. The queen and her evangelical adherents must have had grounds for optimism – the Succession Act of 1534, which named Henry and Anne's issue as heirs, and the executions of Sir Thomas More and Bishop John Fisher all pointed towards a new era.

What, then, did happen to bring about the Pilgrimage of Grace? And to what extent was it religiously motivated? How did a situation arise where such a vast uprising in the region was made possible? What was the perception of Henry's behaviour abroad? Northern power structures will be examined in due course but initially the religious flux in the realm needs to be addressed. To explore the religious motivation, the events preceding the rebellion and the use of rhetoric (from both sides) in harnessing religious sympathy will be identified.

The Act of Supremacy of 1534 is crucial to the Henrician Reformation/ experiment. Clearly the king could not have legally pursued his policies and reformation without it. It is therefore fundamental to an appreciation of the context in which the Reformation was enforced. The king had annexed the power of visitation, the power to discipline the clergy, the right to correct opinion, supervision of canon law and doctrine and the right to try heretics.[3] However, in 1535, Henry delegated his ecclesiastical powers to the Lord Privy Seal, Thomas Cromwell, when he appointed him vicegerent, or vicar general, and Cromwell has become synonymous with the 'policy and police'[4] or the enforcement of the Reformation in the 1530s. According to Bush, 'Cromwell's vicegerency arose from the government's urgent need to conduct a survey of the English Church following the break with Rome'.[5] Whilst this might well be true, it also was typical of Henry to delegate power to a favoured minister, as he himself had such distaste for everyday administration and the minutiae of detail this concerned. As might be expected, Thomas Cranmer, as Archbishop of Canterbury, also had a role to play in the Henrician Reformation, but it is interesting to note that the experiment became synonymous with Cromwell, a layman.

Before examining any evidence for resistance to the Henrician Reformation in these years, it is necessary to highlight the significance of An Act Extinguishing the Authority of the Bishop of Rome[6] and both the First and Second Henrician Injunctions. The 1536 act, extinguishing the 'pretended power and usurped authority of the Bishop of Rome, by some called the Pope', was the final piece of legislation severing England's ties with Rome. The act made it illegal to 'extol, set forth, maintain or defend the authority, jurisdiction or power of the Bishop of Rome' with effect from the first day of August 1536. Anyone guilty of so doing and 'being thereof lawfully convicted according to the laws of this realm ... shall incur ... penalties, pains and forfeitures'. Clearly this statute is absolutely central to the enforcement of the Royal Supremacy and any changes, doctrinal or otherwise, resulting from it. These statutes and the promulgation of the Ten Articles of the Faith of the Church of England and the dissemination of the First Henrician Injunctions underpinned the king's religious policy prior to the autumn of 1536.

In early January 1536, the Imperial Ambassador to Rome, Dr Pedro Ortiz, wrote to Katherine of Aragon that the 'intention of the pope is that ... prayers shall be offered for the Queen and Princess, and the Saints who are fighting for the faith in England'.[7] Dr Ortiz's communications throughout 1536 do appear to be both lively and dogmatic but they are also prone to exaggeration and a scant regard for detail. However, his letter to Katherine as she lay dying at Kimbolton (exiled by Henry and forbidden from seeing her daughter, Princess Mary) does illustrate that the English Reformation was by no means perceived abroad as the abject capitulation of Henry's subjects. This can also be seen in the writings of Johannes Cochlaeus. On 6 January, he wrote to Henry that he was encouraged by the constancy of Fisher and More, whom Henry had put to death, and enlarged on the crimes into which the king has been led by his 'lawless passion'.[8]

The Reformation was disseminated and enforced by injunctions, proclamations and statutes and in February 1536, a draft Act of Parliament was drawn up 'against pilgrimages and superstitious worship of relics'.[9] In March 1536, we witness Cranmer hard at work on the preliminaries. Eustace Chapuys, the imperial ambassador, wrote to Charles V:

> The prelates here are daily in communication in the house of the arch-bishop of Canterbury for the determination of certain articles and for the reform of ecclesiastical ceremonies ... they do not admit ... purgatory ... the use of chrism ... the festivals of the saints and images ...[10]

It would be only natural that fear and uncertainty would have been present within the realm, as previously held certainties and practices were swept away. In February, Chapuys reported that the people were in despair and seeking help from abroad; and in April, a priest in Cumberland was reported to Cromwell for having said that 40,000 would rise up in one day. Henry himself was 'apprehensive of some commotion' in June when the people expected the restoration of the Princess Mary, following the fall and execution of Anne Boleyn in May.[11]

The pace of reform, however, continued. The Act Extinguishing the Authority of the Bishop of Rome was followed by an Act of Convocation for the Abrogation of Certain Holydays, especially during harvest time, which was passed in August.[12] The First Henrician Injunctions were drawn up by Thomas Cromwell and issued in August 1536 and instructed the clergy on the changes in religion – they were an accompaniment to the Ten Articles of the Anglican Church.[13] The clergy in convocation had acquiesced with the Ten Articles and rejected Purgatory, as well as accepting the abrogation of holy days. Purgatory and prayers for the dead had been a central tenet of the medieval Church and were woven into the fabric of local religious culture, which also set great store by the veneration of local saints and pilgrimages.[14] At the same time as these disturbing innovations were taking place, the monasteries were being dissolved (the legislation of empowerment having been enacted in February–April of 1536).[15] The timing of the outbreak of the Northern Rebellions is significant. It surely can be no coincidence that a rebellion which commenced no more than eight weeks after the First Henrician Injunctions would have been motivated by the changes in religion.

It is appropriate, at this juncture, to look at some instances of opposition to the Henrician religious innovations prior to the outbreak of the Lincolnshire and Yorkshire risings. Yorkshire and Lincolnshire were by no means the only counties where dissent was evident; it was indeed a concern in 'every part of the realm'.[16] For example, the Vicar of Stanton-Lacy in Shropshire was examined before the Council in the Marches in September–October 1535 for having failed to delete the pope's name from his service books. Bishop Rowland Lee forwarded the papers to Cromwell but no more was heard of it.[17] Bristol, which had been the base of the evangelical Hugh Latimer, was the setting for what Elton has described as 'violent exchanges' from the pulpit between the old and new.[18]

Preaching was an important tool in promulgating the Crown's religious message throughout the country prior to and after the Pilgrimage. A Friar

Brynstan preached at Glastonbury Abbey in March 1536, and clearly his views would have been at odds with Cromwell's but perhaps more representative of the groundswell of opinion. He spoke about those who embraced the 'new books', calling them 'adulterers' and 'filthy lechers'. He further accused them of being full of envy and malice, whilst being ready to wrong their neighbours. Master Lovell, in Dorset, was reported for disloyal preaching in the summer of 1536. He had encouraged the people to keep holy days and offer candles, as well as cautioning them against heretics and the practice of reading the New Testament in English. A prior in St Alban's Abbey, Hertfordshire, denounced Cromwell and Anne Boleyn as the maintainers of all heresies and asked what should be done about those whose purpose it was to destroy his religion?[19] However, the subprior of Woburn, Bedfordshire, sought pardon for the scruples he had entertained regarding the Royal Supremacy and his erroneous estimation of More and Fisher.[20] The First Injunctions were issued in August 1536 and as early as 30 September, Sir Henry Parker was reporting of opposition in Hertfordshire: the curates and sextons of Stortford and Little Hadham had kept the holy day with high and solemn ringing and singing, contrary to the king's injunctions.[21]

How were events in England perceived outside the realm prior to the Lincolnshire Rising and the Pilgrimage? Charles V and King Francis I of France had done little to interfere in developments in England since the break with Rome. It would be hard to determine a motive for any potential French involvement, apart from wanting to appease the papacy and perhaps stir up some more trouble for their perennial enemies, the English. The 'Most Christian King', Francis, was more than preoccupied with Hapsburg–Valois rivalry and the Italian Wars. Indeed these priorities had led him to form an alliance with Suleiman the Magnificent and the Ottoman Turks.[22]

Certainly a little more surprising was the laissez-faire attitude of the Emperor and King of Spain, Charles V. Charles was, after all, the nephew of Katherine of Aragon and her cruel and shameful treatment at the hands of her husband was both a family and diplomatic matter. For all that, Charles' priorities lay elsewhere. He was embroiled in the Italian Wars and deep-rooted enmity with the Valois and Francis I. His role as Holy Roman Emperor brought him the problems of repelling the Turks and also the religious difficulties which ensued from Luther's stance in Germany.

Moreover, he was responsible for his dominions in the New World. Apart from providing moral support to Katherine and Mary and being a potentially threatening presence, Charles had not become directly involved in the affairs of England.[23]

So, in the period leading up to the Pilgrimage of Grace, there had been no direct or practical involvement from the papacy or European monarchs in the English political or religious scene. Although a second excommunication had been drawn up against Henry in August 1535, a Bull of Deprivation was not finally approved in consistory until January 1536.[24] In the middle of the month, Chapuys reported to Charles V that the people were indignant because of Henry and Anne's gleeful rejoicing at Katherine's death (she died on 7 January). Poison and grief, he suggested, were being blamed for the queen's death. He then advised that, given the people's indignation, the time was ripe for the pope to proceed with the 'necessary remedies'. The following month, whilst reporting on the state of religion in England, Chapuys advised Charles that if the matter were ten times more unjust, none would dare to contradict Henry without outside support.[25] Around this time, rumours were circulating in Scotland that Francis I 'abhorred' Henry's break with Rome.[26] According to Chapuys, the king had determined that curates hearing confessions should not absolve anyone who did not accept that the pope was the Antichrist and the king the Supreme Head of the Church.[27]

Having had experience of religious turmoil in Germany, Charles was aware of potential trouble in England. The emperor informed Chapuys that the withdrawal of Henry from the Church of Rome was truly a matter of great importance, the outcome of which could be division and confusion in his realm. Charles, however, was probably not concerned with internal strife in England. He must have feared a relatively powerful fellow ruler at close proximity to the German Lutheran princes. Reginald Pole (an exile in Italy and a Plantagenet cousin of the king who had refused to agree with the Royal Supremacy) expressed his dissatisfaction with the inertia of the papacy and the emperor shortly afterwards in not enforcing the laws of the Church against Henry.[28]

A few weeks later, in mid-April 1536, Charles showed his hand. He informed Chapuys that he had persuaded the pope to suspend the Declaration of Privation against Henry and the appeal to the secular arm

(Charles in his capacity as Holy Roman Emperor) until Charles advised him to do so.[29] His letter to his ambassador was written in the context of proposed war with France and he desired to demonstrate his amity towards Henry. This suggests that Henry was, in reality, not a player on the chessboard of European politics: the issue of England's break with Rome was clearly not a priority for the emperor. Charles simply wanted to avoid Henry giving any sort of support to Francis I.

At the same time, Dr Ortiz advised the emperor's wife, Isabella, that the English were confirming their heresies by translating the Bible, altering many passages to support their errors. Meanwhile, Charles instructed Chapuys to conduct negotiations with Cromwell with regard to the possibility of Henry's reconciliation with the Holy See. Chapuys continued to inform his master of the developments in England and shortly after advised that the English Church sought to 'usurp' the foundations for the redemption of the dead – the doctrine of Purgatory and the practice of Masses for souls. William Weston of Lincoln College in Oxford felt the need to preach a sermon at the university in which he said that although he had been commanded to avoid mentioning Purgatory, it was a heresy to deny it.[30]

Dissatisfaction with the Henrician injunctions and the direction in which the Church in England was proceeding was clearly not confined to the North. About this time, Chapuys was able to gleefully report of the fall of Anne Boleyn: the people, he said, were joyous at the ruin of the concubine and hopeful of Princess Mary's restoration.[31] Such was the state of affairs in the spring and summer of 1536, prior to the issue of the First Henrician Injunctions in August and the ensuing uprisings at the start of October.

On the domestic front, the disgrace and fall of Anne Boleyn may have given conservative factions grounds for optimism and the possibility of a fresh start. Anne was a figurehead for the evangelical cause and had been found guilty of sexual crimes then associated with witchcraft.[32] Anne's rise and haughty demeanour had not endeared her to many and some were certain to believe slanderous accusations against her. The accusation of witchcraft and entrapment had also been levelled at Henry's grandmother, Queen Elizabeth Woodville, by her detractors. Elizabeth was also a commoner who had been raised up by her marriage to King Edward IV. The fact that the king had been so anxious to be rid of Anne probably had her opponents rubbing their hands with delight and anticipation. However, Henry immediately remarried

– to Jane Seymour – and the First Henrician Injunctions were issued in late summer. The conservatives had experienced a false dawn. At about the same time, the Plantagenet exile Reginald Pole was putting an interesting slant on the Kildare Rebellion in Ireland (1534), when he advised Cardinal Contarini that the Earl of Kildare had been condemned to death for courageously vindicating the pope's authority in Ireland.[33]

In the year which witnessed the deaths of two queens and the crowning of another by mid-summer, as well as a change in religion and dissolution of monastic houses, it is hardly surprising that people were susceptible to rumours. These circulated in England in the autumn of 1536. John Tregonwell reported to Cromwell from Cornwall on 5 September and said that, prior to his arrival, there had been rumours that he was coming to remove crosses, chalices and other 'idols' of the churches.[34] On 19 September, the Duke of Norfolk advised that an organ maker in Norwich deserved death because he intended to organise an insurrection in the shire.[35] Rumours were readily believed in Lincolnshire prior to the outbreak of rebellion there at the start of October.

What then of the North? How was power used in the region? And in what ways did the Crown seek to exercise its authority and enforce religious changes in this peripheral area? Was the region really so remote and backward as to be a refuge for lost causes, as Rachel Reid claimed? The North was not isolated in its displays of opposition to the Henrician religious changes, was it atypical in the exercise of royal power and the structure of its society?

Any discussion of the Pilgrimage and its aftermath in the region, particularly in terms of patronage and reward, needs to be underpinned by an analysis of power. Power, of course, was vested in the person of the monarch, but how was it disseminated? Henry was aided in the enforcement of his policies by the legislative sanction of Parliament and by the Privy Council, the chief executive instrument of the Crown. The council was comprised of members of the nobility and powerful gentry who met with him on a regular basis to offer advice, frame laws and govern the realm. Thomas Cromwell, as Lord Privy Seal, was a pivotal figure. Although, in principle, all land belonged to the king, the ruling elites were the land-owning nobles and gentry who attended both Parliament and Court. They controlled and enforced law and order, government and administration in the localities.

Of course, England's system had been feudal in medieval times but (in common with much of continental Europe) by the sixteenth century the state had assumed more responsibility and the government was becoming more centralised. However, governance in the localities was dependent upon the co-operation of both the ruling elites and an increasingly numerous gentry. In return for their services in office, the gentry received prestige, patronage and the potential for profit. By the use of royal commissions, the king conferred on individuals ad hoc legal powers to perform certain specified tasks in his name.[36] Treasons and felonies were dealt with by sheriffs and Justices of the Peace and the link between Crown and community was maintained.

The 'North' encompassed a proportionately large geographical area, if it is to be viewed as the region north of the River Trent. Yorkshire was the largest county in the region. The northern nobility was comprised of the leading figures of the Earl of Derby in Lancashire, the Earl of Northumberland and the Earl of Westmorland. In addition, there was the Earl of Cumberland, Lord Dacre, Lord Darcy and, further south, the Earl of Shrewsbury. To be a noble was to be prestigious and the gentry continued to serve their superior lords in the 1530s, as an organising feature of northern society. As Hoyle has stated, power was personal, and the nobility had the potential to raise large contingents of troops, particularly if they had deep roots in an area. Local loyalties were an important factor and men were mustered under local noble captains. This situation, however, was not unique to the North: nobles from elsewhere in the realm were equally able to raise and command their tenants during this period and the northern nobility did not present an increased threat to the Crown.[37]

The nobility and gentry thus exercised power in the region and were the conduits between periphery and core. Commissions of the Peace enforced the law and there had been, intermittently, specific councils set up to govern the North. The Council of the North had originated in the private council of Richard, Duke of Gloucester, later Richard III, but this expired with his death and Henry VII did not make specific arrangements for a council in the region. However, a new Council of the North was established in 1525, on the recommendation of Cardinal Wolsey, and was attached to the Duke of Richmond's household. Richmond (Henry Fitzroy) was the king's illegitimate son and was appointed lieutenant. The northern magnates – the

Percys, Nevilles, Cliffords and Dacres – resented the council as an intrusion and by 1530, Richmond was replaced by the Bishop of Durham as president and its jurisdiction was confined to Yorkshire.[38]

The pre-1536 councils served to act on the king's behalf and report back to him but their records have virtually disappeared.[39] The council came to be a significant feature in northern society and governance in the aftermath of the Pilgrimage of Grace, as will be discussed in due course. The Commissions of the Peace, and indeed any councils, had to be staffed by appropriate members of the nobility and gentry. These appointments were important in terms of reward and patronage, as will be discussed in a later chapter. However, it should be acknowledged that Northumberland suffered from administrative problems as a result of the paucity of resident gentry in the county.[40] This dearth of suitably qualified gentry will be examined and discussed when we turn to consider the government of the North in the wake of the 1536 risings. In addition, the far outposts of the region were on the border with Scotland and were governed in a frontier fashion. This area was divided into three marches: the West, Middle and East marches. A warden was appointed to each march in order to defend this militarised area. Another distinctive character of the region was that it encompassed three palatinates: Cheshire, Lancashire and Durham. The king's writ did not run in these areas and they were administratively distinct from the English law court system. The governance of these palatinates was exercised in the name of the lord of each: in Cheshire and Lancashire, the king; in Durham, the bishop.[41]

As Professor Steven Ellis has stated, the North did possess a pronounced regional identity, a varied geographical terrain, a distance from the centre, a land border (with Scotland) and a marcher society. The far north was relatively poor and barren; a land of moorland waste, mountain and forest. The insecurity of a border/marcher region obviously presented special challenges for effective governance. Thus, the Crown was obliged to delegate power in a fashion that was rarely required in lowland England. This had resulted in a mass delegation of power to the region's magnates and strengthened their position as marcher lords. These regional magnates resented the intrusion of the Duke of Richmond's council. These magnates also could call upon their *manraed* (tenants and political affinity) when required. The consequence of all this was that royal governance was not nearly as effective in these areas and the structures of power had evolved differently.[42] The North, broadly speaking, was a case apart and distinct. The far north was certainly a region which swam against the tide of Tudor centralisation and uniformity.

In summary, Henry VIII's religious innovations and the way in which they were enacted and enforced by the government through its power structures up to the autumn of 1536 sets the scene. It has been acknowledged that although the North was a distinct region, distant from the core, and presented its own particular problems of governance, it was by no means alone in producing examples of dissent within the realm. Evidence that Henry's changes were unpopular in other areas of the country demonstrates that the North was not unique in this respect. In addition, the perspectives of foreign commentators have shed light on how Henry's policies were viewed abroad. It will be necessary to analyse developments in England in a wider context given the break with Rome, the influence of Lutheran theology and the general political intrigues in continental Europe.

So, what actually happened to precipitate the Lincolnshire Rising and the Pilgrimage of Grace? The risings will be considered in the subsequent chapter and a narrative of the events is essential in enabling an understanding of the impact of the movement on the North in terms of governance and religiosity: the fate of the protagonists will serve to illuminate how power and religion were intertwined in the region in the aftermath.

2

The Pilgrimage of Grace: A holy Crusade?

A series of revolts against the Crown broke out in the autumn of 1536. What actually precipitated them? It will be argued here that the cause of religion was the paramount motivator for the participants and that the revolts were, in essence, spontaneous and popular. The king's religious innovations were discussed in the previous chapter. In addition to the dissemination of the Ten Articles and First Henrician Injunctions, government commissioners were working in Yorkshire and Lincolnshire in September and October in an 'atmosphere of rumour and alarm'. It was the presence of these commissioners in Lincolnshire, following the first wave of the dissolution of the monasteries, that arguably was the catalyst that unleashed the latent fear and resentment of a huge number of the king's subjects in the North.

Although the Lincolnshire Rising ended by 11 October when the gentry sued for pardon,[1] the revolt had spread to Yorkshire and gathered pace. It is the Yorkshire rising which is correctly referred to as the Pilgrimage of Grace and the title seems to have been devised by the rebel leader, Robert Aske, at York[2] – it is first mentioned in the State Papers on 14 October. The revolt was so large that the Duke of Norfolk referred to it as representing 'all the floure of the north'[3] and it was brought to an end on 8 December when the king's messenger, Lancaster Herald, brought a general pardon and the commons dispersed.[4] A number of renewed revolts broke out early in 1537 and will be discussed in the following chapter; these will be referred to, using Professor Michael Bush's term, as the Post-pardon Revolts.

The first references to a disturbance in Lincolnshire in the State Papers are dated 3 October and refer to 'rebellious knaves' in Lyndsey and a 'great multitude of people from Loweth'.[5] The rebellion actually commenced in Louth on 2 October, when the Bishop of Lincoln's registrar was seized, and it was heralded by bell-ringing and assemblies.[6] This was followed by the murder of the Bishop of Lincoln's chancellor, Dr Raynes, and the burning of his books. The rebels stated that they wanted the suppression of the monasteries to cease and they wanted Cranmer, Latimer, the Bishop of Lincoln and Cromwell delivered up to them or else banished from the realm.[7] The main architects of the rhetoric of reform were thus targets for the rebels.

The religious intent of the first outbreak of trouble at Louth was on Sunday, 1 October 1536 – a yeoman and singing-man, Thomas Foster, stated, 'we shall never follow [the Cross] more' in procession.[8] Lord Thomas Burgh advised the king on 3 October that a sudden great magnitude of people from Louth had come within a mile of him and said that they would not pay any more silver and had caused the church bells to be rung. Sir Robert Tyrwhyt reported on the same day that 20,000 of the king's 'true and faithful subjects' had assembled because it had been reported that all jewels and goods of the churches were to be taken away to the King's Council.[9] The commissioners had been working in an atmosphere where rumours were rife that the Crown intended to appropriate the goods of the parish churches, and it was small wonder that these were believed when everything else in the matter of religion seemed to be changing. The king reproached the Commissioners for the Subsidy early in the rebellion and stated that the removal of the goods of parish churches had never been intended, and he advised Thomas, Lord Darcy on 8 October that it appeared that the insurrection 'grew by crafty persons reporting that we would take the goods of all the churches'.[10]

Lord John Hussey appears to have been the first to have mentioned the Lincolnshire Rising, in a letter to the Mayor of Lincoln, Robert Sutton, on 3 October 1536.[11] Hussey advised Cromwell that the country was becoming increasingly rebellious on 5 October, and the rebels' oath was reported to Cromwell the same day. Its religious tone is illuminating: 'Ye shall swere to be trew to Allmyte god, to crystes catholyke churche, to owr sovereyne Lorde the Kynge and unto the comons of thys realme so helpe you god'.[12] Sir Marmaduke Constable and Robert Tyrwhyt also reported that the rebels' petition was for pardon and that they may keep holy days as in the past and also that the suppressed religious houses might remain. So, even at this early (and less serious) stage of the Northern Rebellions, the rebels were clear that they opposed the dissolution of the monasteries. It is thus hard to see why Dickens could have argued that the 'monasteries should be deleted from religious motives'.[13]

Lord Darcy wrote to the king of the situation in Lincolnshire on 6 October. He spoke of 'seditions' in Northumberland which were dangerous and encouraged by the Scots. The rebels' oath was to suffer neither spoils nor suppressions of abbeys, parish churches or their jewels.[14] In the light of what was to come later, the king's letter to Darcy of 9 October is somewhat curious. Henry praised Darcy's wisdom and diligence and stated, 'what an opinion we must have of your fidelity'.[15] About this time, the king's gentleman usher, Christopher Ascugh, informed Cromwell that the rebels had used 'rigorous' words against the Lord Privy Seal and that the Prior of Spalding had refused to help against the rebels, stating that he was a spiritual man.[16]

Eustace Chapuys, the imperial ambassador, was duly diligent in reporting the events to the emperor. On 7 October, he advised Charles V that there had been a great rising against the king's commissioners over the previous five days. He informed Charles that the uprising was against the demolition of the abbeys and convents throughout England, with the rioters blaming Cromwell. The ambassador also informed his imperial counterpart at Rome, the Count of Cifuentes. Revealingly, Chapuys stated that the rising had no leader of note and cautioned that popular risings of the sort, which at first appeared formidable, often ended in smoke;[17] not exactly the report of an arch-conspirator in the commotions.

Robert Aske is first referred to in a letter of 9 October, when he and others issued a proclamation for all men to assemble on Skypwithe Moor in order to take the oath to be 'true to the king's issue and the noble blood, to preserve the church from spoil and be true to the common wealth'.[18] The following day, the town of Beverley in Yorkshire wrote to the commons of Lincolnshire stating that they too had risen. They stressed that the commons were sworn to their prince but were hostile towards his counsellors. They wished to enquire as to whether the captains and commons in Lincolnshire required their help. At the same time, parishioners and tenants in Northumberland were petitioning their priest, Master Deyn, to pray for the pope of Rome as the head of their mother Holy Church.[19]

The Lincolnshire rebels sued for pardon on 11 October, by which stage the Yorkshire rising was underway. Writing to the empress on 14 October, Eustace Chapuys informed her that a 'great number of men' had risen who 'object to the suppression of churches, wishing ecclesiastical matters to be as formerly'.[20] He also mentioned the position of the princess (Mary) and advised that her cause would be the next important issue for the rebels, after that of the Church. We would expect Chapuys' rhetoric to be anti-heretical and perhaps prone to exaggeration, but the numbers he put the rebels at (30,000–50,000) and his succinct summary regarding religion are indicative of quite an informed and accurate picture of the insurrection at this stage.

This first stage of the insurrection in the North was over by 11 October and it is the uprisings in Yorkshire, led by Robert Aske, a London-based lawyer, which are properly referred to as the Pilgrimage of Grace. On 14 October, the mayor, aldermen and sheriffs of York wrote to advise the king that the commons had rebelliously assembled and that York was 'ill provided' for defence.[21] A copy of a set of rebel articles existed in York at this time, addressed 'To the king our sovereign lord', and these contained five broad grievances.[22] They reveal the religious concerns of the rebels and also their distaste for members of the government. It is worth highlighting three of the articles to illustrate the mindset of the participants:

Item 1: By the suppression of so many religious houses, the service of God is not well performed and the people unrelieved.

Item 4: The king takes of his Council, and has about him, persons of low birth and small reputation who have procured these things for their own advantage, whom we suspect to be Lord Cromwell and Sir Richard Riche, Chancellor of the Augmentations.

Item 5: Are grieved that there are bishops of the king's late promotion who have subverted the faith of Christ, the bishops of Canterbury, Rochester, Worcester, Salisbury, St David's and Dublin.

Robert Aske also issued a proclamation to the City of York between 15 and 16 October, which denied that the rebels had assembled on account of impositions laid on them but because 'evil-disposed persons being of the king's council' were responsible for 'many and sundry new inventions, which be contrary [to] the faith of God ... and thereby intendeth to destroy the church and ... further intending utterly to spoil and rob the whole body of this realm'. The proclamation said that whether what was stated were true or not should be put to conscience but that if those who decided to fight against them should prevail, it would put 'both us and you and your heirs and ours in bondage forever'. The proclamation went on to state clearly that 'we will fight and die against both you and those that shall be about ... to stop us in the said pilgrimage, and God shall judge which shall have his grace mercy ...'[23]

Darcy and the other lords in Pontefract Castle wrote to the earls of Shrewsbury, Rutland and Huntingdon on 15 October and advised that 20,000 men were meeting at York and that they were in no doubt that the commons of Yorkshire and Lincolnshire received messages from each other – 'they increase in every parish and the cross goes before them'.[24] Sir Brian Hastings informed Shrewsbury of Aske's triumphal entry into York on 16 October by letter the following day. According to Hastings, the rebels were present in an area between Doncaster and Newcastle and numbered 40,000. He was of the opinion that Lord Thomas Darcy would surrender Pontefract Castle and the rebels had already taken the abbey.

At this juncture, Hastings advised that Lords Latimer and Scrope had been sworn by the rebels. He implored Shrewsbury urgently to advise the king as he didn't dare trust anyone and confirmed that the rebels had been received at York the previous Monday with a procession at 5 p.m. The momentum was clearly with the rebels: on 18 October, Shrewsbury, Rutland and Huntingdon advised the Duke of Suffolk of the fact that the mayor and commons of Doncaster had been sworn to the rebels' cause: 'never sheep ran faster in a morning owte of their fold than they did to receive the said othe'.[25]

Aske prepared an oath to be sworn by the participants and it appears to be at this stage, whilst at York, that the term Pilgrimage of Grace was devised. The oath is a highly illuminating declaration of the rebels' rhetoric:

Ye shall not enter into this our Pilgrimage of Grace for the common-wealth, but only for the love that ye do bear unto almighty God, his faith and to holy church militant [and for] the maintenance therof, to the preservation of the king's person [and] his issue, to the purifying of the nobility, and *to expulse all villain blood and evil councillors* against the com-monwealth *from his grace and his privy council* of the same. And ye shall not enter into our said Pilgrimage for no particular profit to yourself, nor to do any displeasure to any private person, but by the counsel of the com-monwealth, nor slay nor murder for no envy, but in your hearts put away fear and dread, and take afore you the Cross of Christ, and in your hearts his faith, the restitution of the church, the suppression of these heretics and their opinions by the holy contents of this book.[26]

Aske followed this dazzling early success with an order for the suppressed religious houses to be restored and prepared a draft of protection for the monastery of St Mary's at Salley (Sawley) in Lancashire. The abbot and monks had been reinstated there by the commons on 12 October. The monastery then petitioned Sir Henry Percy, stating that the whole country supported the monks in entering their house and was ready to extend the pilgrimage of Christ's faith. Sawley monastery was a hot bed of dissent and resistance and two revealing documents are to be found in the convent's papers from this time. The first is a paper written in Latin entitled *Summa Summarum*, which stated that it was lawful to fight for faith and country, that men should bear injuries done to themselves, but not those done to God and their neighbours.[27] The second is an example of anti-regime religious rhetoric in the form of a poem which has come to be known as the *Pilgrims' Ballad.*[28] It contains sixteen stanzas of seven lines each; listed here are six of them which serve as an illustration as to the nature of the concerns and grievances of the Pilgrims and will be analysed in turn:

Crist crucifyd!
For thy woundes wide
Vs commons guyde!
Which pilgrames be,
Thrughe godes grace,
For to purchache

Olde welth and peax
Of the spiritualtie.

The crucified Christ is called upon to guide the commons in their pilgrimage. Through God's grace, they believed they would achieve their objective of the restoration of the spiritual peace. We see here the emphasis placed upon the (five) wounds of Christ.

The following stanzas deal with the role of the monasteries:

Gaif to releif,
Whome for amice greve
Boith day and even,
And can no wirke;
Yet this thay may,
Boith night and day
Rusorte and pray
Vnto godes kyrke

Those unable to work had been provided with relief. The fact that the monasteries provided alms for the poor is reiterated in the following stanzas. The poor commons had been prompted into action for the Church's sake. This, it was said, was not surprising because it was clear that the decay of the Church, if allowed to continue un-checked, would be sorely lamented by the poor:

Alacke! Alacke!
For the church sake
Pore comons wake,
And no marvell!
For clere it is
The decay of this
How the pore shall mys
No tong can tell

The succour given to the poor is again highlighted; the abbeys provided the needy and distressed with both ale and bread:

For ther they hade
Boith ale and breyde
At tyme of nede,
And succer grete
In alle distresse
And hevynes,
And wel intrete

The people had been misled by lack of grace into following an erroneous belief:

Thus interlie
Peax and petie,
Luf and mercie,
For to purchache
For mannys mysdeyd,
And wrongfull crede
Most fer myslede,
Throght lack of grace.

The final stanza here contains an explicit reference to Cromwell, Thomas Cranmer and Richard Rich. These three individuals and their 'like' (i.e. adherents) needed to be shown the way by God and to amend their ways. Robert Aske was given the role of undertaking this task, and if he were to be successful, all would be well:

Crim, crame, and riche
With thre ell and the liche
As sum men teache.
God theym amend!
And that Aske may,
Without delay,
Here make a stay
And well to end!

The ballad sheds light on the Pilgrims' perception of the true religion, the role of the monasteries and the authors of their misfortune. The six stanzas above provide a representation of the mindset of the rebels and demonstrate their areas of concern.

The Earl of Shrewsbury sent Lancaster Herald to Pontefract on 21 October and the herald's account sheds light on the views of the commons, the conditions within the castle and the government's rhetoric. He stated that he encountered the commons, in harness, en route to Pontefract and asked them why they were in harness, to which they replied that it was to prevent the Church from being destroyed. The herald described how he was sent for by Aske and had a discussion with him: his description of Aske is (as might be expected) hostile. He referred to him as having an 'inestimable proud countenance' and described him as holding court 'like a great prince' and 'tyrant'. Aske prevented him from reading his intended proclamation at the Market Cross and stated that his people were true to the articles that they must see a reformation or die. When the herald asked what the articles were he was told that one was to go with his company to London on pilgrimage to the king to have all vile blood put from the council. In addition, he sought to have the faith of Christ and God's laws kept and restitution for the wrongs done to the Church.[29]

The herald's intended proclamation stated that the king's subjects had behaved unnaturally and believed false and spiteful inventions devised to bring the country to ruin. They had shown their unnatural behaviour to the king, who had chief charge of both their souls and bodies. It went on to state that the herald was authorised to declare a general pardon in the king's name if he perceived that the rebels were ready to submit.[30] The issue of the king's capacity to have cure of both the bodies and souls of his subjects was obviously integral to the Royal Supremacy and, as Shagan has pointed out, this imposed upon people's religious sensibilities a paradigm of political loyalty. As regards the concept of the cure of souls (in Latin, *Cura Animarum*), and the idea that this function could be possessed by the monarch, these were rejected even by the evangelical Sir Francis Bigod who leapt to prominence in the renewed Northern Rebellions in 1537. Bigod was to write a treatise against the Royal Supremacy and stated that 'the king's office was to have no cure of souls'.[31]

Historians differ with respect to the primary motivation for the insurrection. For instance, Ethan Shagan argues that the issue of the Royal

Supremacy was often crucial, whilst C.S.L. Davies believes that it was probably the least important issue for the Pilgrims. However, both agree that the dissolution of the monasteries was pivotal among the grievances. Shagan is of the opinion that the maintenance of the monasteries was 'an absolute moral imperative' and Davies states that the dissolution was probably the major single cause of the revolt.[32] These views can be sharply contrasted with Dickens, who, as has been shown, stated that monasteries should be deleted from the list of grievances. Thomas Kendall, the vicar of Louth (the birthplace of the rebellions), succinctly summarised the role that both issues played. The people, he said, had indeed long grudged that the king should be head of the Church and were opposed to the putting down of holy days and of monasteries. Kendall was of the opinion that 'if any o[ne would ry] se all would ryse'.[33] The examination of the rebel articles of the Pilgrimage of Grace which follows later will highlight that both issues were extremely important to the participants.

After Lancaster Herald's 'mission' to Pontefract, the rebellion continued with musters taking place in Yorkshire and Cumberland. The Bishop of Faenza, the papal nuncio in France, reported on 23 October that 40,000 were in arms 'on account of the abbeys which the king had suppressed, taking away crosses and chalices and giving away the property to whomsoever he pleased'.[34] The bishop here touched on a point that requires further consideration – the role of reward and patronage in securing obedience in the matter of the king's religious changes. The dissolution of the monasteries and the granting of land and wealth to lay subjects created a symbiotic relationship with the Crown, one that was to have far-reaching implications for the future of both English Roman Catholicism and English society. Thomas Cromwell was central to the award of grants at this time. The issues of reward and patronage with regard to the Pilgrimage of Grace and the North of England will be discussed in a later chapter.

How had a situation come about where a rising of this magnitude had continued unchallenged for over three weeks? By late October, nine well-armed hosts had formed and all regarded Aske as their leader or Grand Captain. The government, it seems, was caught off guard: the king had disbanded an army he had sent northwards to engage the Lincolnshire rebels on 19 October at Ampthill in Bedfordshire, thinking that it was no longer required. The Duke of Suffolk remained in Lincolnshire dealing with the aftermath of the rising there and the Earl of Shrewsbury was still at Nottingham, awaiting the king's orders.[35] Lord Darcy and the majority of the gentry, including Sir Robert Constable and Archbishop Edward Lee, had joined the rebels at Pontefract Castle.

The gentry, nobility and higher clergy all claimed that they had been coerced into the rebellion but, according to Elton, the 'tale rings very false'. Three key figures in the rebellion were Lord Hussey in Lincolnshire, Lord Darcy in the West Riding and Sir Robert Constable in the East Riding, and Elton cited a statement made by Hussey as evidence of manifest planning – Hussey stated that he and the others had agreed among themselves, as early as 1534, that they 'would not be heretics but die as Christian men'.[36] However, it can be suggested that Elton has taken this statement out of context and endowed it with too much weight. In Hussey's letter of explanation to Cromwell of 11 April 1537, whilst imprisoned in the Tower, he stated that a priest in a sermon in 1534 had likened Our Lady to 'a pudding when the meat was taken out' and this had provoked their response at that time. The relatively elderly and conservative lords clearly found such a statement shockingly heretical. That does not mean that they set about organising a conspiracy for rebellion as a direct consequence. The contention that the Pilgrimage was the result of a pre-planned conspiracy will be discussed further in due course.

Obedience was central and crucial in the rhetoric of the king and his government and this obedience now extended to spiritual as well as temporal matters. Henry simply could not comprehend that his subjects were so 'unnatural' as to question his judgement and disobey his will.[37] In this, he was absolutely no different from the other rulers of Christendom of his day, but his blurring of the roles between Church and state was new and distinctly bewildering to his subjects. For all the rhetoric of his right to obedience, he also deployed the weapon of fear and retribution. However, the king sometimes talked a good fight without having the resources to carry through his threats and the Pilgrimage of Grace was undoubtedly one of these occasions.

On 6 October, shortly after the outbreak of the rising in Louth, the king reproached the Commissioners of the Subsidy and threatened retribution against the rebels with a force of 100,000 men. He also demonstrated the cruel and unmerciful dimension of his character. Having described his subjects as 'unnatural', the king stated that he had appointed a great army to invade their countries and to burn, spoil and destroy their goods, wives and children with all extremity to the fearful example of all lewd subjects. Henry's vindictive character and desire for retribution was evident when he instructed the Duke of Suffolk to destroy, burn and kill man, woman and child if there was renewed rebellion in Lincolnshire.[38] The Duke of Suffolk, Robert Tyrwhyt, Archbishop Lee, not to mention Lord Darcy, all advised Henry of the fury and multitude of the rebels and despite this, Henry still stated his intention to 'punish that insurrection to the example and terror of all others'. Towards the end of October, despite the Ampthill force having been disbanded, Henry wrote on three occasions of his personal intention to lead a royal army against the rebels in the North.

The Pilgrimage, however, demonstrated how rebels could utilise the machinery of warning beacons, bells and local musters to raise well-equipped armies which were larger than any Henry could field against them.[39] The king's commanders on the ground obviously had a more realistic grasp of the situation and had to make an assessment as to how to proceed given Henry's intransigence and the logistics of communication. In such circumstances, the Duke of Norfolk and the Earl of Shrewsbury met with the rebels at the First Appointment at Doncaster on 27 October and agreed a truce.

Norfolk gave the reasons for his decision in correspondence to the Privy Council on 29 October, where he described the Pilgrims' army as the 'flower of the north' but displayed an element of apprehension as to how his actions would be perceived by the king. He claimed that he had never served the king as well as by dissolving the enemy's army without incurring losses among the royal forces. He was, however, filled with trepidation as to how Henry would react to the dispersal of his forces. As if to present himself in a more favourable light, he contrasted his actions with Darcy's: 'Fye, fye! upon the lord Darcy, the most arrant traitor that ever was living.'[40] The truce was reached on the understanding that the rebels' first five articles were to be taken to the king by Norfolk, accompanied by two of the Pilgrim leaders, Ralph Ellerker and Robert Bowes.[41] In the light of Norfolk's agreement, Shrewsbury, Rutland and Huntingdon advised Henry on the same day that, following Norfolk's actions, they too had disbanded their army.[42]

The truce held throughout the month of November, although there are a number of references to Henry's contempt for the Yorkshire rebels and it is hard to avoid the impression that he was biding his time, waiting for them to slip up.[43] During this time, Norfolk wrote to Darcy and informed him that the king had answered the Pilgrims' articles 'with his own hand' and advised him to betray Aske for his own preservation.[44] The betrayal of Aske as the sacrificial lamb on the altar of rebellion was also urged by Lord Hussey in a letter to Darcy on 7 November.[45] It is to his credit that Darcy ignored such advice and refused to deliver up Aske (in a letter to Norfolk of 11 November). He also revealed that the people were anxious for the return of Ellerker and Bowes and desired a parliament in the North.[46]

Although Hussey had joined the Earl of Shrewsbury with 200 men, he was summoned to London to give an account of his conduct instead. His answers initially appear to have satisfied the king and he was allowed to return north. He informed Darcy of this in a letter dated 7 November – the same letter where he urged Darcy to deliver Aske to the authorities.[47] However, testimony hostile to Hussey is recorded on 4 November, and the evidence came from one Robert Carre of Sleaford. Carre stated that if Hussey had gathered men for the king as he had done for 'his own pomp' in riding to sessions or assizes, he might have driven the rebels back. Carre maintained that it was Hussey's inaction and lack of leadership which resulted in his tenants joining the rebels.[48]

Meanwhile, Aske was advising the convent of Watton that it was his intention to be a maintainer of religion. Darcy's anxiety about the delay of the envoys' return was echoed by Aske himself when he advised Sir Francis Brian on 15 November that the delay in receiving an answer to the petitions was likely to produce 'serious commotions'.[49] Darcy gave his reasons for his refusal to betray Aske during a long conversation with Somerset Herald sometime in mid-November and maintained that he had been true to Henry VII and the present king and had always believed in 'One God, One Faith, One King'. Discussing the magnitude of the insurrection and the support for its aims, Darcy pointed out that the grievances were not unique to the North – for if the king saw the letters to the captain from all parts of the realm, 'he would marvel'.

Around this time, Darcy was also keen on explaining his involvement in the rising, notably advising Sir Brian Hastings that no man had ever been in such danger as he had been at Pontefract. He continued to try and justify his actions towards the end of November and his language appears to have changed with regard to a section of his fellow Pilgrims: 'I will be no supporter of the commons in their evil acts.' He was writing to the Duke of Norfolk at the time and appears particularly anxious to try to exculpate himself. He advised Norfolk that when Henry knew of his conduct, he was confident that his actions would be justified.[50] It is probable that the enormity of what he had done had started to register with the elderly and conservative Darcy and his words appear to have the desperation of someone who was trying to extricate himself from a dangerous situation before it was too late.

Elton stated that Lord Darcy's actions left no doubt: the implication that he had fully prepared for the rebellion was overwhelming. Three reasons are given for this contention – Darcy's muster book of 1 October 1536; the speed of his surrender of Pontefract Castle; and his supply of the badges used by the Pilgrims depicting the Five Wounds of Christ. It must be conceded that Darcy's muster book does at first lead to suspicion and appears incriminating: why did Darcy feel the need to write the names of knights, squires and gentlemen who had promised to serve the king upon an hour's warning on 1 October, immediately prior to the Lincolnshire rebellion?[51]

Richard Hoyle takes an entirely different view and devotes a chapter in his book, *The Pilgrimage of Grace and the Politics of the 1530s*, to 'Misunderstanding Darcy'. In this view, it is only the date which has led to Darcy's condemnation by historians and Hoyle questions whether the date on the document is indeed accurate.[52] Indeed, having had sight of the document, the date is by no means certain as being 1 October. Hoyle also emphasises the point that Darcy lacked money and munitions and this does indeed seem to be the case as there are numerous letters from Darcy to the king on this subject. Indeed, on 15 October, Darcy stated that he had twice before written to the king, without reply.[53] Darcy's account of the state of Pontefract Castle is corroborated by Edward, Archbishop of York, in a letter to Henry VIII of 13 October and he referred to Darcy as the king's 'true knight'.[54] That the situation was indeed extremely grave is borne out by the letters of Sir Brian Hastings – Hastings wrote that the common people in the North would not be restrained without 'great policy' – and Sir Robert Tyrwhyt, who confirmed that the commons were so furious that the gentlemen were fearful for their lives. The Duke of Suffolk also reiterated the potential danger from the multitude of men in the North.[55]

Hoyle maintains that Darcy was playing for time in difficult circumstances and the fact that he did not act unilaterally against the rebels has resulted in the censure of historians. In such circumstances, it is easy to understand the relative speed with which Darcy surrendered Pontefract to the rebels and this 'rapid conversion' does not automatically prove that he 'must have been involved in the plot'. Nor does the fact that Darcy's badge of the Five Wounds was used by the Pilgrims constitute manifest evidence of advance planning. Darcy had led English troops in assisting Ferdinand of Aragon against the Moors in 1511 and these troops had worn the badge of the Five Wounds.[56] Is it not then possible that Darcy had a stock remaining and these were convenient for the rebels to use in the Pilgrimage?

Elton portrayed Darcy and Aske as the leaders of the conspiracy. The evidence requires closers scrutiny. Aske was in Yorkshire at the start of the Lincolnshire Rising and crossed the Humber into Lincolnshire on 4 October where he was sworn by the Lincolnshire rebels.[57] According to Aske, he had intended to return to London but he was intercepted and sworn; Elton was of the opinion that his whole conduct during the first week of October 'makes sense only on the assumption that he was involved in a conspiracy but was taken by surprise when Lincolnshire broke out before he was ready in Yorkshire'.[58] However, it is exactly that, an *assumption*: there is no hard evidence to support the contention that Aske was involved in a conspiracy prior to his being sworn. Indeed, Aske's conduct in trying to secure an agreement with the government in December and his condemnation of the Post-pardon Revolts of 1537 (which will be discussed in the following chapter), both of which left him open to criticism from the rebels, does not lend credence to such a claim.

The evidence to support a credible claim for a conspiracy simply does not exist. Although Davies refuted the idea of a conspiracy, he does contend that 'many of the nobility and gentry demonstrably played a more active part in the Pilgrimage than they afterwards admitted'.[59] This conclusion would appear to be much nearer the mark. It would seem that, once the rebellion was underway, many acquiesced and used the outbreak to pursue their own agenda – it could, perhaps, be viewed as a conspiracy of inaction once underway – this is a long way from saying that it was all pre-planned.

Indeed, if a conspiracy had led to effective planning, it seems much more likely that the Pilgrimage would have had a greater chance of ultimate success; either a reversal in policy by the Crown or even, perhaps, the deposition of Henry. Davies has argued that the outcome could have been different if the Duke of Norfolk and the Earl of Northumberland had been involved, and by no stretch of the imagination could Norfolk be regarded as evangelical or pro-reform. Reginald Pole was in Rome at the time of the outbreak of the rebellion and was swiftly made a cardinal and sent to Flanders to muster support for the Pilgrims. The idea was that he might potentially go to England at the head of a military force. Whilst he must have been aware of the opportunity it presented, he was, according to the Dodds, 'no crusader' and 'his heart did not leap up at the call to arms'.[60] Pole, however, did not set out on his journey until mid-February 1537, by which time Rome was already aware that the Pilgrimage of Grace was over. In any case, the cardinal had too little money to raise mercenaries.[61] Pole and Rome were reacting to events; they clearly had not planned them.

This reaction to events can also be illustrated in the correspondence of Chapuys' nephew to Queen Mary of Hungary, sister of Charles V, regarding the 'rebellion in the bishopric of Lincoln'. The letter, from mid-October 1536, is illuminating in that it highlights the anti-Henrician rhetoric of the time and displays clarity of purpose about what is required to deal effectively with Henry:

> And now Madame, it appears … that considering the said trouble and they fish so well in troubled water, the time is come (and no such opportunity could be looked for in 100 years) to take revenge upon the schismatic … for … the indignities he inflicted upon your aunt and the innumerable iniquities he has committed against the patient Princess, to restore whom to her rightful estate would require but part of the army which was prepared in Zealand, and that it should land in the river which goes up to York with 2,000 arqubusiers and some ammunition which is what they are most in need of.[62]

On 21 November the Pilgrims' council met at York where Robert Bowes gave an account of his visit to the king at Windsor and reassured them as to the king's mercy. Henry was willing to pardon all but ten ringleaders.[63] There were many among the Pilgrims who hated and distrusted Cromwell, and Aske confirmed this in his correspondence to Darcy. He also stated that the south parts of the country longed for the Pilgrims to arrive.[64] At this time, it appears that the extent of the insurrection was appreciated and its potential to bring about change was being touted on the Continent. Charles V received letters describing the rebellion as being 40,000 'good Christians' strong who used the crucifix as their principal banner. These letters echo Aske's view: 'the other parts of the kingdom wish the men of the north to come on and join them'.[65] Charles was also advised that the pope should send money and could 'easily send Pole'. Count Cifuentes in Rome wrote to the emperor on 24 November and seemed to have additional information. He stated that the pope advised him that he had 'sent them money to succour them by a secret person whom he had in Picardy, and would not desist from aiding them'.[66]

These suggestions are echoed in the correspondence of the Bishop of Faenza: discussing Reginald Pole, he stated that 'he could do great service to God by going there whenever any insurrection may arise'. Faenza also described how the people of England were 'mostly alienated', if not from the king, then at least from all his ministers; chief among these was Thomas Cromwell.

As we can see, these are reactions to the rebellion and suggestions as to how to grasp the opportunity it had presented. They do not provide any evidence of a pre-planned conspiracy. Indeed, Faenza's letter to Monsignor Ambrogio of 12 November succinctly summarises the development of the insurrection: 'these disturbances have been appeased, having been immature and having no head of importance.'[67] This is exactly the case. If there had have been an Aragonese faction conspiracy, as has been alleged by Elton,[68] Pole would have been involved from the start and the leadership would not have fallen to the elderly Darcy and the somewhat obscure Aske.

In any event, the Pilgrims' representatives were summoned to a second appointment to discuss the situation with Norfolk. Prior to this, the king had revealed his feelings to Ellerker and Bowes and his correspondence is characteristic of his righteous indignation and the rhetoric of obedience. He could not understand the ingratitude shown to his royal person in the insurrection, especially by men of nobility. Henry was particularly angry that the rebels 'presume, with force, to order their prince? God commanded them to obey their prince whatever he be.' To underpin this rhetoric, Henry deployed the sanction of retribution: he questioned the madness that had seized the rebels that they were prepared to destroy themselves and utterly devastate the areas (of the country) which they inhabited. The king stated his intention to take measures to cut them off as corrupt members.[69]

Bush has argued that the Pilgrimage can be viewed as a malfunction in the body politic and Henry's thinking appeared to be along these lines when he talked about the removal of corrupt members. Henry used a physician's analogy when writing of the rebels and emphasised the theme of obedience to his ministers, Fitzwilliam and Russell, following the Pontefract meeting.[70]

In the lead up to the meeting, the issue of a free and general pardon for the rebels was to the forefront of the debate. The Privy Council advised the Duke of Norfolk on 2 December that it would not be honourable for the king to grant a free pardon: Henry was of the view that his honour would be gravely diminished.[71] However, the rebels' resoluteness and military strength obliged Norfolk to grant the free and general pardon, and it reserved no one for punishment.[72] Henry attempted to put a positive spin on this decision by advising the Duke of Suffolk that he had granted the free pardon because he had yielded to the advice of his council.[73]

The Pilgrims based their negotiating position on the original five articles given to Norfolk on 27 October and produced the twenty-four Pontefract Articles on 4 December.[74] Of these, ten are undoubtedly exclusively religious grievances and these are the ones which will be considered here. Although the articles can be dismissed as reactionary and somewhat ill-informed (for instance in the treatment given to known continental reformers), they are incredibly revealing. We will begin by examining the articles which specifically attacked heresy – items 1, 7 and 8:

Item 1: The fyrst touchyng our faith to have the heresyes of Luther, Wyclif, Husse, Malangton, Elocampadius, Bucerus, Confessio Germaniae, Apologia Malanctonis, The Works of Tyndall, of Barnys, of Marshall, Raskell, Seynt Germayne and such other heresies of Anibaptist clerely within this realm to be annulled and destroyed.

It is clear that this list is a mishmash of reformers and continental reform ideas, but its intent is clear: the Pilgrims wanted an end to heresy. Martin Luther was the best-known reformer of the day, having precipitated the Reformation and ensuing social unrest in Germany. Indeed, King Henry himself had denounced Luther's ideas in his own work, *Assertio Septem Sacramentorum* (The Defence of the Seven Sacraments), fifteen years prior to the Pilgrimage of Grace. This work went through twenty editions and translations during the century, and Henry was rewarded with the title of 'Defender of the Faith' by Pope Leo X in 1521.[75] Bishop John Fisher and Sir Thomas More had both been authors of anti-Lutheran polemical tracts in the 1520s,[76] but the Defender of the Faith had become the prosecutor of the faith by the mid-1530s and they had paid the price with their lives.

Fisher had also denounced the Swiss reformer John Oecolampadius (referred to in the articles as 'Elocampadius') in 1527.[77] Oecolampadius had been an assistant to Zwingli and denied the Real Presence. Tellingly, Oecolampadius, unlike Luther, gave judgement for Henry when the king had canvassed opinions on his divorce from Katherine of Aragon.[78]

The 'Wyclif' referred to in the Pontefract Articles was John Wycliffe, a fourteenth-century English theologian and university teacher. Wycliffe had translated the Bible into English and his followers were known as Lollards. Wycliffe was declared a heretic by the Council of Constance in 1415. 'Husse' is a reference to the Czech priest and rector of the University of Prague, Jan Hus. Hus condemned indulgences more than 100 years before Luther and was burned at the stake for heresy, again on the orders of the Council of Constance in 1415.[79] 'Malangton' was actually Philipp Melanchthon, a German reformer, professor and theologian, and a close collaborator of Luther's. He was mainly responsible for the *Confession of Augsburg.*[80]

'Barnys', or Robert Barnes, a former Austin friar and doctor of divinity at Cambridge, had been imprisoned after an examination by Wolsey in 1526, before escaping and fleeing to Antwerp in 1528. Barnes returned to England in 1531 and was among Cromwell's associates.[81] 'Raskell' is a reference to John Rastell, a member of Lincoln's Inn and a lawyer and printer who had attacked the practice of paying tithes.[82]

'Bucerus' was actually a reference to Martin Bucer, a Strasbourg-based reformer who had originally been a member of the Dominican order. Bucer had met Luther and agreed with him on the doctrine of *Sola Fide* – justification by faith alone. He rejected the Mass, Purgatory and the pope and emphasised obedience to temporal government. Unsurprisingly, he was excommunicated. His most notable contribution to the theological debate was the notion of *adiaphora*, or things that were indifferent in order to secure salvation. Bucer's ideas were reflected in the Henrician Ten Articles. These articles obviously also reflected Lutheran theology and Henry had opened negotiations with the Lutherans and the German princes prior to their formulation.[83]

Perhaps the Pilgrims missed an opportunity with regard to Article 1. Instead of denouncing a random list of reformers and ideas, they may have fared better if they had concentrated their attack on the ideas and reformers that Henry found so repugnant. Dickens was correct when he stated that the king detested Anabaptists. Yet there is no mention of Thomas Muntzer, perhaps the most notorious 'heretic' of the day. If the Pilgrims had tailored their arguments to suit the king's sensibilities, the item may have been taken more seriously. Having said that, it was indeed a difficult task ascertaining Henry's preferences: they fluctuated on a relatively frequent basis. The one factor that remained a constant was Henry's Caesaropapism (his position as a secular ruler who is also head of the church) and this will be addressed in due course.

Article 1 criticises reformers whose views could actually be interpreted as underpinning the king's position with regard to religious change. For instance, although Tyndale had been burned for heresy in 1535, his book, *The Obedience of a Christian Man* (1528), presented a concept of royal authority over the realm and stated that all people had a duty to submit to the authority of the prince. The work was anti-papal and stressed that the king was the vicar of God: God alone was the judge of kings.[84] This was a view shared by Christopher St German, a 'hard-headed' anti-clerical lawyer, who sought to claim for the Crown authority over the discernment of God's will.[85] The Pilgrims had referred to him as 'Seynt Germayne'. His and Tyndale's views supported the king's Erastian stance (Henry's supremacy in ecclesiastical affairs). Tyndale's main preoccupation had been with the dissemination of the English translation of the Bible. However, Tunstall and the English bishops had ordered its burning as it was riddled with errors and promoted heresy.[86] Of course, Tyndale had just been following the ideas of another 'heretic', Wycliffe, but it is interesting to note that the concern with the vernacular Bible had changed to positive approval when it was promoted by the Henrician injunctions by the end of the decade. The Second Henrician Injunctions of 1538 made it a requirement that every parish church had a copy of the Bible in English.[87]

Item 7: To have the heretiqes, bisshoppis and temporall, and their secte, to have condigne punyshment by fyer or such oder, or els to trye ther quareles with us and our parte takers in batell.

The desire for the punishment of heretics is evident. Death by burning had been the usual method in such cases under the heresy laws, *De Haeretico Comburendo*, 1401.[88] The reference to the bishops, however, does not explicitly name the heretic prelates. This is in contrast to the Lincoln/York Articles of 14 October. These articles listed six bishops as heretics, including Cranmer of Canterbury, Shaxton of Salisbury and Latimer of Worcester. These articles also inferred that the cause of the trouble was the doctrinally orthodox Bishop Longland of Lincoln.[89] It can be suggested that this lends further credence to the view that this was not an orchestrated and premeditated uprising. Sophisticated 'high' politicians and nobles would, perhaps, have 'named and shamed' the Protestant ones in this item in the articles. The temporal heretics undoubtedly referred to the king's 'evil councillors' and would have included Cromwell, Richard Rich and the Lord Chancellor, Thomas Audley. Cromwell and Rich were singled out for notoriety in the *Pilgrims' Ballad*. This is reiterated in Article 8:

Item 8: To have the lord Crumwell, the Lorde Chancelor, and Sir Ric Riche knight to have condigne ponyshment, as subverters of the good laws of this realme and maynteners of the false sect of those heretiqes and the first inventors and bryngars in of them.

This is probably the article that sheds most light on the motivation of the Pilgrims. Not only was heresy deeply unpopular in the North, Thomas Cromwell was seen as its principal advocate and the man responsible, in the main, for providing the king with evil counsel. As Merriman has remarked, the people made Cromwell the author of all their troubles. A crusade against him would not, in their minds, be a revolt against royal authority.[90] They had no complaint against the king, only the influence of the heretical and evil men who had led Henry astray. After all, this was the same monarch who had denounced Luther so passionately that he was rewarded with an exalted title from the pope. Cromwell was not only responsible for the promotion of heresy, he had acted against the body politic by acting against the good laws of the country. This article reflected the perspective that 'ungodly counsellors could and should be removed by monarchs and also reiterated the theme in early Tudor rebellions that the criticism was of the policies and not the person of the prince'.[91]

One could not expect non-theologians to have a complete grasp of the intricacies of theological debate nor a contemporary knowledge of the development of continental reform. Dickens claims that the rebels should have known that Henry disliked Luther and the Anabaptists, but how were they to know this? To the ordinary rank and file Pilgrim, one heretic was the same as another and they lacked the sophistication or training to differentiate between different strands of continental reform. The Pilgrim profile was conservative and consistent in its dislike and distrust of heresy, unlike the monarch who would not be averse to flirting with Lutheranism if he perceived it to be expedient.

It is small wonder that conservative and traditional people should be bewildered and inclined to believe rumours, when everything they held to be true had been turned upside down. Their world view and certainties had been shattered and the actions of the monarch encapsulated this epistemological rupture. If anything, the absence of theological awareness and sophistication lends even more credence to the view that the Pilgrimage was popular, commons led and spontaneous, and not the result of a conspiracy.

Any self-respecting member of an 'Aragonese' noble faction involved in preplanning would have taken the time and trouble to present the argument in a more informed and erudite fashion. Dickens' arguments also fall down when he (rightly) states that there is little evidence of Protestantism in the northern counties until after the Pilgrimage of Grace, but then, paradoxically, argues that 'recorded protests made against heresy do not derive in any remarkable degree from the north, and it would be hard to prove that feeling there was exceptionally intense'.[92] Surely this demonstrates a lack of heretical belief and practice in the North prior to 1536?

One factor remained constant in Henry's religious innovations and this was the Royal Supremacy. The following, however, is the only article which specifically attacks it:

Item 2: the supreme head of the church towching cure animarum to be reserved unto the see of Rome as before it was accustomyd to be, and to

49

have the consecracions of the bisshops from hym, with owt any first frutes or pencion to hym to be payd owt of this realme or else a pension reasonable for the owtward defence of our faith.

Here is the rejection of the Royal Supremacy and the king's capacity to have cure of souls. Royal input in the enforcement of orthodoxy was not new (for example, the 1401 statute had made the secular authorities responsible for the execution of heretics), but prior to the mid-1530s, responsibility for deciding what was heretical had been the preserve of the clerics. The Royal Supremacy invested the Crown with the power to define doctrine and this was indeed radical. After such lengthy, arduous and troublesome endeavours to secure the Act of Supremacy in 1534, Henry was consistently and fundamentally hostile to the papacy and firmly defended his title.

Crucial to the new title's success were the twin foundations of theology and rhetoric. Obedience was emphasised and here the influence of Luther and Tyndale came in useful. It was not just Lutherans who emphasised obedience: even the conservative bishop, Stephen Gardiner of Winchester, wrote a treatise defending the Royal Supremacy, *De Vera Obedientia*, in 1535.[93] However, the Pilgrims were clearly not acquiescent in this regard and probably reflected the views of Reginald Pole, expressed in his *Defence of the Unity of the Church*. To Pole, it seemed absurd that one claiming to be the Supreme Head of the Church could not minister the sacraments but yet could deem himself as the judge of doctrinal controversies.[94] It is worth highlighting that the Pilgrims also took the opportunity to state their preference that first fruits and material wealth would not leave England. Despite clearly expressing a desire for the restoration of communion with Rome, they did not want the first year's income from a new bishop to be paid directly to the Holy See. Perhaps some among the leading Pilgrims had been influenced by the criticisms that wealth from other realms had been somewhat exploited in order to enhance the prestige, aesthetic beauty and power of the Vatican.

Items 4, 6 and 11 deal with the dissolution of the monasteries:

Item 4: To have the abbayes suppressed to be restoryd unto ther howses land and goodes.

Item 6: To have the Freres Observauntes restorid unto ther houses agayn.

Item 11: That doctor Ligh and doctor Layton have condigne ponyshment for theyr extortions in theyr tyme of visitacions, as in bribes of sume religiose houses ... and other theyr abhominable actes bt them comytted and done.

By the autumn of 1536, much of the work of the dissolution of the lesser monasteries had been carried out. The monasteries were part of the fabric of English society and provided education, hospitality, alms, religious services and care for the sick. Those who went on pilgrimages to them could earn indulgences, freeing them from time in Purgatory.[95] Monasteries also had a role as landlords and commanded considerable respect. As Richard Rex has argued, the connection of the dissolution with the Pilgrimage of Grace is undeniable and demonstrates a strong loyalty to local institutions. Merriman has made the point that the sight of an 'army of outcast monks and nuns' passing by people's doors, begging for food and shelter, made the religious changes at the centre real and visible in the North.[96] As early as July 1536, Chapuys had commented that it was lamentable to see legions of monks and nuns: there were '20,000 who knew not how to live'.[97]

Robert Aske emphasised the role of the monasteries in popular loyalty[98] and stated that the commons wanted the suppressed houses to be reinstated. Aske highlighted the 'poverty' of the realm and the North especially. For Aske, much of the relief of the commons of the North was by succour of the abbeys and if this were taken away, poverty would force them to make commotions or rebellions. During his examinations in the Tower in 1537, Aske made a number of points explaining why the Pilgrims called for a restoration of the monasteries. He stated that he grudged against the suppressions and so did the whole country. He also emphasised the fact that the northern abbeys laudably served God by providing alms for the poor.

For Aske, the suppressions meant that the Divine Service of Almighty God was much diminished: a great number of Masses were not said and the consecration of the sacrament was not performed. This, he said, was a source of distress and jeopardised the spiritual comfort of the soul. The 'temple of God' had been pulled down and the ornaments and relics of the church irreverently used. Further, the lands and farms of the monasteries had been given to other 'farmers' for pecuniary gain and advantage. Hospitality had become redundant.[99] The significance of this will be apparent in later chapters when patronage is examined. The dissolved monasteries gave the monarch a much increased pool of wealth with which he could dispense patronage, reward loyalty and purchase support.

The Friars Observant (Item 6) had been founded by St Francis and had opposed the Royal Supremacy. Katherine of Aragon especially favoured the order. The order was dissolved in June 1534 and the most obstinate members were sent to the Tower. Henry and Princess Mary had been baptised at the Church of the Friars at Greenwich,[100] but the friars were to feel his wrath in their theological and spiritual opposition to his new title. They were believed to be the spreaders of active sedition.

One of the friars, John Peto, had preached a sermon in front of the king in 1533 and had strongly denounced Henry and compared him to the Old Testament king Ahab. Ahab's wife was Jezebel and the unspoken implication was that Anne Boleyn was Jezebel. Peto warned that if the king continued on his present course, the dogs would lick his blood, as they had Ahab, after his death. Peto and another friar, Elstow, were reprimanded and banished from the country. Two other friars, Rich and Risby, had been executed in 1534.[101]

The Pilgrims also attacked the commissioners for the dissolution: Dr Leigh and Dr Layton are clearly held to account and the Pilgrims perceived them as having taken bribes.

The following three articles deal with the rights and independence of the Church:

Item 5: To have the tenth and fyrst frutes clearly discharged of the same, onles the clergy wyll of them selvys graunte a rent charge in genrality to the augmentacion of the crown.

Item 18: The privilages and ryghtes of the church to be confirmyd by acte of parliament, and prestes not suffre by sourde on les he be disgradid, a man to be savied by his book, sanctuary to save a man for all causes in extreme nede, and the church for xl daies and further according to the laws as they weeyr usid in the begynning of the kinges daies.

Item 19: The liberties of the church to have ther old customys as the cownty palatyn of Durham, Beverlay, Rippon, Saint Peter of York and such other by acte of parliament.

The benefit of the clergy is stressed in Item 18 and clearly the Pilgrims' desired to see a return to previous practices – those in place at the start of Henry's reign.

As is evident, the above articles are purely religious in nature, but it is worth highlighting the following:

Item 3: We humbly beseche our moost dred sovereign lorde that the Lady Mary may be made legitimate and the former statute therin annulled, for the danger of the title that might incurre to the crown of Scotland.

At this time, in the autumn of 1536, Henry had married Jane Seymour but had yet to produce a legitimate male heir. Both his daughters, Mary and Elizabeth, had been bastardised by the Second Act of Succession in 1536, and the Scottish king, James V, son of Henry's sister, Margaret Tudor, would have had a strong claim to the throne. This would have been disconcerting for the northern people, long accustomed to raids from their perennial enemies. Henry's record in producing children, especially male children, had been less than impressive so it is easy to understand the lack of faith in his ability to do so. Additionally, Princess Mary was a very popular figure in the country,[102] especially the North: her orthodoxy and dislike of heresy and religious innovation was well known. The Pilgrims were obviously seeking to promote a conservative and Catholic potential successor. Elizabeth is conspicuous by her absence.

Item 15: To have the parliament in a convenient place at Nottyngham or York and the same shortly somonyd.

Item 23: That no man upon subpoena from Trent north apeyr but at York or by attorney on les it be directid upon payn of allegeance and for lyke maters concerning the kyng.

The previous two items illustrate the sense of disconnection the Pilgrims felt from the centre of power in the South. A clear geographical demarcation, north of the River Trent, is identified.

Whilst Fletcher and MacCulloch have described the Pilgrims' manifestos as 'highly eclectic',[103] the single issue of religion is by far the most prevalent. The Pontefract Articles do contain other issues, but the nature of protest movements tends to provide opportunities for additional grievances to be 'tacked on'. As a movement gathers momentum, participants are likely to raise other issues in the hope of having them acknowledged and rectified at the same time. It is abundantly clear that the Pilgrimage of Grace's driving motivation was religious. One only has to consider its very title and symbolism to identify its primary *raison d'être.*

On 6 December it was agreed that these twenty-four articles were to be taken to the king. A general pardon was to be granted and the restored abbeys would be allowed to remain. Two days later, Lancaster Herald brought the general pardon and confirmation was given of a parliament which was to convene at York (although no date was specified). The commons dispersed and the gentlemen met with Norfolk at Doncaster to submit and they then tore off their Pilgrim badges.[104] So far as the Pilgrims were concerned, the receipt of the general pardon and the commitment to convene a parliament at York, together with the undertaking that the restored abbeys should stand, must have felt like a mission accomplished. The very fact that King Henry condescended to even contemplate a discourse with the rebels illustrates the sheer magnitude of the insurrection and the potential it displayed to threaten the throne. Thirty thousand men in the field by early modern standards was a huge number. Henry's own father had claimed the throne by conquest with a mere fraction of that number only fifty-one years previously. In sum, the evidence indicates clearly that the revolt was religious in causation, despite arguments by some modern historians to the contrary.

The timing of the risings, hot on the heels of the First Henrician Injunctions and during a period where the monasteries were being suppressed, is surely significant. The Pilgrimage of Grace was undoubtedly a spontaneous, mass public rising and a reaction to change and rumour. It was driven, in the first place, by concerns about the Henrician religious innovations: its very name, the Pontefract Articles and the *Pilgrims' Ballad* illustrate this. It was not the result of a conspiracy but an outburst in opposition to those perceived as heretics: these individuals had influenced the king and made him stray from the right path, in particular Thomas Cromwell.

There has been much debate as to whether Henry ever intended to keep the agreement: to consider the rebels' grievances, to hold a parliament in York and freely to pardon all the protagonists.[105] It is in the aftermath of the Pilgrimage that the king's response will be examined to try and shed some light on his true intentions.

The New Year 1537 brought about the resumption of revolts. Why was this? What role did the leaders play and what was the fate of those involved? The aftermath presents us with an opportunity to explore the king's rhetoric and methods of retribution and reward more thoroughly in the coming chapters.

3

Resumption of Revolts and Royal Retribution

It seems clear that the Pilgrims' rhetoric was dictated, in the main, by religious concerns – but what of the king? Henry's behaviour during and after the Pilgrimage points to a monarch more concerned with politics and obedience than explaining his views on theology and the religious structure of the kingdom. Of course, to Henry, the idea of having to explain himself would have been tantamount to having to justify his actions to mere subjects – this simply was not going to happen. However, his correspondence with his commanders, especially the Duke of Norfolk, reveals his vengeful and duplicitous nature. The king only granted the free pardon upon the advice of the Privy Council and clearly felt that it was detrimental to his honour.[1] What were the terms of the pardon? And how was it perceived by the Pilgrims?

It is necessary to examine the pardon in order to appreciate the ways in which events unfolded, leading ultimately to the resumption of rebellion. The proclamation of the pardon to the rebels would be free and granted under the Great Seal and, in a letter to the Duke of Suffolk of 4 December 1536, Henry wrote that Norfolk had been authorised to consent to a parliament to 'be held at Michaelmas'.[2] Yet on the same day as Lancaster Herald was delivering the pardon, his king was reiterating the message of obedience in his letter to Fitzwilliam and Russell. The Pilgrims had been given to understand that the pardon was free and a parliament in the North would convene at Michaelmas, and indeed Archbishop Lee of York wrote to Lord Darcy at the start of the New Year of this and stated that it would be combined with the coronation of Queen Jane Seymour.[3]

Historians have debated whether the king ever intended to honour the terms of the agreement and the pardon. For Bush and Bownes, the December agreement 'humiliated the crown to the core', but the Pilgrims' rank and file distrusted the gentry leadership and had the perception that the pardon was bogus. The king's correspondence does contain several references to his contempt for the rebels, and it is hard to avoid the impression that he was being disingenuous and waiting for them to make an error which would allow him to dispense with the unpalatable pardon and right the wrongs of their rebellious and traitorous action.

The rank-and-file Pilgrims' distrust of the gentry leadership was probably due in no small measure to the perception that Sir Ralph Ellerker and Robert Bowes had taken too long in returning north after their trip south in the autumn,[4] and was most likely exacerbated by Robert Aske's sojourn with the king at Court over Christmas. In any event, the perception that the king was duplicitous must have been pervasive, for the fact is that plans for fresh uprisings had come to the fore just a month after the pardon and promise of a northern parliament.

One of the leaders of these renewed 'commotions' was John Hallam, a captain at Yorkswold, who was apparently sceptical about the Crown's intentions over the Christmas holidays. One witness stated that Hallam was of the opinion that the gentlemen would deceive the commons and that the king had no intention of granting their petitions. Hallam, it can be said, had a more realistic grasp of politics than the somewhat idealistic Aske.[5]

It was the Post-pardon Revolts which allowed the regime to exact revenge upon the rebellious North and crush opposition so effectively that another uprising was not attempted for more than thirty years. The revolts were relatively easily put down by the Duke of Norfolk, and the events and the ultimate retribution will be discussed in due course.

It is also necessary to examine the rhetoric of the pro- and anti-regime protagonists during the period between the resumption of revolt and the ultimate and indiscriminate punishment handed out by the Crown. What were the feelings of the former Pilgrims after the Doncaster agreement and what rhetoric was expounded in pro-regime circles following the pardon? Firstly, though, it is necessary to set the scene in relation to the discourse between the king and Robert Aske, and to ask how this might have appeared to the latter's fellow Pilgrims.

The king wrote to Aske a week after the pardon on 15 December and stated that he had learned that Aske had repented of his offences in the late rebellion and commanded him to come with diligence.[6] Aske had obviously to comply with the command of his sovereign, but one wonders if he really can have believed that the king was honourable in his intentions. After all, Henry had repudiated his loyal wife of more than twenty years, bastardised his daughter and had had no qualms in executing his long-standing and trusted friend, Sir Thomas More. Can Aske really have thought it possible that Henry was willing to forgive him and honour him with a visit to Court after he had raised 30,000 men in protest against the policies of the Crown? If he felt that Henry was treating him as someone noteworthy and was genuinely interested in his opinions, then Aske was incredibly naive.

Whilst at Court, Aske wrote an account of his involvement in the uprising and stated that he had first become aware of the Lincolnshire Rising upon leaving William Ellerker's house in Yorkshire, intending to return to London. Upon crossing the Humber, he was told of the uprisings by the ferryman and after landing at Barton, he was travelling towards Sawcliffe to stay the night with his brother-in-law, Thomas Portington. En route, he was stopped by a Mr Huddswell who informed him of the commons assembly and made him take the oath to be true to God, the king and the commonwealth. Upon arriving at his brother-in-law's, he found that he too had been taken by the commons and, despite this, Robert attempted to 'take boat' at Wintringham but was 'entreated' by more commons and was 'glad to return to Sawcliffe'.[7]

Aske's account continued until the December agreement and he stated that he had not been in contact with Lord Darcy before he went to Pontefract Castle and claimed that he was not involved in any way prior to his first taking. What is significant is that he ended the account under the distinct impression that there was to be a parliament and requested that the Duke of Norfolk declare to them when and where the parliament should be. He was also given to understand that a further letter, affirming the king's pardon, would be sent to the North.[8] Aske recommended that this letter should be written to Lord Darcy 'to stay' the country about him.

It is surely revealing that Aske was concerned that the pardon be reiterated in writing in order for the North to remain calm. He must have been aware of grave misgivings among the rank and file as to the intentions of the Crown. In any event, Aske must have felt that he had secured the peace, pending the convening of a parliament, and probably he felt that his stay at Court had been a success: the king even gave him a present of a jacket of crimson satin.[9]

In a letter to Darcy of 8 January, Aske was fulsome in his praise for Henry. He stated that the king was a gracious sovereign lord to him and had affirmed his pardon to all the North orally. Again, he referred to Henry's intention to hold a parliament and have the queen crowned at York and stated that Henry was tender towards his subjects and extended his mercy 'from the heart'.[10] Aske must have been subjected to an effective charm offensive and there is no reason to believe that he was at all cynical about it. One gets the impression that he believed that he was actually a player of some significance at this juncture. About this time, he produced what is known as his 'Manifesto' and advised his 'loving neighbours' that the king loved his subjects 'more than any other earthly riches', and reiterated that a parliament was to be held at York to deal with their 'reasonable petitions'.[11] This document was apparently found at Aske's lodging at a later date.

Whilst Aske gave the impression of being pleased with his efforts and was optimistic for the future upon his return north, storm clouds, it appears, were already gathering. On 8 January, Sir Marmaduke Constable wrote to Aske, welcoming him home but advising him that the men of Beverley had been 'excited' by a rumour and imploring him to pacify Beverley in 'all haste'.[12] Interestingly, he observed that this action would lead to Aske being 'better esteemed' for his 'late coming home'.

On the same day, Sir Oswald Wolsthrope pleaded with his neighbours to resist those disposed to 'spoil', i.e. resume disturbances, which would be their undoing in the light of the king's pardon.[13] Aske immediately wrote to Beverley and went there in person, declaring the king's love for the North, confirming the pardon and the intention to hold a parliament, and stayed the town. Sir Marmaduke Constable made Cromwell aware of this on 11 January and also informed him that Lord Darcy had maintained the peace in the parts around Pontefract. Aske dutifully reported to the king the following day that Beverley had been disposed for new commotions, and Lord Darcy instructed the rebellious commons to cease assembling or risk losing their lives, lands and goods.[14]

During this period in January, however, reports of dissatisfaction with the situation continued to grow and the Earl of Cumberland, in a letter to Henry, stated that the people were so wild that there was a danger of further rebellion. The earl reiterated his thoughts in a letter to Cromwell and was even more specific, informing him that the commons 'were so minded against you'.[15] Lady Darcy commented on the volatility in the North to her son, Sir George, on 13 January, and by 16 January it appeared that Scarborough Castle had fallen to the commons. However, what actually happened was that George Lumley, son of Lord Lumley, entered Scarborough with a small band of approximately 120–140 men to mount a guard over the castle and swear the commons. The commons elected two captains, Ralph Fenton and John Wyvell, who were subsequently arrested when Sir Ralph Eure retook the town shortly afterwards.[16]

The 'siege' of Scarborough was orchestrated by one Sir Francis Bigod, and his motivation and behaviour remain somewhat of a puzzle to historians. Bigod did not fit the usual Pilgrim profile, not least because he was a known evangelical and advocate of the new learning and reform. Bigod was a Yorkshire gentleman and he appears to have had no scruples with Henrician religious policy prior to his sudden leap to prominence during the Post-pardon Revolts. In April 1536, he wrote to Thomas Cromwell to 'help me to be a priest, that I may preach the Word of God'. And he appears to have been involved in a festering dispute with the abbot of Whitby in the early part of that year. He reported the abbot to Cromwell early in January for 'disobeying the king's title of supremacy',[17] so his subsequent behaviour in the renewed revolts of 1537 was inconsistent to say the least.

The Royal Supremacy was a prominent item in the Pilgrims' grievances and Bigod had been a defender of the king's stance only a year prior to taking up arms against the monarch. George Lumley stated that Bigod had argued that the king's claim to have cure of his subjects' bodies and souls was against the Gospel.[18] Thus, Bigod's stance on the Supremacy shifted dramatically from his position in early 1536 to his participation in the rebellion in 1537. He even wrote a treatise arguing that the king was not to have cure of souls.

Bigod, it appears, also had severe reservations about the king's pardon and thought it was deficient. In April 1537, after Bigod's detention, he stated in his deposition that he had shown John Hallam a list of the defaults of the pardon.[19] Indeed, Sir Ralph Eure attributed the renewal of rebellion to the commons' perception of the pardon. He maintained that the country had been seduced by Sir Francis and Hallam, who had told the people that the king's pardon was legally insufficient. However, the pardon was not the only cause for concern for Bigod: both the king and the Bishop of Rome, he argued, could be lawfully deprived for heresy. Bigod had explained to Hallam his conviction that the king could have no cure of souls and that the head of the Church ought to be a spiritual man such as an archbishop.[20] This, then, appears to be his motivation for leading the renewed uprisings.

John Hallam had been in conspiracy with Sir Francis Bigod, and he attempted to take Hull (with only twenty men) on 16 January. However, his attempt was a failure and after a skirmish with two of the aldermen of the town, he was captured and imprisoned. According to Hallam, the first insurrection was precipitated by the fact that his local curate had left St Wilfred's Day 'unbidden'. Hallam's ill-fated attempt to take Hull was a disaster and resulted in the execution of the protagonists.

It is worth highlighting here that Sir Ralph Ellerker had gone to Hull to offer assistance to the town and, after Hallam's imprisonment, refused requests for his release from Bigod.[21] Bigod, meanwhile, was attempting to get Sir Robert Constable to join in the renewed rebellion and admitted that the commons had initially been distrustful of him at Pontefract, to the extent that he was in fear of his life. He stated that they were suspicious of his learning at first but now had the greatest confidence in him.[22] This request was met with a decisive rejection by Constable: 'I doo marvell that you doo assemble the comons', and he reiterated the fact that the king intended to pardon them all.[23] Despite this, Bigod's followers swore a new oath to 'prepare themselves to battle against the undoers of Christ's church'.[24]

By 18 January, Aske had advised the king of the commotions and stated that Bigod had not yet taken Scarborough Castle and he had informed the commons that he was astonished that they would assemble themselves with Bigod.[25] The commons, however, had other ideas and argued that the government's stance was actually feigned policy, designed to subdue them. They argued that the suppressed abbeys had not been restored by the December agreement but by the commons themselves, and that Cromwell and other 'evil counsellors' were in higher favour than ever. Interestingly, they were aggrieved that the pardon only extended to those who accepted the king's title as Supreme Head of the Church and believed that, whilst in London, Robert Aske had received rewards to betray them. The distrust between the commons and the gentry is evident in this 'Rebel Manifesto', and it concludes that 'now is the time to arise or else never and go proceed with our pilgrimage for grace, or else we shall all be undone'. The suspicion of the gentry is reiterated: 'And ye shall have captains just and true and not be stayed by no gentlemen.'[26]

The commons were right to have had reservations, as a letter from Sir William Babthorpe to Robert Aske on 1 February 1537 illustrates. Babthorpe, although having been part of the Pilgrimage, advised Aske that both he and Sir Marmaduke Constable had spoken with Norfolk with regard to Aske meeting the duke in the North (Babthorpe's career will be discussed further in the following chapter). Aske was advised not to rendezvous with Norfolk before the latter arrived at York. Babthorpe stated that, although Norfolk would receive Aske 'with no very friendly countenance, you are not to be discouraged, for certain causes he will secretly show you'. He reassured Aske that Constable knew that he had the duke's favour, and that the king and council esteemed his service.[27] Here is evidence of subterfuge: Aske was to expect a cool reception from Norfolk in public, but he was to disregard this as he was a now a trusted confidante of the regime. Aske was soon to discover exactly what the king and council thought of him.

The mayor and aldermen of the town of Hull dealt with the attempted seizure by Hallam, and Sir Ralph Ellerker was one of the examiners of the rebels at the town from 23 January. In a few short weeks, Ellerker had sold out his former Pilgrims and had become an instrument of Crown retribution. Hallam himself was examined on 24 and 26 January. On 25 January, before the examinations were even concluded, the king himself wrote to Sir Ralph Ellerker, senior, and others and instructed them to execute those imprisoned at Hull and to 'send up Bigod with all speed'.[28] The king, it appears, was impatient for vengeance. Norfolk desired to know how many should be executed in his correspondence with both the king and Cromwell on 30 January.[29]

By the beginning of February, things do not appear to have improved much with regard to bringing the commons to heel. Norfolk advised Cromwell of much sedition in the North and informed him that '*lewd persons do not yet cease to speak ill of you*', and he forwarded to the Lord Privy Seal a copy of a prophecy concerning him.[30]

Cromwell's humble origins and rather obscure background did not hinder his rise to power. Like Wolsey before him, it appears that the king had complete faith in his judgement and ability to co-ordinate policy and implement decisions. Henry retained trust in his minister despite the hatred the Pilgrims harboured towards him and the renewed rebellions probably afforded Cromwell the opportunity to settle a score or two. It must, however, have been galling for members of the old nobility to have to report to this 'low-born' minister.

The Duke of Norfolk felt compelled to write to Cromwell in response to certain insinuations in February 1537. On 9 February, he wrote that 'almost' all the gentlemen of the shire 'will bear him witness that he is neither Papist nor favourer of traitors'. Norfolk must have felt that his loyalty was being questioned and the suspicions obviously continued, for he had to write to Cromwell again four days later. He was at pains to point out that he did not deserve a reputation as a papist or as being favourably disposed towards 'naughty' religious people.[31]

Norfolk, however, continued to busy himself with suppressing the residual conflicts and extracting retribution for the Crown. Writing to Cromwell on 13 February from York, he advised that the 'dreadful' execution which had commenced there should be followed elsewhere.[32] Two days later, his advice to Sir Christopher Dacre was even blunter. Referring to Sir Christopher as a true knight to his sovereign lord, as well as being hardy and a man of war, he advised him to 'Pinch now for no courtesy to shed blood of false traitors; and ye be busy on the one side, and ye may be sure the duke of Norfolk will come on the other. Finally, now, Sir Christopher, or never!' He signed this instruction, 'your loving cousin if ye do well now or else enemy for ever'.[33]

Throughout the remainder of February, Norfolk was involved in putting down the post-pardon uprisings and imposing martial law at Carlisle. He discussed the requirement for him to be present at every punishment and the great numbers of prisoners. By 19 February, Norfolk was able to inform Cromwell that he had the 'ill people in such fear', and he confirmed that seventy-four 'principal offenders' had been judged to suffer death in every town where they dwelt, by martial law.[34]

As the risings were put down, martial law declared and people taken in for questioning – such as John Dakyn, rector of Kirkby Ravensworth – it might have been expected that fear and the expedient desire for self-preservation would play its part in diluting the anti-regime rhetoric. Dakyn was subjected to an extensive examination at the end of March and had to answer a comprehensive set of questions devised by the council, some in Cromwell's own hand.

Whilst in prison, Dakyn wrote a petition to Cromwell, apologising for his conduct in the insurrection. In this letter he stated that he feared that Cromwell had taken 'an evil opinion of him' and claimed that he was forced to do as the rebels did, as he was in fear of his life. He acknowledged that he was present at the formulation of the Pontefract Articles, but blamed others such as Dr Marshall and Aske for their content. He also shifted the blame to Archbishop Lee of York and Dr Cliff for murmuring against the abrogation of holy days. Dakyn maintained that the laws made in the king's time were 'just' and the realm was well rid of the Bishop of Rome's authority. He thus appeared to accept the Royal Supremacy and the Crown's legitimacy in spiritual matters, but it must be treated with extreme scepticism, given the circumstances in which it was said.[35] In a similar vein, the abbot of Furness played into the regime's hands on 5 April. Roger, 'knowyng the mysorder and evil lyfe' of the brethren, surrendered all his interest in the house and lands to the king.[36]

Cromwell continued to turn the screw to secure compliance with the regime's policies. In April he issued specific instructions to Sir Marmaduke Tunstall as to how he should behave in his office, responsible to the Lord Privy Seal. Tunstall was ordered to ensure that all curates in the area set forth the king's Supremacy and the usurpations of the Bishop of Rome. Further, if anyone was found preaching or spreading seditious tales, they should be committed to ward, pending further direction.[37] Cromwell's position was extremely secure at this point. Norfolk had cause to write to him yet again with regard to his own behaviour in May. Norfolk was perturbed because he believed that Cromwell had received reports that when he had denounced the Bishop of Rome, he had done so with a heavy countenance and, thus, was insincere. Norfolk strenuously denied such an accusation.[38] This persistent self-justification of a nobleman's own actions to Cromwell illustrates the fact that Cromwell was being regularly informed of news by a network of clients/informers and retained the king's complete confidence. It certainly suggests a belief among the nobility that this was indeed the case.

Despite the evident government crack-down, anti-Henrician rhetoric, as might be expected, continued unabated abroad. Faenza commented that although the English reported that the disturbances were appeased, it was not so, for the people were more irritated than ever because the king had observed none of his promises and put many of them (the people) to death. Cardinal Contarini described his grief that the kingdom of England had been 'torn from this body' and wished that Pole might 'conduct this matter so that the universal Church of Christ, his King and his country of England, may sing praises to God for the fishing of the pearl which was lost and the recovery of the beautiful sheep that had strayed from the fold'.[39] (See also, Chapter 7.)

The sheep, however, were not returning to the fold but were being led into the pen and slaughterhouse by shepherd Cromwell. Norfolk had put seventy-four to death under martial law and investigations and examinations continued in April and May.

The period between the December pardon and the ultimate retribution in May and June – the interrogations and punishments – requires examination. Norfolk himself appears to have been under a cloud of suspicion during this period and one gets the impression that he was almost desperate to prove himself utterly loyal in his beliefs and in his hostility to the rebels. He informed Cromwell at the start of February that unless the commons were soon brought to better obedience, they would lose their lives and goods. He was of the belief that the people had never been so hostile to the nobility.[40]

Examinations of suspected rebels continued into February and carried on until May. Henry was obsessed with bringing Bigod, the architect of the 'new tragedy', to justice. Although Norfolk bravely conceded to the king on 7 February that he could not promise the apprehension of Bigod, he was able to confirm his capture by Sir John Lampley four days later.[41] Lord Lumley's son and heir was examined in the Tower on 8 February by Cromwell and stated that Bigod had argued that the gentry had deceived the commons and that the king should not have cure of souls.[42]

Henry's desire for retribution was unwavering and his instructions became more explicit. Writing to Norfolk on 22 February he ordered that he must administer dreadful execution upon a good number of the inhabitants, hanging them on trees, quartering them and setting their heads and quarters in every town, so as to serve as a fearful warning. He added that Norfolk should tie up the monks, without pity, with no further delay or ceremony.[43]

The attempted use of what Max Weber has described as the state's monopoly of legitimate violence was, of course, not unusual in early modern society and the enforcement of obedience was part of the state's duty. What is interesting to note here, however, is Henry's apparent relish of the task and his graphic descriptions of punishment do lend credence to the perception of him as a blood-thirsty tyrant.[44]

The Duke of Norfolk seemed at pains to emphasise the scale of the Crown's retribution: 'I think the like number hath not be heard to be put to execution at one time.' Tellingly, he advised the king that he had had the vicar of Burgh arrested because he had been a principal maintainer of the Bishop of Rome at the *first* insurrection. However, Norfolk could, by his own admission, get no proof that he consented to the last rebellion.[45] Clearly the pardon had not been binding in this case. The Crown's quest for just punishment involved a degree of subterfuge. Even though Sir Robert Constable had opposed Bigod's rebellion, the Privy Council was still suspicious of him and advised Norfolk to keep a special eye on him. Further, Norfolk was secretly to inform Sir Ralph Ellerker, junior, and Sir Ralph Evers (Eure) of this and order them to secure the ports of Hull and Scarborough to prevent Constable from fleeing.[46]

In the aftermath of the renewed uprisings in the early part of 1537, Lord Hussey was included among those who were under suspicion and interrogated. It can be argued that Hussey's inertia and continuing association with Darcy ultimately led to his downfall. Hussey's servant, Thomas Rycard, was questioned by Sir Brian Hastings on 26 February about alleged comments Hussey had made regarding heresy in Hussey's own garden at Sleaford, Lincolnshire almost two years previously.[47] Once again, Hussey had not been involved in the fresh rebellions. Lord Hussey's role was one of inertia during the risings. His religious qualms have been highlighted and it should perhaps come as no surprise that his wife, Lady Hussey, who had been part of Princess Mary's household at Hunsdon, had been imprisoned in the Tower for a time. This was during the same period as Mary was obstinately refusing to take the Oath of Supremacy.[48] Lady Hussey had been heard to use the title 'Princess' whilst referring to Mary and this was not permitted. The Husseys had conservative and orthodox opinions and old habits die hard – it should be remembered that Hussey was over 70 years of age when the risings began.

Whilst interrogations continued, the fate of the rebels involved in the Lincolnshire Rising of the previous autumn was decided at Lincoln on 6 March. Two lists are given. The first contains those condemned and not executed; the second details the names of thirty-four individuals, including Thomas Moigne and Guy Keym, who were condemned and executed.[49] Sir William Parr (who will be discussed in Chapter 5) confirmed that he had been present at the executions of Moigne and Keym and that thirty-four 'traitors' were condemned in a letter to the king dated 7 March. He stated that he would also attend the subsequent executions at Louth and Horncastle in the following days.[50] Malice and score settling also played their parts in the information forwarded to the regime. One of those condemned at Lincoln who was not executed was Thomas Brumpton of Burton, Lincolnshire. One John Mounson wasted no time in advising Thomas Cromwell the following day that Brumpton had threatened and coerced his neighbours into rebellion and that it was a 'great pity' that he should be pardoned.[51]

It seems from the lines of enquiry being followed by the government that the remit was not strictly to punish those who had violated the pardon: the cases of the vicar of Burgh, Sir Robert Constable and Lord Hussey are testament to this. The momentum for revenge and punishment had been built up and showed no signs of abating, despite any impediments to its implementation. Norfolk advised Cromwell on 8 March that he would sit in justice on the twenty or so rebels at Durham and that none would escape should good evidence be obtained against them. However, the following day, he informed the Lord Privy Seal that Durham was not actually included in his commission, so 'we charged the inquest, *keeping secret our lack of authority*'.[52] The earls of Sussex and Derby were, however, more circumspect. They advised Norfolk that since they had been in Lancashire, they had overseen the executions of the abbot of Whalley and one of his monks,

Sir Richard Eastgate, one of the monks of Sawley, some canons of Cartmell and ten lay persons who lived in the vicinity, who, they stated, had been the principal offenders since the pardon.[53] The details of the ten lay people were not given.

The king sent further instructions to Norfolk on 17 March and specified that he would send for Lord Darcy within a few days, as the duke recommended.[54] Darcy had been an opponent of renewed rebellion, so it can be argued that this instruction was purely a desire to gain revenge on the ageing, conservative nobleman. Norfolk wrote to Cromwell on 22 March and this correspondence highlights the mindset of the regime and points to the direction in which events were heading. He referred to an individual called Boyer as a 'naughty knave', well acquainted with Darcy who would be able to 'tell much'. The friar Dr Pickering would, Norfolk claimed, be able to provide information about the prior of Bridlington and Sir Robert Constable if he was handled with 'fair words'. By adopting this approach, Norfolk was of the opinion that Cromwell would find out whether Lord Darcy or Sir Robert Constable had done anything amiss since the pardon. The duke also stated that Aske was accompanying him on his journey, 'thinking him better with me than at home'. This letter, it can be argued, makes it obvious that Norfolk was duplicitous and was seeking to trap Aske. He advised that the king should lull Aske into a false sense of security by speaking to him as if he had great trust in him. The idea was that Aske might then betray Lord Darcy and Sir Robert Constable by telling all that he knew of them.[55]

At the end of the month, the trial of Dr Mackerell and other Lincolnshire rebels took place. A guilty verdict was returned on all the prisoners and the judgement was the standard for cases of high treason. This basic conceptual distinction, that religion could be treason, was used to legitimate the state's treatment of its Catholic subjects.[56] Their execution was to take place at Tyburn: they were to be hanged, cut down alive, disembowelled and their entrails burned (whilst still alive) and beheaded.[57] Once Catholics, or in this case, those who opposed Henrician religious policy, were identified as 'traitors', they could be treated with 'disgusting violence' and the visual message was that the felon had died a traitor's death, as opposed to a heretic's. The powerful symbolism of the rites of execution was, as Lake and Questier have argued, 'surely intended to operate as a means of ideological control.' Social and ideological energies were released by the rituals on the gallows.

Again, we see evidence of the Weberian idea of the state's use of legitimate violence, and the recurrent theme of the body politic.[58]

In the meantime, the net was closing ever tighter around Lord Darcy. Sir Henry Saville added his poison to the mix in a letter to Cromwell. He recounted that, at the time of the Pilgrimage, the Earl of Shrewsbury had asked Sir Arthur Darcy how many men his father could raise for the king. Sir Arthur had replied that 5,000 could be raised 'if the abbeys might stand'. It was at this point that the Lord Steward (Shrewsbury) began to distrust Lord Darcy.[59] By 7 April, Darcy, along with Constable and Aske, was committed to the Tower for the treasons they had committed since the pardon.[60]

Both Aske and Darcy had been anxious that people return home and not be part of any fresh revolt in January 1537. Darcy expressed his desire that the people keep within the king's pardon and not follow those who assembled with Bigod,[61] but almost immediately there were those who sought to discredit him and sow suspicion. Sir William Fairfax was quick to express his opinion to Cromwell that both Darcy and Sir Richard Tempest were not steadfast, although they soon afterwards began to pretend all they did was with the best of intentions.[62] However, it seems overwhelmingly clear that neither Aske nor Darcy was involved in the outbreak of the renewed revolts and both conducted themselves in a manner displaying complete loyalty to the Crown. Indeed, the king himself expressed his gratitude to them both by letter on 24 January for their 'goodwill' against Bigod's rebellion.[63] It is also clear that, at that time, Aske still had complete faith in the king and his promises and behaved as a dutiful subject.

A number of allegations were made against Darcy, Constable and Aske, and it is obvious that these were framed in such a way as to ensure a guilty verdict. For instance, a letter from Aske to Darcy of 18 January where he asked Darcy to stay the commons until the arrival of the Duke of Norfolk was cited as demonstrating a 'traitor's heart' in that he only desired a stay until Norfolk's arrival. Similarly, Constable and Aske exhibited their 'traitorous hearts' by not having resisted Bigod – this despite the king himself having thanked Aske for his 'goodwill' against Bigod and Constable's clear refusal to join Bigod.[64]

Lord Darcy's words were twisted with one objective in mind – to convict him of treason. The regime seemed at pains to point out that Darcy had offended since the pardon. A letter written by Darcy on 21 January, where he spoke of the Duke of Norfolk's impending arrival in the North and the holding of a parliament, is here portrayed as exposing, yet again, his traitorous heart. He allegedly rejoiced in the parliament, trusting to have his unlawful desires reformed, which was well known to be high treason.[65]

Similarly, Aske was a victim of the clever legal minds who devised the articles against him. He was criticised for his failure to denounce or apprehend Bigod's followers and this evidently made him a traitor. When he returned from his stay with Henry he wrote to the commons assuring them that their reasonable petitions would be ordered by Parliament. So Aske then thought their petitions reasonable, and in writing it, he committed treason.[66] Aske and Constable, like Darcy, were accused of only specifying that the commons should be remain calm until Norfolk's arrival. This was twisted to mean that they would only comply until Norfolk had returned and had the added bonus that if no man should stir, therefore, those who would have served the king could not either.[67]

Included in the articles or items against Darcy, Aske and Constable was an allegation against Archbishop Edward Lee of York. He and the clergy of the North were accused of committing high treason by concluding at Pontefract that the king 'ought not to be supreme head of the church'.[68] Whether Lee genuinely believed this or concurred because of his desire for self-preservation is a moot point. In any event, this quite obviously occurred prior to the December pardon and it may be that fact which saved Lee from being condemned as a traitor, or the fact that the desire for retribution was focused on Darcy, Aske and Constable. Similarly, the Earl of Northumberland was accused of high treason for 'maintaining Aske' by surrendering his castle at Wressle in the East Riding of Yorkshire in November. Cromwell himself had written opposite this item, 'Before the pardon'.[69] It is worth pointing out that the earl had gained the enmity of his brothers by having named the king as his heir. In any event, the earl did not suffer the same fate as Darcy, Aske and Constable.

On 8 April, the king wrote to Norfolk instructing him to seize the goods of Darcy, Constable and Aske, who were committed to ward, and for inventories to be taken so that they might be forthcoming to his use if Lord Darcy, Sir Robert Constable and Robert Aske were not acquitted of the treasons of which they were accused.[70] Clearly there is here a presumption of guilt prior to their trial – guilty until proven innocent.

Aske, Lord Hussey and Darcy were interrogated on 11 April and 106 questions put to them. This extensive set of questions included a number with regard to bishops of the 'New Learning' and they were asked whether they favoured the insurrection in order that those bishops might be punished? They were asked whether they grudged against the king's title of Supreme Head. Darcy was asked why he yielded Pontefract Castle when the rebels had no artillery to besiege it and the king's army was not far off. He was also asked about the badges of the Five Wounds and whether or not they had been newly made or were left over from his time in Spain.[71] Their answers to each specific point are not recorded at this juncture. Hussey, however, stated that he was not privy to the rebels' acts and had not led them.[72]

Aske was examined in the Tower of London on 11 April before Dr Leigh, Dr Petre and the Lieutenant of the Tower. During this examination, Aske maintained that the suppression of the monasteries was the greatest cause of the insurrection. In his own hand, he explained that the suppression meant that the service of God was much diminished: a great number of Masses were left unsaid, the temple of God pulled down and the ornaments and relics of the Church irreverently used.[73] With regard to the Royal Supremacy, Aske stated that all men murmured at it and said it could not stand with God's law and that it would result in England's division from the unity of the Catholic Church.[74] Aske answered the questions with regard to the bishops specified in the list of 106. He stated that the bishops were reputed to be of the new learning and maintainers of Luther and Tyndale's opinions and were noted as such at the time of the Lincolnshire Rising in October. He also said that he did not know the difference between a heretic and a schismatic but could see that they varied from and preached against the old usages and ceremonies of the Church.[75]

It is indisputable that the nature of these questions referred to the original Pilgrimage of Grace and not the post-pardon uprisings. It is thus evident that the so-called pardon counted for nothing and that doubters such as Bigod and Hallam had been correct in their assessment that the pardon was just a ruse. If the pardon was bogus, then so was the promise of a parliament in the North and the Crown's word was meaningless – the regime had revealed its true colours. The king was affronted and vengeful; neither he nor his councillors were to be trusted.

Whilst the interrogations in London were continuing, Norfolk was busy in the North visiting retribution on behalf of the Crown. Sixteen offenders were adjudged at Durham to be hanged in chains near their dwellings.[76] Aske was examined yet again on 15 April,[77] and William Colyns, the bailiff of Kendal, was accused by three individuals in depositions of being true to the rebellious commons.[78] Examinations and confessions continued to ensue and one Ninian Staveley of Massam in Richmondshire confessed to consenting to gather a company to destroy the Duke of Norfolk so that their abbey might stand and Holy Church to be as it was in Henry VII's days.[79]

Percival Cresswell, servant to Lord Hussey, and Nicholas Tempest of Craven were examined in late April.[80] Nicholas Tempest was accused of being an organiser of the first musters and principal architect in the later rebellion and to have procured the late abbot of Sawley to raise the king's people. He and Sir Stephen Hamerton were accused of raising the commons in Lancashire, in Burnley and Whalley against the lords of Derby and Cumberland.[81] It was also alleged that since the pardon, Tempest had maintained the abbot of Sawley in his possession against the king. Similarly, William Wood, the prior of Bridlington was named as a principal protagonist in the first insurrection and of being heavily involved in the second. He and Dr John Pickering had allegedly rejoiced at the insurrections and Dr Pickering had composed a rhyme of treasons.[82]

Dr Pickering's depositions included the names of the 'learned men' who attended Pontefract and he maintained that Aske had said that the Bishop of Rome was head of the Church of England and that he was prepared to die in the quarrel. He stated that apart from a friar of Knaresborough, he did not know any religious men involved in the rebellion and blamed Aske, Darcy and Constable. Pickering said that when he was at Pontefract, he did not think that the king could be head of the Church but had since changed his mind and confessed this on oath before Norfolk. He did, however, confess to composing the rhyme 'O faithful people'.[83]

Meanwhile, more 'evidence' was being gathered against Darcy. Mr Magnus, having returned from making an inventory of Darcy's goods, informed Norfolk that he had discovered a book, which, though written 'long ago', showed that Darcy had long been dissatisfied with the governance of the king's affairs.[84] Soon after this discovery, one Marmaduke Waldby alleged that Constable, Aske and Darcy had wanted him to send a message to Flanders to Charles V's sister, requesting money, arms and horsemen. Further, he alleged, a message was to be sent to the pope to have absolution for all offences. Waldby said he went to Hull, but whilst there, 'Darcy sent word that he should tarry, and not go'.[85]

Other depositions were obtained in late April prior to the prosecutions. Sir John Bulmer confessed that at the time of Bigod's uprising, he sent Robert Hugill to the vicar of Kirkby to inquire if the commons would rise again. His 'wife', Margaret Cheny, was accused of having enticed Sir John to raise the commons again. Sir Francis Bigod confessed to having sent Hallam to Hull and to his own attempt to take Scarborough. He reiterated the defaults in the pardon and said that he had made an oration to the people declaring the faults in it. George Lumley admitted that he had met Bigod, heard his oration and raised the countryside with the aim of taking Scarborough Castle, entering Scarborough with 600–700 men. Sir Thomas Percy confessed to having received a letter from Bigod, which asked that he raise Northumberland and to having, since the pardon, received a supplication from the abbot of Sawley 'concerning the saving of that house'.[86]

Further allegations were made against Darcy. Sir Henry Saville reported him for having said, at the time of the Lincolnshire rebellion, 'Ah! They are up in Lincolnshire. God speed them well! I would they had done thus three years past; for the world should have been better than it is'.[87] James Cockerell, the quondam prior of Gisburn, confessed that he had read Bigod's book against the title of Supreme Head but denied the allegation that he had commended it, whilst the prior of Malton, William Todd, admitted to having shown Bigod a prophecy that the king should be forced to flee the realm.[88] Prior to the prosecutions of Aske, Darcy and the others accused, Norfolk remained busy in the North and reassured Cromwell that all in Yorkshire had been 'hung in chains'. He denied displaying any compassion by allowing those hanged in Westmorland and Cumberland to be taken down and buried.[89]

A few days before the trial, John Husee wrote to Lord Lisle in Calais of the forthcoming proceedings and of Darcy, Hussey and the other northern men in the Tower. He was of the opinion that there was only one outcome possible and wished that God would have mercy upon them and 'send them grace to repent'.[90] On 15 May 1537, twenty people were tried as 'false traitors' who had conspired to 'deprive the king of his title of Supreme Head of the English Church'. These included Darcy, Aske, Constable, Bigod, Sir Thomas Percy, Sir John Bulmer, Lord Hussey of Sleaford and the friars discussed previously. They had been participants in a number of insurrections and had 'traitorously assembled to levy war' at Doncaster on 20 October 1536.[91] Both Darcy and Hussey were tried by their peers and pleaded not guilty but were convicted by a unanimous verdict. The judgement was specified as being the standard in cases of high treason and their executions were to take place at Tyburn.[92]

Aske wrote to the king on 16 May and asked for forgiveness and requested that Henry would make restitution for his debts.[93] Constable wrote to his son, Sir Marmaduke, in an attempt to ask the queen to intercede with the king to secure his pardon and said that he would spend the rest of his life lamenting his offences. He stated that what they did was 'for lak of furnyture and fear of owr lyves. Yet we dyd good service at Doncaster … Bygod was clerly stayd by me.'[94] The plea for his life was futile. Constable, Bigod and Aske pleaded not guilty, whilst Percy, Sir John Bulmer, Margaret Cheny and Sir Stephen Hamerton pleaded guilty. Constable, Aske, Lumley and Bigod were found guilty and ordered to be executed at Tyburn along with John Bulmer, Hamerton, Nicholas Tempest and the four abbots, one canon and one priest. Margaret Cheny was to be drawn to Smithfield and burned.[95]

About this time, Pole remarked that Henry was very insolent after his success in subduing the realm and that his cruelty increased with his success.[96] Norfolk, however, wrote to Cromwell that the two lords (Darcy and Hussey) and Constable 'will be little regretted'.[97]

At the end of May, Darcy and Hussey were still in the Tower, awaiting their fate. On 24 June, the king wrote to Sir William Parr to advise that he was sending Constable and Aske 'to be executed in Yorkshire where they committed their treasons'.[98] Three days later, in a letter to Suffolk, Henry offered an insight into his mindset and was even more specific. He had determined to have Constable, who held Hull during the rebellion, hanged in chains there and also to have Robert Aske, 'the grand worker of that insurrection, hanged at York where he was in his greatest and most frantic glory'.[99] He also confirmed that he was sending Lord Hussey 'to be beheaded in our city of Lincoln'.

By 8 July, Cromwell could confirm all the punishments – the traitors had been executed, Lord Darcy at Tower Hill and Lord Hussey at Lincoln, Aske hanged upon York Castle, Sir Robert Constable hanged at Hull and the rest at Tyburn, 'so that all the cankered hearts are weeded away'.[100] Once again, the body politic imagery and preoccupation with social pathology is apparent.

The post-pardon uprisings did indeed, in the king's own words, constitute a 'new tragedy'.[101] The king's retribution appeared to be complete and the realm was, on the face of it, tranquil and obedient. In all, 178 people had lost their lives as a result of the Lincolnshire Rising, the Pilgrimage of Grace and the 'new tragedy' of the aftermath. Of these, seventy-four were the victims of Norfolk's declaration of martial law. These people were victims of what Elton has conceded was the king's 'ferocious personality' and 'self-righteous and vindictive temperament'.[102]

It is clear, having looked at the evidence and sequence of events, that the December pardon was, in fact, meaningless and must be regarded as a ploy to delay the Pilgrims' momentum and allow the regime to regroup and plan its strategy for retribution. That Darcy, Constable and Aske had played no part in the resumption of the revolts was obviously irrelevant as far as the Crown was concerned. Similarly, there was no proof that Sir Thomas Percy had instigated or agreed to the new uprisings. According to Hoyle, Percy 'was clearly a marked man, if only because of his charisma and popularity with the commons'.[103] It is also worth highlighting that legal process was not strictly adhered to. One only has to look at Norfolk's admission of his defective commission in Durham to realise this. The king and the regime seized the opportunity which the Post-pardon Revolts presented and capitalised on it. Momentum for revenge was built up and the main movers in the Pilgrimage were going to pay, irrespective of their conduct in early 1537. Bigod and Lumley were undeniably guilty of raising a new insurrection, but the majority were not.

The thirst for scapegoats and retribution did not end with the victims already discussed. The king's desire for vengeance appeared to take on a life of its own. It was not enough that some individuals who had not violated the pardon had been punished. The desire for retribution even reached the king's own servant, who was, demonstrably, not a Pilgrim – Lancaster Herald. The herald, named Thomas Myller, was dispatched on a mission to Aske and Darcy at Pontefract on 21 October 1536 and described Robert Aske as having a proud countenance and behaving like a tyrant. He also told how Aske had prevented him from reading his proclamation at the

Market Cross in Pontefract. However, in the summer of 1538, a number of articles were drawn up against Thomas Myller, 'otherwise called Lancaster Herald of Arms'. The herald was accused of having encouraged the rebels at Pontefract on 20 October by kneeling before Robert Aske. He had promised the rebels that the Lord Privy Seal would be delivered to them and, in addition, his lies had resulted in false and detestable rumours against Cromwell. He had shown the king's counsels to the rebels and had told them that their other demands would be granted. Myller had discouraged the king's army at Doncaster by exaggerating the numbers of rebels and stating that 10,000 of them had horses. In addition, it was alleged that he had referred to the Northern Rising as a marvel and implied that God had helped the rebels.[104]

Myller then wrote to Cromwell, praising him for his charitable goodness and stating that the allegations made against him were false and made out of malice by Somerset Herald. Myller stated that he trusted that Cromwell would 'take pains' to ensure an indifferent trial in the matter.[105] On 2 August 1538, Christopher Jenney wrote to Cromwell from York and advised that Lancaster Herald had been arraigned. He informed the Lord Privy Seal that the evidence against Lancaster was handled by Mr Clarencieux and his fellows honestly and not of malice, and, although Lancaster had alleged the contrary, he was unable to prove it. As a form of perverse retribution, Jenney appears to have relished informing Cromwell that he had arranged for the herald's head to be 'set up' next to Robert Aske's body.[106]

On 6 August the Council of the North confirmed the assizes held at York against Lancaster Herald. On 20 August, the acting president of the Council of the North, the Bishop of Llandaff, wrote to Cromwell advising him of the outcome of the assizes held at York between 22 July and 17 August. He informed the Lord Privy Seal that eighteen people had been put to death, three on the charge of treason. One of these was the unfortunate Lancaster Herald.[107] This outcome was reiterated in a letter to the king two days later from the Council of the North. The assizes at York Castle were attended by the justices along with Lords Scrope and Latimer, both of whom had been in attendance at the Pilgrims' Council at York on 21 November.[108]

It seems, then, that the Post-pardon Revolts can be attributed to the perception of the Pilgrims that King Henry had been duplicitous in granting the pardon and promising a parliament in the North. It also appears that this perception must have been latent at the time of Lancaster Herald's promises in December. After all, it was just over a month before the simmering distrust manifested itself in the North, and, allowing for the Christmas holidays, this was insufficient time for the Crown to have 'addressed' any of the issues in the Pontefract Articles, nor to have made plans to convene a parliament in the North.

The distrust which existed between the Pilgrim rank and file and the gentlemen in the movement was ably exploited by the king. Firstly, Ellerker and Bowes had attended Court and this must have caused suspicion among the Pilgrims – being, as they were, so far removed from the centre of the action. Secondly, Aske's stay at Court for the festivities must have left a sour taste in the mouth of those who had lauded him as their great captain and hero. This was undoubtedly exacerbated by the length of his stay, and Marmaduke Constable had advised Aske that his return was to be welcomed, as there had been murmurings of suspicion and discontent.[109]

When Bigod and Hallam expressed their misgivings about the king's motives and actions, some Pilgrims were only too ready to concur and were roused into action and renewed revolts. The king was undoubtedly duplicitous: he had played the Pilgrims false to stop the momentum of the rising and seize an opportunity to regroup and plan a strategy for their ultimate defeat and his own retribution. This is precisely what happened. A parliament in the North was never convened. Indeed, Henry did not even visit the North until five years later. The Pilgrim leadership suffered retribution for their temerity and deep affront to this most vainglorious monarch's honour.

The victims were vanquished. What, then, of the victors, those who had remained loyal to the Crown? What was their reward for their compliance and service at such a pivotal stage in the reign? Those who had been steadfastly loyal to Henry throughout the crisis will be examined in due course, but before discussing these individuals and the issue of reward, attention must be given to the impact the events had upon the society, religiosity and power structures in the region.

An examination of those individuals who became reconciled to the Crown, such as Ralph Ellerker and Robert Bowes, will be undertaken in an attempt to analyse how they managed successfully to rehabilitate themselves from Pilgrims in the original uprising, to loyal servants of the king in the aftermath. What was their motivation and that of others such as Sir Thomas

Tempest, Sir Christopher Danby, Sir William Babthorpe and William Stapleton? How did these renegades manage their successful rehabilitation and how were they rewarded? What were the implications for their families? Why was such a disingenuous and vengeful monarch prepared to forgive and forget in these cases? And what were the benefits to the Crown? These issues will be explored in the following chapter.

4

Rehabilitated Rebels and Reward

'This Grace is disposed to give gifts and rewards to his true servants',[1] wrote a Halifax priest, Robert Holdsworth, in May 1537 after having described the execution of some of the rebels and the incarceration of others in the Tower. The Pilgrimage of Grace and its aftermath in the North can be used as a snapshot to illuminate and explore issues of reward and patronage and the role they played in securing compliance with Henrician religious policy. Reward is not examined in isolation and is interlinked with the regime's policy of retribution; a carrot and stick approach aimed at achieving cohesion, obedience and uniformity.

The role played by Thomas Cromwell in implementing Crown policy is widely recognised and has been discussed by Geoffrey Elton in detail.[2] However, Richard Rex has identified a need for Cromwell's specifically ecclesiastical patronage also to be surveyed[3] and David Loades has acknowledged that Cromwell's success depended upon a network of local patronage and that this in turn brought about a slow transformation in northern politics.[4] Patronage will be discussed in more detail in the following chapter and it should be noted at the outset that there are inherent difficulties in attempting a study of patronage. As Sharon Kettering has pointed out, such studies can appear to be a 'bewildering heap of examples, piled one upon the other'.[5]

The requests for confiscated lands addressed to Cromwell began during the Pilgrimage and continued thereafter. But before examining Cromwell's relationship with some of the individuals loyal to the Crown during the rebellion and the successful rehabilitation of others, in particular, Ralph Ellerker and Robert Bowes, it is necessary to set the scene by highlighting the tone of requests forwarded to the Lord Privy Seal.

In October 1536, one Anthony Curteys was named as a great offender in the Lincolnshire Rising and was recorded as having been given bail, but his name was then crossed out. On 18 November, the Duke of Suffolk requested that Cromwell give Curteys' lands to his kinsman and George Harper, but two days later, in a letter to the king, he described Curteys as a kinsman of Robert Aske who had offered to go and kill him![6] It would seem reasonable to deduce that Curteys had been implicated in the Lincolnshire Rising and had subsequently been able to preserve both his life and lands by turning against his kinsman, Aske. Thomas Hattecliffe displayed a similar opportunism to Suffolk on 18 November when he informed Cromwell about one Lionel Rathby of Lincolnshire. He requested that if Rathby were to be attainted, he should have his lands and goods as a 'rewourde'.[7]

The opportunism characteristic of Suffolk and Hattecliffe was by no means unusual nor confined to the Lincolnshire situation. Sir Ralph Eure (also known as Evers) was very quick off the mark on 11 February 1537 – after Bigod's capture by Sir John Lampley – when he wrote to Cromwell and told him that he wanted Sir Francis Bigod's lands. He desired to have the lordships of Setterington and Bursdal.[8] Similarly, Sir Ralph Ellerker (whose career will be discussed further below) wrote to Cromwell the following day, stating that the bearer, John Fowberry, had been the first to inform of Hallam's traitorous intentions at Hull. Ellerker was of the opinion that Cromwell should help Fowberry, perhaps by granting him a farm of Hallam's at Watton and other land worth 5 marks.[9]

The executions of high-profile Pilgrims such as Lord Darcy, Lord Hussey, Robert Aske, Robert Constable, Francis Bigod and John Hallam have been discussed, but a brief exploration of the reprisals taken against some other members of the gentry and nobility and an identification of the impact this had upon their heirs is necessary. An exploration and analysis of the rehabilitation of other individuals and the benefits they gained will then follow.

Sarah Bastow has made the point that the involvement of Sir Christopher Danby, Sir William Stapleton and Nicholas Fairfax indicates a strategy of involving second sons in the Pilgrimage, thereby safeguarding the families' land and inheritance.[10] However, this contention would suggest a premeditated plan to protect wealth. Older sons were obviously vulnerable because they were heirs to the family estates and wealth. Bastow's hypothesis does not take into account the involvement of Lords Darcy, Hussey, Lumley and Sir John Bulmer. The Pilgrimage was not pre-planned and such tactics were clearly not uniform among the nobility and gentry.

Bastow also contends that there was a Tudor tactic of ensuring financial ruin and exclusion from office for the entire family following disobedience and that this was a deterrent to the gentry. This, as we shall see, was demonstrably not the case. The reconciliation of Ellerker, Bowes, Stapleton, Danby and Fairfax proves otherwise: it is apparent, as shall be discussed in the next chapter, that Sir Arthur and Sir George Darcy went on to prosper, despite their father's execution for treason. The Crown could simply not afford a complete 'harrowing' of the northern gentry, however much the king thirsted for retribution. The region was not as attractive a proposition for the ambitious, qualified gentleman as the South and suitably qualified candidates, possessed of local knowledge and experience, were, relatively speaking, in shorter supply. Bastow is correct, though, in that the Danbys, Fairfaxes and Stapletons were to form a core of Catholic gentle families in the area.

Whilst Hussey was being interrogated for his participation in the Pilgrimage, Lord William Grey wrote to Cromwell, requesting his lands (11 April 1537). Here again is clear evidence of the link between retribution and opportunism: the request was based upon a presumption of guilt. Hussey was indeed executed and his estates were seized for the Crown. He had made his will on 22 October 1535. It mentioned his wife, Lady Anne, his sons, Sir William, Thomas, Gilbert and Sir Giles Huse, and his brothers, Sir William and Sir Robert. Hussey had many manors, lands and tenements in Lincolnshire, including Grantham and Old Sleaford.[11] His forfeited lands were worth approximately £5,000 a year and although Hussey's eldest son, Sir William Hussey (d. 1556), did not gain his inheritance, he was restored in blood by statute of 3 Edward VI, and his other sons and daughters by a further statute of 5 Elizabeth I.[12] The restoration in blood was vitally important to peers (e.g. lords and barons) who claimed themselves 'ennobled in blood', meaning peerage could only be removed three ways: by an Act of Parliament; on the death of all heirs to it; or on forfeiture for treason or felony. Of some irony is the fact that one of Lord Hussey's daughters, Bridget, married Sir Richard Morison (d. 1556) of Cassiobury – Henry and Cromwell's chief propagandist, whose works will be discussed in more detail in Chapter 6. This is an example of political calculation and strategy: the forging of a dynastic alliance that was mutually beneficial. Lord Hussey's noble birth enhanced Morison's status and gave him the standing he quite obviously craved. At the same time, such an alliance had the advantage of banishing any lingering doubts about the Hussey family.

John, 5th Baron Lumley became involved in the Pilgrimage of Grace and although, like many others, he claimed to have been coerced, his Catholicism was probably a motivating factor. Although he was involved with the rebels in the initial stages, he came to terms with Crown policy and was one of the negotiators at Doncaster between 2 and 4 December 1536. He suffered declining health in his later years and avoided further trouble until his death in 1545. However, he had had to look on as his son and heir, George, became embroiled in the resumption of revolts in early 1537. George said in his deposition that he had heard Francis Bigod's oration and was commanded to go and take Scarborough Castle, mustering men as he went.

Lumley was to meet a traitor's death at Tyburn on 2 June 1537.[13] Lord Lumley's estates were eventually settled upon his grandson, John Lumley, 1st Baron Lumley (*c.* 1533–1609), a committed Catholic and the son and heir of George. John became involved in the intrigues of Mary, Queen of Scots and the Ridolfi plot and was imprisoned for over a year from 1571. He eventually died in 1609 and was buried at night – probably with Catholic rites.[14] It is interesting to observe that the Lumleys obviously retained Catholic sympathies from the time of the Pilgrimage until at least 1609 – some seventy-three years later.

Sir John Bulmer was executed at Tyburn by 8 July 1537. Bulmer was obviously a gentry rebel leader and it is illuminating that both Sir Robert Bowes and Sir Thomas Tempest, his former fellow rebels, escorted him (among others) to London for interrogation. By May, Bowes and Tempest were appointed to a special commission at York to indict rebels including Darcy,

Aske and Robert Constable. This was, as Christine Newman has argued, the government's way of achieving the 'ultimate show of loyalty from reconciled rebels' – forcing them to condemn their fellow conspirators.[15] Sir John's son, Ralph, was his heir and remained loyal to the Crown until his death in 1558.[16]

Sir Stephen Hamerton and Nicholas Tempest were found guilty of having been involved in the renewed revolts in 1537. As such, both were guilty of treason. They thus met their fate and were executed at Tyburn on 8 July 1537.[17] Nicholas Tempest (younger brother of Sir Thomas) had a son called Richard, according to *The Visitation of Yorkshire in the Years 1563 and 1564*, and an Elizabethan hand confirms that Nicholas was attainted with Sir Stephen Handlon in 1537. Sir Stephen Hamerton, son and heir of John Hamerton, was married to a daughter of Ralph Bigod but no issue is recorded. He was survived by his brother, Richard, who was in turn succeeded by his son, John.[18]

The link between retribution and reward needs to be examined and it will be revealed how former Pilgrims demonstrated their loyalty by prosecuting their erstwhile allies. The poachers had effectively turned gamekeepers. Firstly, the careers of two men who had been prominent figures in the Pilgrimage of Grace, sworn by the rebels and the bearers of their petitions to the king, Sir Ralph Ellerker and Sir Robert Bowes, will be considered. Both managed successfully to rehabilitate themselves and consequently furthered their careers and finances. How did they achieve this?

On the same day that a general pardon was issued to Lord Darcy (18 January 1537), Robert Aske advised the king that the commons were 'wildly' disposed to new commotions and that Francis Bigod was assembling and swearing the commons, although he had not yet taken Scarborough Castle. The following day saw Sir Ralph Ellerker advising Henry that he hoped to meet with Bigod that day. However, Ellerker had to inform Henry on 20 January that he could not confirm what had happened to Bigod or Lumley, but he had sent out spies.[19] By 23 January, Ellerker was one of the examiners into Hallam's rebellion at Hull, and Henry was expressing his gratitude to both him and his father for their conduct in the pursuit of Bigod a couple of days later.[20]

It is quite remarkable that this erstwhile Pilgrim should have been endeavouring to establish the whereabouts of Bigod approximately six weeks after the December pardon. Ellerker's transformation was so rapid and complete that he was able to deploy spies in the hunt to apprehend Bigod and Lumley in the service of the Crown. To underline his new-found loyalty and commitment to Henry, he was playing the role of examiner into Hallam's conduct before the first month of 1537 was even out.

Following the collapse of Bigod and Hallam's renewed revolts in the New Year, Norfolk was able to restore order and peace in the North. Trials were held and guilty verdicts were reached in the cases of the Lincolnshire rebels. However, an interesting trial at the end of March sheds some light on the interlinked themes of retribution and reward. Witnesses were examined in relation to Bigod and Hallam's ventures and one witness, William Levenyng, was brought to trial. It is recorded that some of the jury thought the accused guilty of felony upon the evidence given at the bar by Sir Ralph Ellerker, but seven others held to the contrary and stated that Ellerker had given evidence out of malice because the king had given him part of Levenyng's lands.[21] The result was that Levenyng was acquitted. But it is interesting to note the perception of the jurors as to what Ellerker's motivation was and also to consider the fact that Henry appears to have deprived Levenyng of some of his lands based upon a presumption of guilt.

By mid-May, Ellerker was firmly established on the road to rehabilitation and presented himself in the guise of trusty, loyal servant to the king. He was one of a small number of men appointed to the Yorkshire Commission for the trial of Lords Darcy and Hussey 'to take in the counties of York, city of York, and town of Kingston upon Hull indictments of all treasons ... lately committed'.[22] Cromwell recorded that Ellerker had informed him that he had discharged the garrison at Hull and that he had incurred £68 3s 3d in unpaid expenses. Ellerker sought to gain Strangwich for his brother, who had served without wages, and requested a letter for the stewardship of Watton, previously held by Sir Robert Constable.[23] Ellerker was clearly looking to be reimbursed for his expenses at the garrison in Hull but he also took the opportunity of obtaining favour for his brother, Thomas. The specification of Robert Constable's lands also illustrates the link between retribution and reward.

By early June, Ellerker was hard at work on his commission in Yorkshire. He was sent by the Duke of Norfolk (also on the commission) to arrest one Thomas Strangewyge, who had been Lord Darcy's steward.

Norfolk confirmed this in a letter to Cromwell and also stated that he had asked Ellerker to search for writings concerning the king. Ellerker had apparently found such writings and had forwarded them to Cromwell. Ellerker's diligence and attention to detail were soon to be rewarded for, within a couple of weeks, Norfolk had recommended him to the king for a position on the Council of the North. This recommendation was reiterated in a letter to Cromwell with the additional suggestion that Ellerker receive a pension of £40.[24]

In July, Ellerker was appointed to assist Sir William Eure, Deputy Warden of the East and Middle Marches, and was granted a fee of £20 per annum. Norfolk was still championing Ellerker's cause when he wrote to Cromwell from Sheriff Hutton with regard to Sir Thomas Tempest. He also mentioned Sir Ralph Ellerker and Robert Bowes who, he said, were short of money when it was advisable that they be rewarded and encouraged for diligent and careful service. Ellerker was confirmed as a member of the Council of the North with a fee of 100 marks per year, and we see him performing his duties in October at York Castle when, together with John Uvedale, he examined one John Petenson for sedition, with the result that Petenson was indicted and subsequently executed for treason.[25]

This newly re-constituted Council of the North covered the five northern counties of Yorkshire, Durham, Northumberland, Cumberland and Westmorland. It exercised executive authority and was the Supreme Court of Justice north of the Trent. The council was to investigate the grounds for the insurrection and its ringleaders and 'to make every effort to secure the ringleaders or captains, if these had committed any offence since the pardon'. The Bishop of Llandaff became lord president of the council and was required to summon the council for four general sessions a year for the administration of justice. The maintenance of order, good governance and the implementation of the king's religious, social and economic policies were what Henry required of the council. The Privy Council forwarded directions for the apprehension and examination of suspected criminals and all royal proclamations were made through the Council of the North.[26]

The very fact that Ralph Ellerker was a prominent member of such a body within a year of his being sworn by the rebel Pilgrims is a telling indication of just how speedily and effectively his rehabilitation had been achieved. Ellerker was demonstrably diligent in the pursuit of his duties on the Council of the North. In December 1537, he was present at York when charges were made against the Vicar of Mustone, Sir John Dobson, including the charge that he had not prayed for the king for over a year.[27] The following spring, Ellerker examined suspects accused of anti-regime sedition, including Mabel Brigge who, together with the Vicar of Mustone and another priest, John Ainsworth, was found guilty of treason on 7 April and subsequently executed.[28] Ellerker was also busy throughout this period surveying castles in the region, including Pickering and Scarborough castles.[29]

He received further reward in June when he was appointed chief steward of the king's possessions in Lincolnshire and Yorkshire, which came about because of the attainder of Sir Robert Constable with a fee of £5 a year. Thus Ellerker's request for recompense was granted. Sir William Eure and Lord Clifford were also appointed as chief stewards of the possessions of the abbot of Jervaulx and Sir Stephen Hamerton respectively, which had been forfeited by attainder. The link between retribution and reward is clearly highlighted here.

The following month, Ellerker and his brother, Thomas, were appointed as Justices of the Peace for Yorkshire. Here is clear evidence of Ellerker's success as a broker. Ellerker was a busy man and was entrusted with further responsibility, together with Robert Bowes, when given a commission in October to hold an Inquisition Post Mortem on the possessions of Walter Calvery, and was in attendance at Carlisle in December to keep the sessions.[30]

In 1539, he succeeded his father, Sir Ralph senior, as head of the family on the latter's death. In August, Ralph remained the steward of Sir Robert Constable's lands, with a fee of £5 and also had a fee of £56 13s 4d per annum as a member of the Council of the North. On 2 June 1540, Ellerker was granted the house and site of the late priory of Haltamprice, Yorkshire, with various lands in both Haltamprice and Cotingham.[31] A Pilgrim who had appeared, ostensibly at least, to be concerned with the role of the monasteries was now the beneficiary of the demise of such an institution.

In September 1541, together with Robert Bowes, he was entrusted with the task of surveying the borders and estimating the expense of fortification against future Scottish raids. The king wrote of his approval of their proceedings in October. Ellerker was granted the house, lands, buildings and church of the Grey Friars in Beverley, Yorkshire, the following April. August 1542 saw Ellerker appointed Marshall of Calais and he was involved in the siege of Boulogne between July and September 1544. He was subsequently made Marshall of Boulogne after its capture. In March 1545, Sir Ralph was given a grant of Grange Farm in Beeford, Yorkshire.[32]

Ellerker died whilst on service abroad, following a French ambush on 26 April 1546. The Earl of Hertford (Queen Jane Seymour's brother) reported that a witness saw him lying dead on the sands after being wounded through the stomach.[33] He was succeeded by his son, yet another Ralph.[34] Sir Ralph Ellerker made his will in June 1545 and although the preamble is traditional in form, it is interesting to note that there are no provisions made for Masses for his soul.[35] The Inquisition Post Mortem which survives was taken in 1547.[36] Sir Ralph's successor, his son Ralph, only outlived his father by four years.

In the space of a decade, Ellerker had managed the transition from prominent rebel to trusted and loyal servant of the Crown. He was able to rapidly rehabilitate himself; he became a member of the Council of the North and featured in the prosecutions of his former Pilgrim adherents. It is difficult to assess the ramifications for his successors, as his son and heir only lived for a further four years.

Ellerker's career is intertwined with that of his companion and reformed Pilgrim, Robert Bowes. Bowes' service to the Crown began with his appointment to the Duke of Richmond's council in 1525 but he surrendered Barnard Castle to the Pilgrims without resistance and delivered the rebels' petitions to the king.[37] Bowes had something in common with Sir Francis Bigod, in so far as his motives are something of an enigma to historians.[38] As Bowes had Cardinal Wolsey to thank for his promotion to the higher echelons of northern administration, it may have been that he was not overly enamoured of Thomas Cromwell. By 1536, Bowes, like many of the northern gentry, had cause for dissatisfaction with the Crown's policies, but perhaps it was the passage of the Second Succession Act, with the provision that the Crown could be bequeathed by will, which was of paramount importance to Bowes, given his legal training.[39]

It is highly unlikely that, in Bowes' case, the cause of religion was the catalyst for his initial rebellious stance. Bowes had studied at the Inns of Court and the Protestant inclinations of the Inns influenced the religious thinking of many figures of the English Reformation, including Thomas Cromwell. By the time the Pilgrimage broke out, it is arguable that Bowes' paramount concern was the fear of a Scottish succession as opposed to the king's religious innovations. Indeed, Newman argues that by the time of the uprisings, Bowes may well have held Reformist views which were subsequently to 'fuel the Streatlam family's remarkable attachment to Protestantism, in an age when much of northern society remained notoriously conservative in religion'.[40]

As will be seen in due course, Bowes initially supported the plot to put the Protestant Lady Jane Grey on the throne in 1553 and his niece actually married the Scottish reformer John Knox.[41] At any rate, Bowes' stance as a rebel was relatively short-lived and his visit to Court with Ellerker appears to have been a decisive turning point. The pragmatic Bowes appears to have been motivated by his own survival and the prospect of political advancement in the North. As Newman has put it, 'the Pilgrimage proved to be the movement which propelled Bowes firmly into the political limelight and served to determine the course of his subsequent career'.[42]

As with Ellerker, we soon witness Bowes portraying himself as a loyal and trustworthy servant and playing the role of peacemaker. In the aftermath of Bigod and Hallam's futile risings, Ralph Sadler wrote of Bowes' conduct in a letter to Cromwell on 28 January 1537. Bowes, he advised, was based at Durham but went about the countryside to ensure its quietness. Revealingly, he was of the opinion that if Bowes and the other gentlemen had behaved in this manner at the start, an insurrection would not have occurred.[43] Sadler's comments, however, could be construed as a back-handed compliment and perhaps left room for lingering doubt as to Bowes' integrity.

John Dakyn, the rector of Kirkby Ravensworth, went some way to casting doubt with regard to Bowes' conduct in a statement made in March. Dakyn was examined with regard to the formulation of the Pontefract Articles and stated that Mr Robert Bowes was the most influential.[44] Notwithstanding this, by the end of April, Cromwell was disposed to include Bowes in a list of individuals to be remembered for their service, and in May Bowes, together with Ellerker and others, was given a special commission to examine all indictments of treasons in the county of York, the City of York and Kingston upon Hull. This was followed by Norfolk recommending Bowes for a position on the Council of the North in a letter to the king. Again, Norfolk reiterated this suggestion to Cromwell with a suggestion that Bowes receive a pension of £20.[45]

Norfolk was mindful of Bowes and Ellerker's importance in securing the peaceful governance of the North and desired Cromwell to be a good lord to them, as they should be recompensed in order that they be encouraged to 'take pains'. Norfolk continued to value Bowes' ability and this was evident a few months later when he advised Cromwell that he was sending up the bearer, Robert Bowes, as he promised the king. He requested that Cromwell dispatch him in time to arrive the following Monday night, as on Tuesday, Norfolk would have matters of importance requiring his help. Bowes' membership of the Council of the North was confirmed and his fee is recorded as being 100 marks per annum (the same as Ellerker's). He was subsequently appointed as a Justice of the Peace for Yorkshire in November.[46]

Bowes set about discharging his duties and he was part of a panel which examined Sir William Bulmer (brother of John Bulmer, previously executed) in March 1538. He was also among those who found the unfortunate Mabel Brigge, John Dobson and John Ainsworth guilty of treason. Bowes requested a place for his nephew, George Bowes, in the king's service in November 1538 – here we see an example of him seeking patronage for another – and by early December, Robert was busy, engaged in the sessions at Carlisle. He was also involved in the apprehension of three Scots who had been found in possession of a 'suspicious' letter in March 1539. Bowes was returned as a Knight of the Shire in 1539; he was subsequently returned in 1542, 1545 (for Newcastle), 1547 (for Westmorland) and 1553 (for Middlesex). Bowes was granted an annuity of £100 in March 1544.[47]

Bowes was appointed Warden of the Middle Marches in March 1545, following the death of Sir Ralph Eure (Evers), and a number of letters from him to both the Privy Council and King Henry from this period survive.[48] Following the death of Sir Cuthbert Ratclif, Constable of Alnwick Castle and steward of the king's lands in Northumberland, Hertford, Tunstall and Sadler petitioned the king on Bowes' behalf, stating that he did not have any patrimony in the locality. Approximately a week later, the Privy Council confirmed that Bowes should be appointed to all Ratclif's offices.

In December, Bowes received a payment from the king of £25. Despite this, Bowes was still bemoaning his poverty to the council the following May and requesting that his very small living be increased. To justify his claim he stated that all on the Borders agreed that no Borderer had achieved so many great adventures for the king's honour. By showing him favour the council would be doing a good deed and encouraging those who earnestly served there. Here, Bowes reveals that he was acutely aware of the fact that loyalty should be rewarded. In January 1547, the month of King Henry's death, Bowes was granted a further £50 annuity out of the manor of Bothall, Northumberland, together with various lands and the wardship of Robert, Lord Ogle in Northumberland.[49] It is indicative of his advancement and standing in the locality that he was given the wardship of a peer: there were nobles in the area who would most probably have expected to undertake this role.

Bowes was obviously well acquainted with frontier society, and after the accession of Edward VI he became Warden of the East March in April 1548. However, he appears not to have acted in this role after 1551, the same year as he compiled a more comprehensive survey of the Borders. Bowes concluded that the 'whole countrey' of Northumberland was 'much given to wildnes'.[50] He was, however, appointed as one of the commissioners who negotiated a Treaty of Peace with Scotland in 1551,[51] and was made a Privy Councillor, residing in London in the autumn of that year. Bowes had been trained as a lawyer and was subsequently appointed to the position of Master of the Rolls in 1552.[52]

In 1553, Bowes was a member of the council and signed the letters patent to facilitate King Edward's 'device' bypassing Mary and Elizabeth, with the objective of allowing Lady Jane Grey to succeed to the throne. Bowes' family, by this stage, had become closely associated with John Knox so his actions were, it could be construed, both religiously and politically motivated. However, it appears that when he realised which way the wind was blowing during the crisis which ensued in July, he signed the council's order for the Duke of Northumberland to disarm. However, he was obviously compromised and could not initially remain in office, although he received a general pardon in October. The queen still required his expertise in Anglo-Scottish affairs and as such, Bowes soon regained the favour of Queen Mary and on 27 April 1554, he received a present of £100 from her, and was then sent north and was active in Berwick, surveying the town's defences and organising musters. He died there on 28 February 1555 whilst reviewing the garrison defences.[53]

Bowes' children had all died in childhood and his heirs were the three daughters of his nephew, George Bowes. Unfortunately, a copy of his will has not been located but his inventory describes his possessions, which included a gold chain valued at £109 17s.[54] His wealth was valued at £188 2s 4d,[55] hence he was a wealthy country gentleman.

As Newman has argued, Bowes benefited from the administrative predicament in which the government found itself in relation to the North – as a penitent ex-rebel he was only too eager to display his loyalty to the Crown.[56] Like Ellerker, Bowes had managed a totally successful rehabilitation. In his case, the evidence suggests that, although pragmatic, he probably had Protestant leanings: his niece's marriage to John Knox illustrates the Reformist tendencies of some of the family. His initial rebellious stance may well have been due to his legal concerns with regard to the succession and a distrust and distaste for Cromwell's growing influence. A man of such legal and administrative competence was just the sort of individual the Crown required for the efficient government of the North. This former Pilgrim managed to navigate his way through three reigns as a servant of the Crown and attained high office as both a Privy Councillor and Master of the Rolls. The former rebel ended up being a frequent correspondent of the Scottish monarch[57] – a man given a second chance who seized it and capitalised on the opportunities it presented.

The successful political rehabilitation of Sir Ralph Ellerker and Sir Robert Bowes, two of the most high-profile individuals involved in the Pilgrimage of Grace, has been examined. It is now time to investigate the roles played by a number of other men in the aftermath of the Pilgrimage and seek to identify the ways in which they sought to achieve rehabilitation and demonstrate loyalty to the Crown. Some managed the transition and benefited materially as a result. The impact this had upon their successors will also be discussed.

Sir Thomas Tempest, a Member of Parliament in 1536, was also based in County Durham and he was implicated, together with Robert Bowes, in the Pilgrimage of Grace. He had attended the Council of Pilgrims in York in November 1536. By late October, the Tempests and their faction had declared for the Pilgrimage at Halifax. Thomas' brother, Nicholas, subsequently marched down the bank of the River Ribble to Whalley, with approximately 400 men and administered the Pilgrims' Oath to the abbot and eight of the brethren. Nicholas was examined on 23 April 1537[58] and a memorandum written before the trial stated that he was instrumental in the first musters and a principal protagonist in the second insurrection. It was alleged that he had encouraged the resistance at Sawley Abbey and had given the monastery a fat ox and other things. Nicholas was found guilty of treason and executed in July 1537.[59]

Thomas Tempest was a trained lawyer and had been a member of the Council of the North since 1530.[60] The fact that his kinsmen, Nicholas and Richard, were implicated in the Pilgrimage – Nicholas was condemned as a traitor and Sir Richard died in prison in August 1537[61] – did not impede his subsequent career. Indeed, by April 1537, Cromwell had recorded that Tempest was to be 'remembered' for his service,[62] and June found Tempest reminding Cromwell that he had served the king from the beginning of his reign 'in all his notable wars in these parts', and requesting compensation.

As in the case of Ellerker and Bowes, Norfolk drew attention to Tempest's service in July and asked Cromwell to be a good lord to them, in order to encourage their efficient service in the future. Tempest was rewarded with the lease of Synningthwaite Priory near York and the following year he purchased the freehold title of the property. Tempest was appointed as a Justice of the Peace for the West Riding of Yorkshire in November 1537 and was confirmed as member of the Council of the North, following a recommendation from the Duke of Norfolk, with a fee of 100 marks.[63] He remained an active member of the council until his death in 1544 and his heir was his daughter, Anne. Tempest survived and prospered despite his initial involvement in the Pilgrimage and the punishment and disgrace of his relatives.

Another former Pilgrim who managed successfully to secure his rehabilitation was the lawyer William Stapleton. The Stapleton family of Wighill, near Tadcaster, were followers of the Earl of Northumberland and had a position of standing in the locality. William Stapleton's long 'Confession' provides a detailed account of the rising at Beverley and the siege of Hull.[64] William stated that he had been about to depart for London for the beginning of the law term when news of the Lincolnshire Rising prevented him. He said he was reluctant to leave his infirm brother, Christopher, amidst all the turmoil. Christopher, he said, was extremely scared, feeble and weak, and thus unable to escape nor offer resistance. According to William, both himself and Christopher were coerced into taking the oath and the people cried that 'Master William Stapleton shall be our captain'.[65] Stapleton maintained that, as the mob was so wild and dangerous, he believed his safest course of action was to accept the leadership. He continued in this role during the uprising and liaised with Aske.

Stapleton was present at the First Appointment at Doncaster in late October and had prevented his company from launching a spontaneous, surprise attack on the seemingly ill-defended and vulnerable town.[66] He subsequently visited the depressed Earl of Northumberland, along with Robert Aske, at the start of November.[67] The earl had fostered the resentment of his brothers, Ingram and Thomas, as well as his clientele by naming the king as his heir. Stapleton had cause to be fearful for the earl's life, as he tells us in his confession that he had heard the commons call for his head to be cut off in order to replace him with Sir Thomas.[68] Having said that, the Percy brothers had the sympathy of both Aske and Stapleton, as well as Stephen Hamerton and William Babthorpe.[69]

However, William was also the brother-in-law of Sir Thomas Wharton and it is most likely that this relationship saved him from the retribution of the Crown and facilitated his rehabilitation. Stapleton, then, appears to have been reprieved due to the influence of his patron, Wharton. In his confession Stapleton claimed that he had acted under duress but had preserved property and discipline among his host. He concluded the confession by stating that he was very sorry for his offences against the king, and had confessed all the details he could remember, before submitting to the king's mercy.[70] Stapleton was indeed fortunate that his explanation was accepted and he subsequently benefited from Wharton's rapid rise. Indeed, Wharton may have secured Stapleton's return as burgess for Carlisle to Parliament in 1539. We do know that he was definitely returned in 1542.[71]

His reinvention was not to last long. He was suffering from ill health in early 1544 and made his will on 30 March and was dead by 7 May. Astutely, he besought:

> The holie churche to pray for me as God hathe appointed it aftre the manner as is sette forthe by the kinge's Booke to Gode's glory and my body to be buryed amonges Christian men in the churche or churche yarde where God shall call me to his marcy.[72]

Stapleton left one third of his goods to his son, who was still a minor, and the remainder to his wife, Margaret. He requested that his 'cousin', Wharton, and nephew, Robert Stapleton, care for them.

Stapleton's rehabilitation appears to be due to his family's connections and the appeals to the king's grace, and was politically motivated. Having survived one scare, he was evidently not going to risk any behaviour that may have been perceived as dubious. Even when in ill health, he erred on the side of caution. His will demonstrates that he was hedging his bets so as not to alienate his family from the whims of the monarch of the day or jeopardise their position.

Two northern gentlemen by the name of Fairfax went on to prosper following the Pilgrimage of Grace – Sir William and Sir Nicholas. However, they behaved differently at the start of the insurrection. The Dodds have described Sir William as the 'stingy farmer' of Ferriby Priory, and said that he was quite unusual among the northern gentlemen in not joining.[73] Riding through Wakefield around the 22 October, William was approached to take the oath but declined and rode off home. However, both he and his cousin Nicholas are recorded as being present at the Pilgrims' Council at Pontefract which sat between 2 and 4 December 1536.

Sir William had advised Cromwell during Bigod's rebellion in January 1537 that he was of the opinion that Darcy had not been steadfast during the Pilgrimage. In the same letter he stated that, where archbishops, bishops, abbots and spiritual persons had rule, the people 'are most ready at a call'.[74] In July, Fairfax had been entrusted with the responsibility of delivering the Earl of Northumberland's goods to the king in compensation for a debt of £82. On 2 November, William was rewarded for his loyal service. Cromwell appointed him to the Council of the North with a fee of £20 and instructed Tunstall to allow him to come and go at his liberty.[75]

Sir Nicholas Fairfax, who had served a term as a Sheriff of Yorkshire by 1536, shared the command of a large group of rebels with Sir Thomas Percy during the Pilgrimage of Grace. However, by Christmas he was on his way to Court with a letter of recommendation from the Earl of Northumberland. He was obviously fortunate to make his peace with the king and subsequently was involved in the proceedings against Lords Darcy and Hussey. The Duke of Norfolk then recommended him for a pension of £20. Fairfax was returned to parliament for Scarborough in 1542 and Yorkshire in 1547 and 1563.

In 1554, Fairfax was the head of a household with thirty to forty servants and had an income of at least £1,000 per year.[76] He was also appointed to the stewardship of the lands of St Mary's Abbey some twenty years after the Pilgrimage, in the reign of Mary on 24 June 1557 'in consideration of his service'.[77] This was his most lucrative office and his career is an example of a man who, initially enthused with the zeal of the Pilgrimage, managed to rehabilitate himself with comparative ease.

Sir William Babthorpe, based in the East Riding, was a trained lawyer and served on the Duke of Richmond's Council in the North from 1525 until the duke's death in 1536. He was also one of the Earl of Northumberland's councillors from 1533.[78] Babthorpe was appointed one of the commissioners for surveying the lands and goods of the dissolved religious foundations in the East Riding in April 1536. However, in October he joined the leaders of the Pilgrimage of Grace.[79] This decision most probably owed much to the influence of his kinsman, Robert Aske. Babthorpe's name appeared on Aske's proclamation dated 10 October 1536 and it was probably with his assistance that Wressle Castle became the rebels' headquarters. He was with Darcy at Pontefract, and on the morning of Thursday 19 October he assembled with Darcy, Archbishop Lee, Robert Constable, Sir George Darcy and many others in the state chamber of the castle to hear Robert Aske make the case for the Pilgrimage of Grace. After Ellerker and Bowes returned from their meeting with the king in London, they met with the Pilgrims' chief captains at Pontefract on Saturday 18 November. Babthorpe was present, alongside Lord Darcy, Sir Robert Constable and Robert Aske. The king had stated that he was to send the Duke of Norfolk to discuss their grievances further and Darcy was of the opinion that the king's offer should be accepted. The other captains, Babthorpe included, felt that the matter should be put before the full Pilgrims' Council which had been summoned for only a few days later – 21 November.[80]

On Tuesday 21 November, the Pilgrims' Council assembled at York, including Babthorpe, but Darcy was not present. He had been excused because of the difficulty he had in travelling. At this meeting, Sir Robert Constable was against the proposal of a conference with Norfolk, but Darcy and Babthorpe were in favour and Babthorpe spoke on the side of peace.[81] Babthorpe was also present at the council at Pontefract between 2 and 4 December 1536 and made a written contribution to the Pontefract Articles, which were read out to the whole assembly. In fact, Babthorpe's opinions appear to have related primarily to heresy.[82] His opinions on heresy appear to have been genuine and he was doctrinally orthodox, as is apparent in the behaviour of his heirs, which will be discussed in due course. William obviously retained Catholic loyalty but outwardly conformed as it was politically expedient to do so. After the formulation of the Pontefract Articles, William appears to have taken a back seat and when it became clear that the uprising had failed, he changed sides. In January 1537 he sought to prevent another uprising in the East Riding by 'staying' the commons.[83]

On 15 May he was appointed as one of the special commissioners given the task of processing the indictments against his former associates.[84] His initial sympathies and actions did not do him long-term damage: he continued as a member of the Council of the North and was able to purchase a considerable amount of monastic property, including the manor of Flotmanby (which had previously belonged to Bridlington Priory) in Yorkshire in August 1543. He was also granted rents, lands and woods in Wistowe and Fenton, in Yorkshire, which had been part of Selby Monastery. In addition, Babthorpe was given the lordship and manor of Newhey, Yorkshire (previously in the possession of Drax Priory), with rents and lands of numerous tenants.

Thus, despite his Catholic sympathies, he had a vested interest in maintaining the Henrician status quo. Babthorpe clearly blossomed into a politically influential and important figure in the region. This is demonstrated by his election to the parliaments of 1547 and April 1554 as one of the Yorkshire knights of the shire. At the coronation of Edward VI in 1547 he was made a Knight of the Bath. William died on 27 February 1555 and his heir was his eldest surviving son, another William.[85]

Sir William Babthorpe's opinions on heresy at the time of the Pontefract Articles must have been genuine, and although he quite obviously conformed for the remainder of his life, his religious sentiments were transmitted to his heirs. In fact, the Babthorpes became one of the leading Yorkshire recusant families in the subsequent reigns, culminating in the forfeiture of their property in the reign of James I (1612) and their decision to move abroad.

As a suspected recusant, Sir William junior (1529–81) was under a cloud. In a report compiled in 1564 on the Yorkshire Justices of the Peace, Sir William was described as a man who was not in favour of the Elizabethan religious settlement.[86] However, when the Northern Rising broke out in 1569 Babthorpe demonstrated his loyalty to the Crown by joining the royal army under the Earl of Sussex. His loyalty to the Protestant Elizabeth overrode any sympathy he may have harboured for the Catholic Mary, Queen of Scots.[87]

A man whose actions and subsequent reactions in some way mirror Babthorpe's was Sir Christopher Danby. Danby was briefly involved in the Pilgrimage of Grace after he and his brother-in-law, Sir John Neville, 3rd Lord Latimer, were taken and sworn by the commons in mid-October 1536. Danby is mentioned as one of the captains who favoured a truce agreed at Doncaster at the end of October. However, he was still listed as among the knights present at Pontefract between 2 and 4 December. Danby managed to escape punishment for his disloyalty and even acted as foreman of one of the grand juries involved in the subsequent trials, including that of his cousin, Lord Darcy.[88] After this episode he became heavily involved in public affairs, serving as a commissioner for musters and a Justice of the Peace. It is probably revealing that his only election to Parliament came in April 1554, in the reign of Mary I, as one of the Yorkshire Knights of the Shire, alongside Sir William Babthorpe.[89]

During Elizabeth's reign, Danby's Catholic sympathies caused suspicion in official circles. In a report on the Yorkshire Justices of the Peace which the Archbishop of York forwarded to the Privy Council in 1564, he and his son Thomas were described as men who were no favourers of the established religion. His younger son, Christopher, was described as being 'one of the chief rebels for religion' in 1569 and eventually fled abroad.

Sir Christopher Danby eventually died on 14 June 1571. His heir was his son, Sir Thomas (*c.* 1530–90). Like Sir William Babthorpe junior, Sir Thomas Danby must have taken the politically expedient decision to fight for the Crown against the northern rebels, putting aside his Catholic convictions and family connections with the Earl of Westmorland (he had married the daughter of the 4th Earl, Ralph Neville). However, during the early 1570s, Sir Thomas was faced with the attentions of the Council of the North with regard to his religious loyalties. In March 1573, he was ordered to receive Communion three times a year, and afterwards he seems to have conformed sufficiently to avoid further suspicion.[90]

Of the fourteen rebels studied in this chapter, five were executed for treason – Lord John Hussey, George Lumley, Sir John Bulmer, Nicholas Tempest and Sir Stephen Hamerton. They joined the high-profile victims Robert Aske, Lord Darcy, Sir Robert Constable, Sir Francis Bigod and

John Hallam. In total, 178 people lost their lives due to their involvement in the Pilgrimage. However, nine of the perpetrators of the revolt – Sir Ralph Ellerker, Sir Robert Bowes, Sir Thomas Tempest, Sir William Babthorpe, Sir Christopher Danby, Lord Lumley, William Stapleton, William Fairfax and Nicholas Fairfax – managed to survive and even thrive. And, in the cases of Ellerker and Bowes especially, completely turn their careers around.

For the gentry in the region, social rank would inevitably continue to exist, but a man's abilities could now potentially overcome barriers to advancement. As beneficiaries of the new order, they were anxious to legitimise their own rise and were anxious to maintain the privilege.[91] It was not just rehabilitated gentry who benefited from new-found loyalty and service, nor was it the preserve of the some of the nobility. Edward Lee, Archbishop of York had been under suspicion due to his conduct during the Pilgrimage, especially at Pontefract. Proof that his loyalty was now above question came in the form of a significant grant of lands, manors, woods and priories in Yorkshire to the prelate in February 1543.[92]

It should be emphasised that the practicalities of governing the North required suitably qualified officials and the limited number available in the region was a question which the Crown had to consider. Professor Ellis has made a similar point with regard to the governance of Ireland in the wake of the Kildare Rebellion.[93] Total retribution in the aftermath of the Pilgrimage, involving a 'complete purge of gentlemen rebels from the region's government', was out of the question as so many royal officials had participated in the uprisings. As Christine Newman has argued, the Crown needed to impose order in the region in the aftermath, so it is hardly surprising that many former rebels regained their positions in the administration. The rebellion of men like Robert Bowes made the Crown only too aware of the necessity of effective and centralised control of the North and this could only be achieved by the compliance of this northern elite.[94] The former rebels who then collaborated with the regime separated themselves from their more radical neighbours and this, in turn, abetted the success of 'heresy' in England.[95] It is interesting to note that four of the rehabilitated rebels were lawyers by profession – the type of gentry potentially useful in the government and administration of the North.

In all of the cases of rehabilitated Pilgrims discussed, it is evident that the restoration of loyalty and appeals to the king's grace were politically motivated.

Individuals such as William Babthorpe and Christopher Danby were rehabilitated, despite retaining Catholic sympathies. This must have been a source of inherent tension for themselves and their families. At the time, however, self-preservation was paramount and these men were evidently not of the stuff of which martyrs are made. They were, in reality, cautious and pragmatic. Conversely, King Henry could not possibly have foreseen that their descendants would retain papist sympathies – they could not have done so themselves with any certainty, given the state of religious flux they were living through.

Returning to the immediate aftermath of the Pilgrimage, it would probably be fair to say that the king satisfied his desire for retribution in a more restrained fashion than he would have liked, by the execution of the prominent ringleaders. However, the imperative was the successful governance of the North and the objective of fostering such conditions which would prevent an attempt at a further rising.

This aim was clearly not achieved, as is demonstrated by the 1569 rising. The Crown's continuing religious innovations in the reign of Edward VI and Elizabeth I and the intermediate false dawn of the Marian reaction only served to confuse people even more. At the time, religious belief was in a state of constant flux and Catholics, as well as Protestants, would have had grounds for optimism at different stages. It is, however, important to emphasise that divide-and-rule tactics were deployed effectively and the adept use of patronage created a gentry with a vested interest in a stable northern society – whatever they may have felt in their private consciences.

The relationship between the Crown and the Church had become explicitly enshrined in statute by virtue of the Royal Supremacy legislation. An individual's faith came to be a symbol of loyalty and a prerequisite for advancement, power and patronage. The legislation of the Crown was expected to be adhered to and, on the surface at least, respected. The Crown's powers of retribution were to be feared, and outward compliance became a matter of expediency, not only for the gentry but for the populace as a whole.

What may to us appear as apathy in the North for the remainder of Henry's reign and into Edward VI's was, in reality, practicality and self-preservation. Pragmatism was imperative if one were to survive unscathed, let alone prosper during this period. Notwithstanding, Catholic sympathies remained in the North, as illustrated by the Northern Rising. J. T. Cliffe has contended that more than half of Yorkshire gentry families were Catholic in 1570[96] but that most Catholics continued to attend Protestant services.[97] It is, though, beyond the scope of this book to examine the details of the 1569 rising or to offer a study of the recusancy in the region thereafter.

In the next chapter, an analysis of how power and patronage were distributed in northern society and an examination of the careers, gains and religious leanings of the men who had been loyal to the Crown from the outbreak of the Pilgrimage, and the legacy this bequeathed to their heirs, will be undertaken.

5

Loyalty and Patronage

In the previous chapters the retribution of the Crown against some rebels and the successful political rehabilitation of others were discussed. It is now important to turn our attention to a more extensive exploration of power and patronage in the latter part of Henry's reign. The events of the Pilgrimage provide an opportunity to highlight and analyse issues of power, patronage and clientage – focusing, in this case, on the North of England. Who held power? Who were the patrons? And who were the clients? How were loyal clients rewarded in the period following the Pilgrimage of Grace?

The study of power and the associated themes of clientelism and patronage have occupied political scientists and sociologists for decades. However, writing in 1986, Sharon Kettering was of the view that historians have undertaken surprisingly little work on patronage.[1] The exploration of power, patronage and clientelism is essential to aiding an understanding of how northern society recovered from the tumultuous events of 1536–37 and how good governance in the region was restored. In this chapter, numerous examples will be given of how a client's loyalty during the period resulted in his reward.

At the outset, it is necessary to give a brief appraisal of the concepts and definitions of power, patronage and clientage. At its most basic, power is the control of the behaviour of others. It may rest upon the potential for physical force, the control of economic resources or the existence of social prestige. Power may manifest itself directly as coercion, or indirectly as manipulation or influence. Patronage is an indirect type of power: the patron manipulates his clients by granting or withdrawing benefits and favours. In this way, he rewards compliance and punishes disobedience. The patron can assist and protect his clients. He can provide them with offices and opportunities for career advancement. He has the power to distribute wealth and resources, in particular, political office. Clientage, conversely, is the service and loyalty the client owes a patron in return. The client acts as an obedient, reliable subordinate. He provides information and can secure places for other dependents. Clientage is the patron–client relationship characterised by the fact that it is unequal, personal and reciprocal.[2] As Steve Gunn has recognised, nobles built up clienteles or affinities to serve their purposes in local government and court politics in England.[3]

Patronage was the lord's contribution to the personal relationship between he and his man and, conversely, service was the man's – the relationship was mutual. Service was also underpinned by the ingrained duty of obedience. It was also performed so as to result in some return, e.g. a grant (of fee, office or land). Horrox summarised the reciprocal relationship when discussing late fifteenth-century England: medieval kings had relied heavily on the co-operation of their subjects in implementing their wishes, especially with regard to regional governance. Geographical specialisation meant that men were ideally employed in areas where they possessed influence and knowledge. This strategy was deployed by Henry VIII in the aftermath of the Pilgrimage, particularly with regard to Ellerker and Bowes. That men of local standing served the Crown in this way was necessary for effective royal governance.

When discussing loyalty and examples of reward in the aftermath of the Pilgrimage of Grace, it is important to bear in mind the nature of patron–client relationships. These relationships were dyadic (two-person), personal, unequal and reciprocal. There is a superior, the patron, and an inferior, the client. Thus, they are unequal in rank. For this study, although the ultimate source of power and patronage was quite obviously the monarch, King Henry, the patron mainly under consideration is the Lord Privy Seal, Thomas Cromwell.

With regard to the evidence, we need to add the caveat that the operation of patronage is difficult to observe because patrons often veiled their activities. This is exacerbated by the distance of nearly 500 years and reliance upon written documentation. The three basic types of evidence that Kettering accepts as indicators of a patron–client relationship – letters, requests for patronage and expressions of gratitude – are all present with regard to Cromwell. It is fortunate that much of his correspondence survives. There are also the monthly lists of grants, which have been carefully scrutinised for evidence of reward.[4]

Cromwell's role was of particular importance in the enforcement of the king's policies. It is not the place here for a discussion of Cromwell's career and rise to power. Suffice it to say that he is an example of both patron *and* client. His own career prospered despite his 'low-born' and obscure background. On 2 July 1536, he replaced Anne Boleyn's father, the Earl of Wiltshire, as Lord Privy Seal and six days later he was elevated to the peerage as Baron Cromwell of Wimbledon. He was made Earl of Essex on 18 April 1540, shortly before his fall.

What is important here is the consideration of him in his role as a patron and how adeptly he fulfilled it. Henry VIII, unlike his father, had little interest in the day-to-day bureaucracy the governance of a kingdom entailed and had a particular aversion to writing letters.[5] The second Tudor monarch entrusted the minutiae of correspondence to ministers who were both able and shrewd. Cardinal Thomas Wolsey was the main influence upon the king until the ascendancy of Anne Boleyn. After Wolsey's demise in 1530, Thomas Cromwell fulfilled the minister's role. Thus, Henry's inattention to detail gave more scope to these ministers to maximise their roles and power – and to dispense patronage.

Cromwell himself had been a client of Wolsey's. Cromwell was to acquire a reputation for generously rewarding those who served him and thus he could exercise power because he had the potential to reward compliance and influence behaviour.[6] D.M. Loades is also of the opinion that Cromwell's success depended upon a network of local patronage.[7] The blatant deference and requests contained in some of the correspondence cited here suggests that some were undoubtedly motivated to inform by the possibility of some sort of reward. What strikes the reader in the reports sent to Cromwell is the sycophantic nature adopted by the informants.

On the evidence to be presented here, it would be difficult to concur with Elton's assessment that the vicegerent did not use spies. It is impossible to categorically state one way or the other, but one has to be at least open to the possibility. Examples of this occur in the middle of the Pilgrimage. Cromwell was informed by Sir William Pykering that he had been spying on the Dean of Lincoln and revealingly went on to beg 'remembrance of his late suit'. Similarly, William Wood of Stamford, Lincolnshire, reported information regarding the missals in his church and revealed that he would be willing to provide further information 'that it may please your honourable lordship'. He informed Cromwell that he lived at 'great cost' and was 'but of small substance'. The king himself instructed the Earl of Derby to secretly search for sedition in a letter dated 27 November 1536.[8]

In October 1538, Robert Ward began his report of the papist misdemeanours of John Adryan, a parish priest in Suffolk, by thanking him for past favours received. John Freman in Lincolnshire wrote to Cromwell that he remembered his kind words when the two last met at Windsor. He desired help and living which, he said, would not be possible without Cromwell's help. He asked Cromwell to move the king's 'highnyse to be a good lorde unto me' in order to obtain the demesnes of Hawnby Abbey, in Lincolnshire, which he had in farm for £36 7s.

In November of the same year, Thomas Elyot wrote twice to Cromwell. The first was a letter of compliments in which Elyot appealed to Cromwell's recollection of their past friendship since they first met twenty-one years previously, and to Cromwell's good opinion of his learning.[9] This letter was followed immediately by one which offered Cromwell 'all hearty love and service'.[10] Elyot went on to request that Cromwell would obtain for him from the king a portion of the suppressed lands on which he could live.

Sir William Waldegrave lamented his 'heartburn' for informing on his grandmother, but also took the opportunity to ask Cromwell to 'put the King in remembrance of me to have something given me one day'.[11] Horrox has identified the fact that the possibility of patronage may have motivated service, and the examples of Elyot and Waldegrave support that contention. Indeed, the provision of an opportunity to serve might in itself be a form of patronage.

As will be discussed in a later chapter, the Crown via Cromwell also deployed propaganda as a weapon in the battle to win hearts and minds. Theology and obedience were themes for rhetorical works within the realm, and here, too, Cromwell emerges as a benefactor with his hands on the purse-strings. The Scottish Lutheran, Alesius, denounced the monasteries, the cruelty of the rebels and stated that the real cause of the rebellion was 'papistical doctrine'. On the same day (5 November 1536), he wrote to Cromwell asking for money.[12]

Richard Morison, author of two tracts against the Pilgrimage of Grace, wrote frequent letters to Cromwell and the request for money was a common feature. Morison's two tracts were the only ones printed, apart from the royal admonitions, and as Zeeveld has stated, through them his future was secure. By December 1537, Morison was able to write of his gratitude to Cromwell for his 'goodnes towards me'. The next sentence continued in Italian: 'Thanks to your bounty, I have no cause to complain of fortune.' Here we see an expression of gratitude for favours granted – a characteristic feature of a patron–client relationship. It illustrates how a man with few resources of his own was a dependent client, aiming to perform service which would please his patron whilst being beneficial to himself.[13] Morison's rhetorical works will be examined in the following chapter, but it is important to note that a man of such apparently meagre means became a highly regarded member of the administration and was to enhance both his wealth and prestige as a result.

Morison was to benefit materially from his loyalty and service to the Crown and his career survived Cromwell's fall. In April and June 1540, he was granted various lands in London (the late priory of St Mary, Bishopsgate, Covent Garden and tenements and buildings in Shoreditch), as well as various properties in Worcestershire and Yorkshire. The following March, he was granted a number of lands in Yorkshire. In April 1544, the propagandist who had regularly complained of his impoverishment was granted £587 5s and various lands in Yorkshire.[14]

Events in August 1545 must have pleased Morison immensely. He was granted manors in Quenyngton, Gloucestershire and Lustbye, Lincolnshire, as well as Bardney Monastery. However, a more spectacular grant rapidly followed. This consisted of manors in Yorkshire, Worcestershire, Warwickshire and Somerset; five rectories in Yorkshire and another in Worcestershire; nineteen woods; Reading Monastery in Berkshire; St Alban's Monastery in Hertfordshire; the lordship and manor of Cassiobury in Hertfordshire; Montague Priory and Christchurch Priory in London.

This was an impressive portfolio, extending across a number of counties. In addition to this, Morison was appointed collector of customs and subsidies in the Port of London. Morison had indeed come a long way thanks to his rhetorical gifts. He was a special ambassador to Denmark between 23 December 1546 and March 1547, serving as Henry's delegate in Holstein for the peace conference held there by the Duke of Holstein and Christian III, King of Denmark. Here is clear evidence that service resulted in an enhancement in social standing.[15]

Rhetoric and suggestion were not the exclusive preserve of known propagandists such as Morison and Starkey. Many sought Crown patronage or received it as a reward for loyalty during the rising, or for the expectation of diligent service and information to come. Alesius attempted to gain pecuniary favour by denouncing the Pilgrimage and, in January 1536, one John Parkyns suggested the reorganisation of the universities along evangelical lines as a remedy for dissent – he then proceeded to beg Cromwell for money repeatedly.[16] It is worth highlighting that Cromwell was involved in the patronage and protection of evangelical preachers.[17]

The dissolution of the monasteries, which was a precipitative factor in the outbreak of the Pilgrimage of Grace, caused the avaricious to contact Cromwell with a view to enhancing their financial status. Lady Elizabeth Ughtred, a sister of Queen Jane Seymour, wrote to Cromwell on 18 March 1537, seeking to have one of the farms from a monastery if they were dissolved, and went on to say that Cromwell had promised her his favour when she was last at Court as her living was insufficient to entertain her friends and described herself as a poor woman alone. In June 1537, Sir William Gascoygne implored Cromwell to plead for either Bridlington or Jervaulx Abbey. He stated that he had but a small living. Darcy's lands were up for discussion before he had even been charged or tried: Thomas Dalaryvere petitioned Cromwell in February 1537 for the monastery of Rastall in the North Riding and Fosse in the same region 'now in the hands of Lord Darcy'.[18]

Despite the Duke of Norfolk being at pains to reassure Thomas Cromwell of his diligent service in early 1537, the king appeared pleased with his efforts in February and told him that his services would not be forgotten. Henry was glad to hear how the duke advanced the truth and how discreetly he painted 'those who called themselves religious in the colours of their hypocrisy'. Revealingly, he went on to state that Norfolk was to ensure that the lands and goods of those attainted should be given to those who had truly served him.[19]

Sir William Parr (whose subsequent career will be examined below) was very active in drawing attention to his loyalty and service at every given opportunity. On 7 March 1537, he advised the king that he was present at the executions in Lincolnshire, and the following day he asked Cromwell for the attainted Guy Keym's goods for William Tyrwhyt 'in recompense for part of his expenses'. Similarly, on 12 March, he asked for allowances for five men in Lincolnshire as 'they have done good service'. On these occasions, he was obviously interceding on behalf of others: this is an example of a client attempting to secure favours for other dependents. Parr was a frequent correspondent of Cromwell's and used this relationship to further his own career and financial resources. For example, he then asked Cromwell for the farm of Barlinges for his own use on 18 March. Parr was praised as having handled himself 'wisely' by the Duke of Norfolk on 24 March.[20]

Parr was by no means unique in petitioning for the spoils of the confiscated lands of rebels or dissolved monasteries. Sir William Leylond wrote directly to the king requesting certain lands of the abbot and convent of Whalley, together with the parish church of Eccles and the chapel of the former dean of Whalley. Sir Thomas Wharton was able to confirm the state of affairs in Cumberland and advised Cromwell that the 'goods forfeited of those traitors amount to a good sum'.

William Lord Grey asked Cromwell for some of Lord Hussey's property in Lincolnshire while Hussey was in the Tower in April, whilst Sir Thomas Wentworth was to be remembered for Bamborough, following an order taken of all Darcy's offices in the North. Here we see the shrewd and calculating opportunism of some of the northern gentry. Hussey and Darcy were imprisoned but not yet executed and vultures were circling around for prey. Norfolk also desired Cromwell's favour for one Roger Myddelwode 'who was in company with Gregory Conyers in pursuit of Bigod'. Sir George Lawson who had been loyal throughout the rebellion was also anxious to draw Cromwell's attentions to his needs and said that he trusted that Cromwell would succour him in his old age.[21]

The names of those who had been loyal to the king during the northern risings continued to be brought to Cromwell's attention and on 1 May 1537, Norfolk praised three individuals and sought the minister's favour. Thomas Barton was described as having served the king 'right well' and Norfolk was of the opinion that he deserved thanks for his conduct at Beverley during the Bigod rebellion. John Eland of Hull, he said, did good service in the apprehension of Hallam and his accomplices and Hugh Ascue was held in good estimation in the locality.

By mid-May, Norfolk had switched his attention and praise further north to the Borders and requested that Cromwell be a good lord to the 'four brethren of the Greymes' (Grahams) who, he said, had served the king well on the Borders. They had, he stated, attacked the rebels at Carlisle. Norfolk sent a similar letter with regard to Robin Gase, 'otherwise Robert Greme', praising him for his efforts at Carlisle and stating that he was one of the best spies in Scotland.[22]

Sir John Neville shed some light on the state of affairs in the North in his letter to Cromwell and ended his description with a request for some reward. Neville stated that the country had never been as quiet since the king granted his pardon. He said he would like Richard, Cromwell's nephew, to be there, so he could hear the people for himself and finished by asking Cromwell's favour in his 'grete suit to the kyng'.[23]

In the period following the collapse of the risings, it is clear that those who had remained loyal wanted to emphasise the fact that stability had been restored whilst, at the same time, impressing upon Cromwell's mind their diligent service and request for some recompense. In addition, individuals who had not featured prominently in the proceedings obviously saw opportunities for self-aggrandisement and sought to benefit from the disloyalty or misfortune of others. Thomas Hall of Lincolnshire was quick to stake a claim to Lord Hussey's mills at Sleaford in a letter to Richard Cromwell on 26 June, and covetous eyes were also trained on some of Hussey's other lands. One Richard Gresham asked for the lease of the manor of Wytheham and the parcel of Barkele's lands 'which Lord Hussey had'. Darcy's demise also brought the speculators to the fore and one John Babington told Cromwell that he trusted he would be remembered in his suits for Lord Darcy's lands in Lincolnshire.[24]

The Dukes of Norfolk and Suffolk recommended individuals for reward as a result of loyalty to the Crown and the Earl of Shrewsbury also adopted this strategy on occasion. He wrote on behalf of Sir Henry Sacheverell who, he stated, did very good service with him during the recent insurrections. Sacheverell was en route to the king, and Shrewsbury requested that Cromwell grant him access to the king's presence and to instruct His

Highness of his services.[25] The Earl of Shrewsbury was not averse to furthering his own ends as well as those of his clients; in October 1537, he contacted Cromwell seeking some of Darcy's lands and was granted 'various lands in Yorkshire and Lincolnshire' that same month.[26]

Norfolk continued to further the causes of loyal men into July, in correspondence with the Lord Privy Seal, and he desired him 'to be good lord to' John Horseley who had been one of the best defenders of Northumberland during the uprisings. Around this time, in August, Norfolk was seeking clarification from Cromwell with regard to the possessions of Lord Darcy, Sir Robert Constable and the Bulmers. He went on to plead in favour of Sir George Lawson: 'I require you to be good lord unto George Lawson concerning th[e] offer that I wrote unto you of before'.[27] These examples serve to highlight the link between retribution following the Pilgrimage of Grace and the rewards gained by those who served the Crown. Those who had demonstrated their loyalty were opportunistic – they seized the chance for wealth, gain and material advancement. They benefited from the disloyalty or, depending on one's perspective, misfortune of others.

It is worthwhile considering those individuals who had remained steadfastly loyal to Henry during the Pilgrimage, despite having close family members who had chosen the path of rebellion. We have already examined the role played by Sir Robert Constable in the Pilgrimage of Grace and his subsequent demise. We can now turn our attention to his younger brother, Marmaduke. Marmaduke had established a junior branch of the family at Everingham by his marriage to a local heiress, the daughter of Sir John Sothill.[28] He did not follow in his brother's footsteps and participate in the Pilgrimage of Grace, thus remaining loyal to the Crown. By the summer following the Pilgrimage, in June 1537, Norfolk had suggested Marmaduke for a place on the Council of the North, and confirmed this to Cromwell, specifying that Constable was to have four servants and £20. His membership of the council and fee of £20 was confirmed in October 1537 and he is referred to as Sir Marmaduke Constable 'the elder', so as to differentiate him from yet another Marmaduke Constable (the son of the executed Robert). On 12 November, he was present at the funeral of Queen Jane Seymour.[29]

Like Ellerker and Bowes, Constable duly took his seat on the Council of the North and began to discharge his new-found responsibilities in an efficient and loyal manner. March 1538 saw Constable undertake surveys of Pickering and Scarborough castles with Sir Ralph Ellerker, and he was one of the examiners of Sir William Bulmer at York. Constable was also involved in the proceedings against Mabel Brigge, John Dobson and John Ainsworth, who were found guilty of treason. On 22 April, Tunstall wrote to Cromwell of 'owre felowe Sir Marmaduke Constable th[e] elder'. Tunstall stated that Constable was 'faithfull and substaniall' and 'at the tyme of the late commotion fleede frome hys brodyre Sir Robert for hys malice'. He praised Marmaduke for his 'indifferencye and wisdome' and stated, 'I humbly beseech yo[ur] good lordship to be a good lord to hym'.[30]

Together with Ralph Ellerker and John Eland (among others), Constable was then appointed to the Commission of Sewers for Yorkshire in July 1538. He was also appointed as a Justice of the Peace for Yorkshire, North, East and West Ridings – this illustrates an enhancement in social standing and an increase in influence – and on 22 July he was rewarded handsomely. He was given a grant of £200 of the house and site of the dissolved priory of Drax in Yorkshire. This included the church, steeple, churchyard, lands and the fishery of New Hey, with a house and lands attached. The annual value was listed as being £21.[31] Although Drax Priory had been founded by his wife's Sothill ancestors and this probably explains his desire to acquire it, it must be viewed as a reward for his loyalty.

Like Ellerker and Bowes, Constable kept the sessions at Carlisle in December 1538 and, as a member of the council, dealt with a Scottish ship which was stranded at South Shields as a result of high winds in the spring of 1539. On board the ship were an English priest, Sir Robert More, and two Irish monks. The council sent the men, their letters and More's examination to Cromwell. Soon afterwards, Constable signed a letter to Cromwell from the council to advise him of the apprehension of three Scotsmen and the discovery of a suspicious letter. These examples illustrate the diligence of the members of the Council of the North and the vigour with which they, Constable included, discharged their responsibilities. Constable continued to serve the Crown until his death on 14 September 1545, including participating in the Scottish campaign of 1544.[32]

Although Marmaduke's brother had been one of the most high-profile leaders of the Pilgrimage, he himself had steered clear of involvement. It may be that the brothers were not particularly close or that they shared the same opinions on the great matters of the day. Marmaduke evidently threw himself into the cut and thrust of northern government in the aftermath of the Pilgrimage and was, perhaps, all the more eager in an attempt to display loyalty and compensate for Robert's disgrace.

Although George Darcy had been present with his father, Lord Darcy, at the council at Pontefract in early December 1536, both he and his younger brother, Sir Arthur, displayed coolness towards the revolt. By February 1537, Arthur had emerged as a staunch supporter of Norfolk's mission to subdue the North and he 'gained considerably in the king's and Cromwell's favour as a result'.[33] Lord Darcy had obtained a general pardon on 18 January.[34] Four days later, in a letter to his father, Arthur revealed something of his own character and his assessment that fidelity must inevitably lead to reward: 'Old Sir Ralph Ellecarr is likely to be rewarded for his service against Sir Francis Bygod.' He stated that he did not doubt that his father would also prove himself a true knight.[35]

In April 1537, whilst his father was languishing in the Tower, Arthur was busy making enquiries as to the offices Lord Darcy held and what the king's intentions were in respect of them. At the beginning of May, Arthur wrote directly to Henry and reassured him that the country was in 'good quietness' despite the fury of the late commotion. He went on to enquire whether his father's acts condemned him and if he could exchange his lands for lands in the South. Arthur wrote that his house was in the middle of the countryside where there had been 'pestilent commotions' and that he would never be happy living there.[36] Perhaps Arthur wanted to distance himself as much as possible from his father's legacy of disloyalty and so reinforce his own credentials of fidelity. His use of the word 'pestilent' in relation to the Pilgrimage suggests more than distaste for the movement that Lord Darcy stood for. It may be that his father's former allies in the movement, especially those of the lower social orders – the mere commons – harboured a lingering resentment against the gentry. How much more so towards the son of one of their leaders who could have been perceived as betraying his own father? In any event, Arthur was clearly unhappy and uncomfortable in his northern surroundings at this time.

On 8 June, Arthur wrote to Cromwell to confirm that he was present at the suppression of Jervaulx Abbey. He also stated that he felt he was wasting the king's money at Pontefract, as the areas in the North were never in a more dreadful and true obedience. He ended his report by beseeching Cromwell to be a good lord to him.[37]

Arthur was obviously on reasonably good terms with Queen Jane Seymour's family, as he petitioned the queen's sister, Lady Ughtred, in June to intercede for him to obtain the parsonage of Askyrth. He was of the opinion that just a word from her would result in the king granting the request. As for himself, he stated, he would be happy to tarry in the North if she were to remain with him, but he was aware of the possibility that some Southern lord would make her forget the North.[38] Here again, we see evidence of Arthur's hankering for the South and the fact that he perceived a clear geographical demarcation between North and South.

On 12 November, Sir Arthur was present at the queen's funeral and had been granted the office of steward of Galtres Forest, Yorkshire, a few weeks before.[39] In May 1538, Arthur was granted lands, the extent of which is quite astonishing and thus needs to be listed in order to appreciate its magnitude. He was granted three dissolved monastic properties: the monastery of St Mary in Sawley, the abbey of Coverham and the priory of the Holy Trinity, all in Yorkshire. Coverham came with various lands, three messuages and Scraston Grange. In addition, Darcy was granted twenty-five manors, mainly in Yorkshire, with some in Lancashire. The manor of Gisbourne also included a forest. At least fifteen other messuages and other lands were also granted, as were two granges: one in Sonderland, Lancashire, and the other in Glingtorpe. To top this off, he was granted the advowsons and rectories of Tadcaster and Gargrave in Yorkshire, with an annual rent of 53s 4d.[40] This grant is really quite spectacular when one considers that it came about eighteen months after the end of the Pilgrimage of Grace and a mere eleven months after Darcy's father was executed as a traitor. Clearly, the king did not believe that the sins of the father should be visited on the son and Arthur's shrewd perception that loyalty was the key to advancement had been borne out.

In January 1539, he was granted, in addition, over 500 acres of land in Conysthorp, North Yorkshire.[41] Overall, he was, as R.B. Smith has stated, the recipient of the largest 'political' grant that the king bestowed on those who had been loyal during the Pilgrimage of Grace.[42] Sir Arthur and his brother George were also on the reception committee for the arrival of Anne of Cleves at the end of 1539. The following December, he received a grant of a priory, lands and a vicarage in Yorkshire and in December 1541 he was granted the priory of St Andrew's in York. The following August, Arthur was the beneficiary of yet another grant of £236 12s 6d and additional lands that had previously belonged to the convent of Charterhouse, London.[43]

May 1543 provides an indication of how diverse Arthur's property portfolio was – he and his wife obtained a licence to alienate (sell or transfer) some of his property. These were the house and priory of the late priory of Clementhorpe and other lands in Burneholme, Yorkshire, and, interestingly, a 'mansion' in London to his brother, George. The following month he was the recipient of a licence to purchase lands and tenements in Aldgate, east London. Yet another grant of a manor, that of Nappaye in Yorkshire, was bestowed upon him six months later in January 1544 and the following year he received the manor, wood and fisheries of Gonby, and Selby Monastery in Yorkshire. He was also given the manor of Talertheg.

The Book of Augmentations for 1546 also reveals that Arthur was in receipt of the tithes of Whitgift Chapel, Yorkshire.[44] Although Arthur may have been disappointed with regard to Lady Ughtred, he went on to marry Mary, the daughter of Sir Nicholas Carew of Bedyngton, Surrey, and was based at Brimham, North Yorkshire. Together they had ten sons and five daughters, including his heir, Henry, who in turn married the daughter of Sir Robert Tyrwhyt.[45] Tyrwhyt, as will be seen in due course, had remained steadfastly loyal to King Henry during the Pilgrimage and its aftermath and had gained both materially and in status as a result.

Whilst Arthur was evidently handsomely compensated for his loyalty and fidelity in Yorkshire, his elder brother, George, Lord Darcy's son and heir, does not feature as prominently in the sources from the time of the Pilgrimage and does not appear to have gained as much. George had been in attendance at Pontefract with his father in December 1536 but appears to have kept a lower profile from then on. His presence at the Pilgrims' Council, as Darcy's elder son and heir, does not support Bastow's theory that only second sons were involved in rebellious activity.[46]

Richard Pollard wrote to the Lord Privy Seal with regard to George the following August and stated that he understood that Cromwell had been a good lord to Darcy. This provides evidence that George Darcy was involved in a patron–client relationship with Cromwell. We are not told in what way Cromwell had been a good lord but the fact that it was acknowledged, and by a third party, is surely illuminating. Perhaps Cromwell had displayed another characteristic of a patron? Maybe he had protected George despite Lord Darcy's rebellious actions? Pollard sent George to Cromwell with this letter and enclosed the value of the late Lord Darcy's lands.[47] Some of these lands were granted to Sir Thomas Hennege in May 1538: the house, manor and the advowson of the parish church of Knayth, Lincolnshire. The Lord Privy Seal duly recorded George's name in his (Memorandum of) Remembrances.[48]

In September 1539, George was granted a manor in Gloucestershire, and he accompanied his brother to the reception for Anne of Cleves at the end of that year. The grant of an annuity of £56 3s 4d was to follow three years later, but a more extensive reward was bestowed in June 1543 when he was granted eleven manors and six rectories. His most significant grant was in April 1545 when he was given the manors of Hamylton, Acaster Selby and Stillingfleet in Yorkshire. In addition to this, George received the possessions of Selby, St Oswald's, Gysborne, Pontefract and Worksoppe monasteries, as well as Helaugh and Basedale priories and St Leonard's Hospital.[49] The elder son does not appear to have gained the extensive rewards of his younger brother, but he was restored as Baron Darcy and he married Dorothy, the daughter and sole heir of Sir John Melton of Aston.[50] His heir was John, 2nd Baron Darcy of Aston.

In 1536, Sir William Parr could not have envisaged the possibility of his niece, Katherine, becoming Queen of England; not least because she had married for the second time, her husband being Sir John Neville, Lord Latimer, who was involved in the initial stages of the Pilgrimage and present at the Pilgrims' Council between 2 and 4 December.[51] When the Lincolnshire Rising broke out in the autumn, Parr was steadfastly loyal to the Crown and was designated, among others, to take command in the event of the Duke of Suffolk being absent.[52] Parr appears to have relished the opportunity to be involved in the restoration of peace and order in the North. His correspondence with both the king and Cromwell in the aftermath of the Lincolnshire Rising and the Pilgrimage of Grace is both abundant and informative.

In early March 1537 Guy Keym and Thomas Moigne were among the ninety-two rebels condemned as traitors at Lincoln and among thirty-four sentenced to death. Parr wrote to advise the king that he had been present at the proceedings and at the executions of Keym and Moigne – he reiterated these details in a letter to Cromwell the same day.[53] The following day, 8 March, saw Parr advancing the cause of the sheriff, William Tirwhit, who wished to have the goods come to the king by Guy Keym's attainder, in recompense of his expenses. Four days later, in a letter to Cromwell, Parr confirmed that he had attended the executions at Louth and Horncastle and stated that he thought the people sorry for their late ill demeanour and that no county was now more peaceful. He went on to request allowances for Sir John Villers, Sir John Markham, John Herrington, Thomas Neville and Sir William Newnham, as they had performed good service.[54] It is hard to avoid the impression that Parr wished to cast himself in the role of both loyal and diligent servant of the king and benefactor to the local gentry – a conduit between Crown and countryside. Here we see clientage in operation – Parr was endeavouring to secure favours for other dependents in the locality.

Having initially sought reward for others, Parr had obviously endeavoured to promote his own advancement and reward. On 18 March 1537, he wrote to Cromwell thanking him for speaking to the king about the farm of Barlinges. He said that if he were to be granted it, he could do the king good service in the locality.[55] Unfortunately for Parr, he was to be disappointed in this request for the Lincolnshire abbey, but he received manors, lands and rents through grants in the same month. He received the manor and hundred of Rothwell, Northamptonshire, on a forty-year lease, which had reverted to the king as a result of the attainder of Edward, Duke of Buckingham (in 1521). In addition, he was granted five manors in Westmorland (Kirby, Croftwaite, Lithe, Heslington and Sampole) as well as two in Lancashire (Weresdale and Clevely).[56]

By mid-May, he was writing to Cromwell with regard to Lord Hussey's indictment and, revealingly, stated that he hoped that Hussey's offices would be given to those who would ensure the order of the countryside and that he wished them for himself.[57] Parr was part of the Yorkshire jury panel annexed for the trial of Constable, Bigod, Percy, Sir John Bulmer, Cheny, Hammerton, Aske and Ralph Bulmer at Westminster on 16 May 1537,[58] and by the end of that month he was writing to Cromwell, reminding him of his recent visit to London during which he had asked the king for the preferment of Jervaulx Abbey if it were to be suppressed. He reminded Cromwell of his promise of a favour, saying that if he failed to gain preferment of the abbey, of which he was the founder, he would consider it a great reproach.[59] The outcome of this request will be noted in due course.

Parr continued to press not only for his own advancement but ostensibly that of others as well. In August, he informed Cromwell that he wanted the lands of the two abbeys in the City of Lincoln for the people of Lincoln.[60] He followed up that request in a letter to Wriothesley in September when asking for the executed Lord Hussey's lands for himself and asking what Cromwell intended to do with regard to Barlinges.[61] He continued to be vigorous in his search for sedition and the maintenance of order, and told of a secret meeting which he suspected was against the king's peace in the area of Brigstock. He duly had those in attendance arrested and pledged that he would continue to apprehend persons who held secret assemblies.[62] A picture emerges of Parr as a rigorous and enthusiastic member of the loyal gentry in the North and one gets the impression that he rather relished his power, local standing and opportunity for wealth and self-advancement. He seems, more than any other, to have been at pains to point out his efficient service on a frequent basis.

In early 1538, Parr reminded Cromwell yet again that the situation with Barlinges had not yet been resolved and repeated his request that the City of Lincoln might have the attainted lands there which belonged to the two houses, in recompense of money and plate which he had taken out of the city for the king's use.[63] Although disappointed in his request for Barlinges, Parr was appointed as the chief steward of possessions in Lincolnshire, Rutland, Nottinghamshire and the City of Lincoln, 'which came to the king by the attainder of John, Lord Hussey and Thomas Moigne' with fees of £6 a year. During the summer, Parr was appointed to a Commission of Oyer and Terminer for Treasons for Northamptonshire, Warwickshire, Leicestershire, Rutland, Nottinghamshire, Derbyshire, Lincolnshire and the cities of Lincoln and Coventry, as well as the towns of Leicester and Nottingham. Parr was also granted Brayfield Rectory in Northampton in 1538.[64]

William Parr's star continued to rise and he was granted leases of ex-monastic property, including Pipewell Abbey and a number of granges. In 1539, he was elected to Parliament for the last time.[65] In September of that year, Parr was granted an annuity of £3 6s 8d from the attainted lands of Jervaulx Monastery; so his previous request was, in part, satisfied.[66] John

Hussey wrote to Lord Lisle on a couple of occasions in March 1539, stating that he had learned that Parr was to be made Lord Fitzhugh.[67] Although Hussey was premature and had got the title wrong, Parr must have been a very proud man when he was created Baron Parr of Horton on his elevation to the peerage in 1543 after his niece Katherine's marriage to the king. The ceremony took place on Sunday, 23 December at Hampton Court.[68]

Baron William Parr became chamberlain to the queen's household and took his seat in the House of Lords on 17 January 1544. The following month, he received a significant grant of property – priories, rectories, manors, farms and windmills in various counties.[69] The king appointed him a member of the regency council to advise Queen Katherine whilst he was abroad, but Parr was absent from the Lords during the last of Henry's parliaments. Parr made his will on 21 June 1546 which made provision for his wife and relatives, including his grandson, Ralph Lane. (Parr and his wife had four daughters.)[70] The following November, he was appointed as keeper of Rockingham Park, Northamptonshire, and keeper of the deer in Corby Woods.[71]

His loyalty to the Crown and energetic service had proved lucrative, and when he died on 10 September 1547, his wealth was approximately £1,500 in bequests and plate.[72] He was thus a wealthy man. Parr's career is an example of how enhanced prestige and power could be attained by loyal service: he profited from the patronage of a grateful monarch and the defeat of that monarch's enemies.

Sir Ralph Eure (also known as Evers) was the son of Sir William Eure of Witton, County Durham, and predeceased his father. Both were active members of the northern gentry and are not recorded as having participated in the Pilgrimage of Grace. Ralph Eure appears on the East Riding Commission in April 1536 and was in command of Scarborough Castle during the Pilgrimage.[73] Eure wrote to Sir John Bulmer in January 1537, praising the king for forgiving the Pilgrims both in writing and in his heart. He also kept Henry informed of the activities of Bigod and Hallam.[74]

Eure wasted no time in requesting Bigod's lands in a letter to Cromwell of 11 February, before Bigod had even been to trial.[75] The Privy Council displayed faith in both Eure's and Ellerker's abilities in March when it instructed Norfolk to 'keep a special eye' on Sir Robert Constable: 'You shall secretly inform Sir Ralph Ellerker and Sir Ralph Evers of this matter and let them take order of the parts of Hull and Scarborough to prevent him stealing away to outward parts.'[76]

By April, Cromwell had noted that 'Raffe Evers' was to be remembered, among others,[77] and in May Eure was busy taking the inventory of the goods of the attainted Sir James Cockerell, formerly of Gisburn. In June, Norfolk recommended Eure for a pension of £40 a year[78] and Cromwell made a further record of Eure's entitlement to some acknowledgement in his Remembrances for 1537.[79] It is interesting that Ralph's servant was one of the accusers of the Vicar of Mustone for his failure to set forth the Royal Supremacy.[80] Eure's servant was clearly not only loyal and obedient to him, but also to the king's religious policies and the vicar was subsequently executed for treason. The loyalty that Eure fostered in his servant was mirrored by his own behaviour towards the regime and he was duly rewarded, as he had requested, in April 1538. Eure was appointed chief steward of possessions in Lincolnshire and Yorkshire, 'which came to the king by the attainder of Sir Francis Bigod', with a fee of £5 a year.[81] This example again illustrates the link between retribution and reward.

Ralph's father, William, had been a member of the Council of the North since 1525, and was suggested as a member for the newly constituted council set up by the Duke of Norfolk in the aftermath of the Pilgrimage in 1537.[82] William, a man of 'moderate fortune', was appointed as one of the king's lieutenants in the marches; Deputy and, subsequently, Warden of the East March.[83] In June 1537, he was involved in a 'device' for the keeping of the East and Middle Marches, alongside Ellerker. Eure was given 200 marks per year and Ellerker £20. Eure was also paid £20 per annum as a member of the Council of the North and was appointed as a Justice of the Peace for the West Riding of Yorkshire in November 1537. He also received an annuity of £20 from the manor of Barmeston in Yorkshire from January 1542.[84]

William's offices included Escheator of Durham, Steward of Pickering, Whitby Strand, Sir Francis Bigod's lands and Jervaulx. He was also Constable of Scarborough and Captain of Berwick, in addition to being Warden of the East March. The pinnacle of his achievement came in March 1544, when he was created a baron, 1st Lord Eure, and had his patent as Warden of the East Marches renewed.[85] In January 1545, William was also granted the lordship of Stritton Grange, Northumberland.[86] In this case, a man of moderate fortune had reaped handsome dividends for his loyalty throughout the Pilgrimage.

However, his pleasure in his success must have been tempered by the death of his son and heir, Ralph, the following year. Ralph had been active on the border and participated in the Earl of Hertford's invasion of Scotland in 1544, for which he received Henry's thanks, but he then fell at Ancrum Moor on 27 February 1545 at the hands of the Earl of Angus.[87] Lord William was appointed as chief steward of the lands in Lincolnshire and Yorkshire (previously Sir Francis Bigod's) the following May. He was also made Constable of Scarborough Castle (these offices had been Ralph's) and received a grant for life of the manor of Northstede in Yorkshire.[88] Ralph's will was made on 6 May 1544 and his offices passed to his father, William.[89]

When William Eure died three years later, he was succeeded by Ralph's son, William, who in turn became 2nd Baron Eure. Both father and son had benefited materially and in status as a result of their unwavering loyalty during the Pilgrimage and its aftermath. William made his will shortly before his death – it is dated 25 February 1548.[90] William's elevation to the peerage was the zenith of their achievements and Ralph would have expected to inherit the title as 2nd Baron Eure. However, the price he paid for his steadfast service on the Borders was that the title did not pass to him. Instead, his son, William, continued the family's line in the nobility.

Sir Robert Tyrwhyt (or Tyrwhitt) of Lincolnshire played a role in suppressing both the Lincolnshire uprising and the Pilgrimage of Grace. On 15 October 1537 he is recorded as being present at Prince Edward's christening.[91] Between 1536 and 1547 he was rewarded with two dozen grants and leases. His first grant was the dissolved monastery of Stainfield in Lincolnshire: he received the house, site and 662 acres of land in 1538.[92] John Freman expressed his disappointment to Cromwell in October that the farm of Bardney, Lincolnshire – which he had sought for himself – had been given to Tyrwhyt.[93] In July 1538, Tyrwhyt was appointed as Justice of the Peace for Lincolnshire, alongside Sir William Parr.[94] In December of the following year, Tyrwhyt was granted the former priory of Unforth in Lincolnshire and many other farms and lands, together with the rents from the tenants. Tyrwhyt advanced at Court and was a gentleman of the Privy Chamber by 1540. He acquired a number of other lands, manors and grants in Lincolnshire and Peterborough in August 1542. The following year, Tyrwhyt was appointed steward and bailiff of various properties, in addition to receiving life grants for a number of lands and a water mill in Bedfordshire.[95]

Like William Parr, Tyrwhyt benefited from a family connection with Queen Katherine Parr, was knighted and was the queen's Master of Horse by 1544. At the end of that year, he was also appointed as steward and bailiff of Kimbolton in Huntingdonshire. Tyrwhyt was elected as Knight of the Shire for Lincolnshire in 1545 and on 12 July 1546, he was given the responsibility of keeper of Thornton manor, including the 'mansion', park and all the deer therein. Shortly before King Henry's death, Tyrwhyt was granted an annuity of 58s 2d out of lands in Nottinghamshire and Lincolnshire which were in the king's possession as a result of the minority of William Coggan. Tyrwhyt was given the wardship.[96]

Tyrwhyt was subsequently returned as Knight of the Shire for Huntingdonshire in 1554 and 1559. Thus he continued to prosper during the reigns of Edward VI (he purchased Leighton Bromswold, a manor of Lincoln Cathedral and 2,400 acres of land, pasture and marsh), Mary I and Elizabeth I. He acquired further property in Huntingdonshire and sat at Elizabeth's first parliament before retiring to Leighton Bromswold where he died in May 1572.[97] Tyrwhyt had gained a good deal in material wealth and enhanced status. From a member of the Lincolnshire gentry, he rose to become a gentleman of the Privy Chamber, the queen's Master of Horse and a Knight of the Shire. His social prestige was significantly raised as a result. His daughter married Henry Darcy, Sir Arthur's heir. Here we see evidence of loyal gentry families consolidating their positions and demonstrating their unwavering loyalty and reliability in the region.

Following the Lincolnshire Rising and the Pilgrimage of Grace, John Uvedale, who was loyal throughout the Pilgrimage, was appointed to the newly constituted Council of the North as its secretary and was the keeper of a new, specially designed signet.[98] In May 1537, he was sent to survey Bridlington and Jervaulx abbeys and as a member of the council assisted Norfolk with the examinations of those accused of sedition and treason, including the Vicar of Mustone in December 1537.[99] Around this time, however, on 10 December, he wrote to Cromwell assuring him of his old and steadfast friendship. Uvedale requested that he might be allowed a position at Court, under the king or Prince Edward. He stated that he would rather serve in that capacity for £40 a year than in the North for £100. Here, like Arthur Darcy, is evidence of Uvedale's dissatisfaction with life in the North. The lure of the South, or the Court, was obviously a characteristic in the personalities of some members of the northern gentry. We also see a clear indication of a patron–client bond. Appealing to Cromwell's evangelical tendencies, he maintained that he might be able to set forward some of Cromwell's good and godly purposes.[100] This plea fell on deaf ears, apparently, for Uvedale was to spend the remainder of his career based in the North. Uvedale and Darcy were obviously required to remain in the North as part of the northern gentry necessary for the effective governance of the region.

In 1538, he was part of the council under the Bishop of Llandaff, and in 1539 he was appointed a commissioner to supervise the surrenders of five priories in Yorkshire.[101] In April 1540, shortly before Cromwell's fall, Uvedale wrote to the Lord Privy Seal thanking him for the gift of a stallion (a characteristic expression of gratitude). He wrote another letter to Cromwell around this time congratulating him on his creation as Earl of Essex. Uvedale stated that he rejoiced in Cromwell's increase in honour.[102] Here the use of effusive language is manifest evidence of the patron–client relationship at work. Uvedale asked Cromwell for a house and parsonage at Marrick and was eventually granted this request, together with other lands in 1541, interestingly after Cromwell's demise.[103]

John Eland, Mayor of Hull, had been instrumental in capturing John Hallam in the renewed revolts in January 1537 and he advised the king of the 'very truth of the taking of that traitor'.[104] At the end of January 1537, he expressed his delight at the king's benevolence in a letter to Cromwell. Eland confirmed that he had received the king's letters, together with £20 for capturing the traitor Hallam and his accomplices. He reassured Cromwell of his best efforts in subduing anyone who misbehaved after the king's pardon. He stated that the king's aid to the town of Hull was 'so abundant' and his letters so 'comfortable' that the town would 'doubt not' to keep it surely.[105]

In May, the Duke of Norfolk sent Eland to Cromwell with a letter stating that nobody had been of better service in the apprehension of Hallam and requesting favour for the bearer.[106] Eland was subsequently knighted. Here is a clear example of Eland being bound to Norfolk by virtue of his knighthood.[107] The following July saw Eland appointed as a Justice of the Peace for Yorkshire; he was also granted the parcel of Elley Rectory in Hull. In 1540 and 1541, he and his wife were granted tithes in Analby and Wolfreton.[108] He was also appointed as overseer of the king's works in Hull in 1541 but died on 6 May the following year. His will, made shortly before his death, gave his wife a life interest in his lands in Lincolnshire and Yorkshire and goods worth £112 – his heirs were five of his kinsmen.[109] Thus Eland died a wealthy country gentleman. From being Mayor of Hull and loyal during the risings, he amassed wealth and land. His enhanced status as a knight and Justice of the Peace can be attributed directly to his conduct in 1537.

John Dudley's conduct during the Pilgrimage of Grace may well have been a contributory factor in laying the foundations for his family's advancement well into the reign of Elizabeth (despite his own fall and execution under Mary I). In November 1534, Dudley was Knight of the Shire for Kent in Parliament. When the Lincolnshire Rising broke out, he was appointed as one of fifteen commanders under the Duke of Norfolk and in charge of 200 men.[110] He was appointed sheriff in Staffordshire in October 1536 and was another who was part of the reception committee to greet Anne of Cleves in late 1539. He received grants of lands, including a priory and rectories in Staffordshire and lands in Northamptonshire, in 1541.[111] Dudley was subsequently sent to Calais as deputy to Arthur Plantagenet, Viscount Lisle (an illegitimate son of Edward IV). Further grants of manors and lands ensued in 1542, and in March of that year he was elevated to the peerage and created Viscount Lisle, following the disgrace and death of Arthur Plantagenet, with a grant of 20 marks a year.[112] With tensions rising with the Scots in the autumn of 1542, the king decided to send Dudley to the Borders and appointed him Warden of the Marches.[113]

Dudley continued his political career and loyal service for the remainder of Henry's reign and was granted manors and lands that had previously belonged to Queen Jane Seymour in August 1543.[114] This was followed with an enormous list of grants in May 1544. These included a hospital and manor in Burton, Leicestershire, and the hospital of St Giles in the Fields, London. In addition, there were three lordships and manors and a rectory in Derbyshire; two manors and lordships in Norfolk; a rectory, four manors and lordships in Lincolnshire; the rents out of two rectories in Leicestershire; and a rectory in Feltham, Middlesex. Dudley was also granted Everley Wood in Staffordshire – which had previously belonged to George, Duke of Clarence, Edward IV's brother – in June 1545.[115]

Dudley was a pivotal figure in the manoeuvre or 'device' in attempting to interfere with the succession on Edward VI's death, with the objective of preventing Princess Mary from succeeding to the throne. He failed miserably and was executed for treason on 22 August 1553. His wealth at death was land to the value of approximately £86,000 and an inventory of goods worth £10,000.[116] Dudley was a spectacularly wealthy nobleman, who had been minor gentry at the time of the Pilgrimage. His rise was meteoric: he was, after all, a relatively minor figure in the autumn of 1536. It may be stretching the point, but the fact that he was demonstrably loyal at a crucial time perhaps laid the foundations for his future advancement. He was a man, perhaps fortuitously, in the right place at the right time, and obviously a man of undoubted ability. He was appointed as sheriff as a result of the rising and then became a peer, Lord High Admiral, Privy Councillor, Knight of the Garter, an earl, a member of the regency council and, finally, a duke. He eventually overreached himself, but had risen to become an incredibly wealthy noble by the time of his death.

Thus far, the role, reward and rehabilitation of the northern gentry has been concentrated on. It is now time to examine the parts played by some leading nobles and ascertain what benefits their loyalty to the Crown during the rising may have brought them.

Although Lord Thomas Darcy was the most outspoken of the northern nobility, he was by no means the most powerful. The five powerful and influential northern earls were Northumberland, Westmorland, Cumberland, Derby and Shrewsbury, and none were directly involved in the Pilgrimage. Their positions were, in reality, ambivalent and it can be argued that they decided on a policy of inertia at best. The Earl of Northumberland died in 1537. His nephew, Thomas Percy (son of Sir Thomas who was executed following the Pilgrimage) was restored to the peerage and became the 7th Earl of Northumberland in 1557.[117] However, he inherited his father's Catholic beliefs and somewhat reckless, or brave, characteristics.

Percy was one of the prime movers in the 1569 Northern Rebellion and was prominent in the restoration of the Mass at Durham and Ripon. It is not the place here to discuss the details and chronology of this rebellion, but it was a failure. Northumberland fled and was eventually captured by the Scots who delivered him to York, where he was beheaded on 22 August 1572.[118] Sir Thomas Gargrave reported Northumberland's last profession of Catholic faith and refusal to ask Queen Elizabeth's forgiveness. Percy was advanced as a martyr by the English Catholic bishops and beatified by Pope Leo XIII on 13 May 1895: the grounds were primarily his Catholic declaration on the scaffold.[119] So, although the Earl of Northumberland was loyal to the Crown in 1536, his heir revealed himself as very much his executed father's son in his religious and rebellious behaviour.

The Neville Earl of Westmorland did not involve himself in the Pilgrimage but his son, Lord Neville, did march from Durham to Pontefract and finally to Doncaster. He is recorded as being present at the Pilgrims' Council in early December 1536, together with Lords Darcy, Lumley, Scrope, Latimer and Conyers.[120] As the earl himself was not involved, Smith has argued that he was able to use his influence to save Neville clients and supporters from serious harm. Thus, Westmorland was fulfilling his role as a patron by protecting his clients. Among this group were Robert and Richard Bowes, as well as John, Lord Latimer and his brother, Marmaduke.[121]

A stand-out name among this group must be Lord Latimer; he was, at this time, married to Katherine Parr who came to be known for her evangelical sympathies. It is most unlikely that her husband, nineteen years her senior, shared his wife's convictions in 1536, as is revealed by his attendance at Pontefract and his will – he instructed that a priest should sing for his soul for forty years. He also bequeathed alms for 'poor folks'.[122]

The Neville Earl himself remained aloof and used his loyalty in a bid to further enrich himself. In April 1538, he wrote to Cromwell asking for a farm and nunnery in Yorkshire that had previously belonged to Sir John Bulmer and was worth £50 a year.[123] Sir John had been attainted and executed for his part in the Pilgrimage. Here again, we see the link between retribution and the possibility of reward. The earl followed this up with another request in February 1539 for Blauncheldone Abbey: the earl stated that he was aware that Sir Reynold Carnaby and others were going to petition for it, but he wanted it for himself.[124] He was, however, unsuccessful in this regard. Westmorland died in 1549 and was succeeded by his son, Henry, the 5th Earl (d. 1564), a prominent supporter of Mary I, and in turn by Charles Neville, the 6th Earl. Charles, raised a Catholic, brought a degree of infamy to the family name through his undoubtedly significant contribution to the Northern Rising in 1569.[125] As in the case of the Percys of Northumberland, a loyal peer in 1536 did not guarantee a loyal noble in 1569.

Edward Stanley, 3rd Earl of Derby was the grandson of Thomas Stanley, 1st Earl of Derby, whose intervention at the Battle of Bosworth Field had been critical in securing Henry Tudor's victory. The earl was about 27 years old at the time of the Pilgrimage of Grace and the commons of Lancashire expressed sympathy with those in Lincolnshire. It was generally perceived that the 'young' earl was of the same religious persuasion. Smith has described Derby as 'intriguing' in that he gave no indication of his political views and appeared to waver at the start of the Pilgrimage; this, again, appears to be an inherited family trait. He was, though, married to the Duke of Norfolk's daughter and in the end, Lancashire did not rise.[126]

On 10 October 1536, the king informed Derby of the traitors assembled in Lincolnshire and stated that, although prepared for them and confident that they would be subdued, the earl should be prepared as the outcome was uncertain![127] Mixed messages indeed: if Edward ran true to the Stanley form (waiting on the sidelines in order to see the most likely victor), he might well have wavered and been tempted to join the Pilgrimage.

According to the Dodds, Thomas Stanley, a priest who was related to the earl, used all his influence to persuade Edward to join the rebels. The Dodds maintained that it was believed that the priest had been successful in his efforts 'for a time' but that when it came to it, he 'chose to serve the king'.[128] This is exactly what happened and it can be argued that the rest was mere speculation and supposition. Derby remained steadfast and loyal to the Crown, and on 19 October Henry informed Derby that, contrary to previous instructions to join up with the Earl of Shrewsbury, he was to proceed immediately to Sawley to repress an insurrection there. Derby was to apprehend the captains and have them executed immediately or sent to Court. Derby was instructed to take the abbots and monks with violence and have them hanged in their 'monks apparaul' and ensure that no town or village began to assemble. 'And doubt you not but that we shall remember your charges and service.'[129] Here again, Henry appears to have relished the retribution at his command – the reiteration of the link between loyalty and reward.

Derby obviously fulfilled his duties conscientiously, as is demonstrated in a further letter from the king on 28 October. Henry thanked Derby for his diligence and wrote that he would remember him and that his posterity would rejoice; manifest evidence of the patron–client relationship between sovereign and vassal. Henry gave explicit instructions as to how the earl should proceed in the event that he found the abbot and monks restored again at Sawley. They were, he said, to be hanged on long pieces of timber or from the steeple. The king emphasised the fact that he wanted the ringleaders to be made an example of and the remainder reminded of the king's mercy.[130]

Derby, however, was not inundated with grants from the Crown in the years following the Pilgrimage. There appears to be only one record of a grant in 1542 of a monastery with woods and pastures in Leeke, Staffordshire.[131] It seems apparent from this survey that it was the loyal gentry who were the main beneficiaries of material reward.

Thomas Manners, 1st Earl of Rutland, possessed Plantagenet blood through his mother and was one of Henry's favourites from early in the reign. During the Lincolnshire Rising and the Pilgrimage of Grace, Rutland was entrusted with the defence of Nottingham Castle. He was appointed to a joint command with the earls of Huntingdon and Shrewsbury and he duly marched promptly to Nottingham and on to Newark, Southwell and Doncaster. However, he was moved to petition Cromwell for additional money in order to carry out his orders. Manners wrote that his base at Nottingham Castle was very expensive and that he had spent almost all of his own money at Doncaster. He stated that although the Duke of Norfolk had sent him £500, a large portion had been spent on paying for gunners at Nottingham and Newark. As a result, he had a little over £300 remaining and had to spend money on the castle on a daily basis. He begged Cromwell to obtain some money from the king.[132]

Manners' stewardship of many monasteries, together with his ancestral claims to the foundation of certain houses, as well as his proven loyalty, worked to his advantage in the wake of the dissolution. By a grant of March 1539, in return for the sale of land to the king, including Elsinges, he received at least fourteen manors (mostly in Leicestershire) and several abbeys, including Rievaulx and Beverley, Yorkshire, and Belvoir Priory and Croxton, Leicestershire.[133] Rutland was lord chamberlain to Jane Seymour and was also named as one of those appointed to receive Anne of Cleves in November 1539, together with the Earl of Derby, Sir John Dudley, Arthur and George Darcy, William Parr and Sir Robert Tyrwhyt. He was also appointed chamberlain to Anne of Cleves and Katherine Howard.

Following the fall of Thomas Cromwell, Rutland acquired his former offices of warden of the forests beyond the Trent and steward of Halifax manor, Yorkshire, for which he received an income of £100 a year.[134]

Rutland continued as a Justice of the Peace for Lincoln during this period and received considerable grants of lands in March 1541 – seven lordships and manors, six rectories, the hospital of St Giles in Beverley and a priory in York. In addition, he was granted a long list of lands throughout the Midlands, including the monastery of Garadon in Leicestershire. This was followed a couple of months later by the grant of a manor and lands in Grantham and Barrowby, in Lincolnshire, and further lordships and manors in Leicestershire, Northamptonshire and Yorkshire. Grants of priories in Lincolnshire and Yorkshire were again made in July 1541.[135] It should be acknowledged, however, that Rutland's main sphere of influence was the Midlands – much closer to the core of power, the Court. He thus did not fit the profile of an 'over-mighty' peripheral magnate of the far north.

When the king made his long overdue visit to the North in the summer of 1541, Rutland was in attendance when Henry entered Lincoln on 9 August.[136] The following summer saw Rutland sent north to the Scottish border, together with Sir Robert Bowes. In August 1542, he was appointed warden of all three marches. The following month, Rutland was the beneficiary of yet further grants, including one of £183 12s 6d.[137] In April 1543, the earl received another grant of lands, chapels and a pension.[138] This was the last recorded grant before his death in September 1543. Indeed, Rutland's 'intrusion' into the power structures of the far north, especially the marches, reveals that the king must have trusted him more than the traditional regional magnates and thus sought to sideline them.

George Hastings, the Earl of Huntingdon was the grandson of William, Lord Hastings, trusted companion and councillor to Edward IV, who had been executed by Richard III in 1483. The Pilgrimage of Grace afforded Hastings the opportunity of demonstrating his loyalty to the Crown. In early October, at Ashby-de-la-Zouch, when news came of the risings in the North, he was swift to indicate that he was ready to raise troops against the king's rebellious subjects. Alongside the earls of Shrewsbury and Rutland, he joined the forces headed by the Duke of Norfolk, remaining in Yorkshire until the dissemination of the royal pardon in December. In May 1539, his son was rewarded: Sir Francis, Lord Hastings was granted an annuity of £20 from the manors of Goodeby and Overtonquartermarshe, Leicestershire.[139] Hastings continued in favour and in royal service until he died on 24 March 1544.

Although George Talbot, 4th Earl of Shrewsbury was a conservative and unimpressed by Anne Boleyn, he remained steadfastly loyal to Henry during the Lincolnshire Rising and the Pilgrimage of Grace. Once informed of the disturbances in Lincolnshire, on 4 October, he mobilised his servants, tenants and friends, raising men on horseback. Shrewsbury stated that the king's subjects had risen in great numbers, 'contrary to their duties and allegiance'.[140] A week later, the earl wrote to Lord Darcy stating that he heard that Darcy's neighbours had begun to rise, as they had in Lincolnshire. He advised Darcy to remain in his country.[141] He was to write to Darcy again on 1 November, praising him for having stayed the commons: in his opinion, a good and honourable deed.[142]

Shrewsbury followed this up in the New Year with a letter to the king, advising the sovereign that he should write a letter of thanks to Lord Darcy.[143] Henry responded three days later and confirmed that he had indeed written a 'gentle' letter to Darcy, in accordance with Shrewsbury's recommendation. The king stated that he trusted that Darcy would now do his duty and he, the king, would regard this favourably, as if nothing had happened to the contrary.[144] This exchange of correspondence is somewhat surprising given Darcy's subsequent execution for treason. This appears, once again, to be evidence of Henry's duplicitous nature. Talbot was obviously attempting to steer Darcy clear of suspicion and trouble and had demonstrated his own loyalty to the king. He was, it seems, of the opinion that Darcy was inherently honourable and wanted to make Henry aware of this. As Talbot had proven his loyalty to the Crown and was an important noble and commander north of the Trent, it would appear that Henry sought to appease him by acquiescing at this point. The evidence suggests, however, that Darcy was a marked man in the king's eyes from early in the Pilgrimage (see the king's letters of admonition) and was biding his time in order for the opportunity to punish him to arise.[145]

After the rebels captured York and Pontefract Castle and began to threaten the town of Doncaster in October 1536, Shrewsbury marched north to prevent its capture. Shrewsbury and Norfolk were outnumbered and forced to negotiate with the Pilgrims. Shrewsbury's actions halted the momentum of the rising. The rebels did not march on London and their way was blocked by the area of influence of the Earl of Shrewsbury, centred on Sheffield and extending southwards through Derbyshire to Nottinghamshire. The earl's loyalty to Henry VIII was therefore crucial to the failure of the Pilgrimage.

In the aftermath of the Pilgrimage, Shrewsbury both added to and developed his estates. He acquired the lands of the former monasteries of Rufford in October 1537, which included the manor of Worksop and the lordship of Rotherham. The annual value was £246 15s 5d with rent of £46 15s 5d.[146] Following his death on 26 July 1538, his income was assessed at £1,735[147] and he was succeeded by his son, Francis, as the 5th Earl. Shrewsbury's role in the crisis was pivotal – if the rebels had managed to secure his support, they might have achieved their goals.

Thomas Cromwell assured Shrewsbury that he was the 'most woorthye erll that ever servyd a prince and suche a chefftayn as ys worthye eternall glorye'.[148] Henry and Cromwell, it appears, were well aware of the strategic importance of keeping Talbot onside. Shrewsbury had the potential to raise his retinue and clientage. Given his geographical landed base, Talbot had the means to have tipped the balance of power during the Pilgrimage from stalemate to a decisive outcome in favour of the Pilgrims. Had he taken this stance, other nobles may well have followed suit.

Henry Clifford, Earl of Cumberland's loyalty to the king is seen clearly during the Pilgrimage of Grace. He was initially instructed to lead a force to Hexham, Northumberland, where the monks had barricaded themselves in the monastery in defiance of the commissioners sent to suppress it. He attempted to fulfil this command but must have been forced to retreat to his castle at Skipton. Cumberland was trapped there by an insurrection of his own tenants, who attacked his houses and killed his deer. At the Pilgrims' Council at York on 21 November 1536, a letter was sent to the earl, requesting that he surrender Skipton Castle[149] – a request he obviously ignored.

Cumberland's son, Henry, Lord Clifford, also managed the defence of Carlisle against the commons. On 12 January 1537 Cumberland advised the king that the commons were wild and that there was a danger of further rebellion and informed Cromwell that the people were against him.[150] The earl tried to capture the rebels' captains around Westmorland, in accordance with the king's instructions. His illegitimate son, Thomas Clifford, and Sir Christopher Dacre routed the commons outside Carlisle Castle on 16 February 1537. The earl was elected to the Order of the Garter on 23 April 1537 to reward his loyal service. Henry, Lord Clifford was duly rewarded in June 1538 when he was appointed chief steward of the Yorkshire possessions of the king which had come about as the result of the attainder of Sir Stephen Hamerton.[151] Here again is the link between retribution and reward. In April 1542 the earl was granted the Craven estates of Bolton Priory, a house traditionally associated with the Cliffords. However, he died on 22 April 1542.[152]

There is an abundance of evidence to support the contention that Henry's loyal subjects undoubtedly benefited from their behaviour, either during or in the immediate aftermath of the Pilgrimage. The upper echelons of the nobility – the likes of the dukes of Norfolk and Suffolk – have been omitted from this aspect of the study, as the Pilgrimage did not really afford them the advancement and material gain that the other loyal protagonists coveted. However, some peers, such as the Earl of Shrewsbury, profited from the acquisition of ecclesiastical property. Whatever their private convictions, such men capitulated to the new order.

The most striking example of meteoric rise and spectacular financial reward during this period is, perhaps, John Dudley, but the material gains and wealth acquired by others, in particular, Arthur Darcy and Richard Morison, are illuminating in terms of demonstrating how conformity resulted in patronage and enhanced social prestige. This is not to say that loyalty during the Pilgrimage was solely responsible. Other factors, such as individual ability and serendipity, must also have been contributory factors in advancement. Richard Rex has emphasised the role that the dissolution of the monasteries played in facilitating grants and rewards. The dissolution, he stated 'transferred the patronage of hundreds of benefices into lay hands, with the king emerging as far the greatest gainer'.[153]

It is hoped that this study has shown that the patronage of the Crown in the North was essential in securing loyalty and compliance. Such patronage was an important tool in the defeat of the Pilgrimage of Grace. Thomas Cromwell's role in this process, throughout the risings and in the following years until his fall in 1540, was critical and the many examples given here have had to be included to demonstrate just how the Lord Privy Seal operated.

It is, however, interesting to note that Cromwell was ultimately a mere patron and broker, with an effective network of clients and informants.

Many of his former clients continued to prosper despite his demise. The void left by Cromwell was filled by other administrators and patrons acting on behalf of the Crown – he was replaced as secretary jointly by Wriothesley and Sadler.[154] Patronage and power were ultimately the preserve of the monarch and continued to be disseminated based upon the evidence of a subject's service and loyalty. The watershed moment, it can be argued, came here. From this point, religion was inextricably linked with service as a way of demonstrating that loyalty.

The links between retribution and reward have also been examined and it seems apparent that one man's misfortune was, inevitably, another man's gain. Evidence of opportunism, 'tale-telling' and avarice has been presented. As Horrox has remarked, subjects were called upon to provide information in a mutually beneficial relationship. It is hard to avoid an impression of vultures circling on the lookout for carcasses. As Kettering has stated, the practice of clientage concealed the cold, hard reality of men and their ambitions coming together.[155]

The Pilgrimage of Grace and its aftermath provide an illustration of how patronage and clientage were used in a mutually beneficial way. Henry retained the loyalty of men who were crucial in the movement's ultimate demise, whilst these clients were rewarded materially and socially, and so fulfilled their personal ambitions.

It is now time to consider the demise of the Pilgrimage under another spotlight. The rising was defeated on the ground, but how were the ideas and rhetoric it espoused quelled? Or were they? We turn, in the next chapter, to examining perceptions of the Pilgrimage and to analysing the methods the Crown used to attempt to discredit and defeat the ideals which led the Pilgrims to rebel in the first place.

6

Perceptions and the Pilgrimage: The Crown's Response

Wherefore I cannot think that the putting down of abbeys, that is to say, the putting away of maintained lechery, buggery and hypocrisy, should be the cause of this rebellious insurrection.[1]

Richard Morison was unequivocal in his condemnation of the Lincolnshire Uprising in October 1536, and the purpose of this chapter is to examine the varying perceptions of the Henrician religious innovations before, during and after the Pilgrimage of Grace. Of course, Morison's pro-regime perspective can be challenged by other commentators, and in this and the following chapter, attention is focused on the diametrically opposed perceptions of the Pilgrimage of Grace and, more widely, the Henrician religious experiment.

How were the Henrician religious changes enforced? We will examine the Crown's responses to the Pilgrimage: an approach which deployed the use of propaganda, preaching, the king's personal involvement and the use of sanction and punishment. An examination of the rhetoric and language of the official Henrician position, including proponents such as Morison and Thomas Starkey, will be used in conjunction with the other methods the Crown used to seek to defend and justify its position. We will begin by attempting to gauge opinion in the period prior to the outbreak of the trouble in October 1536.

Richard Layton, who became one of the hate figures in the Pilgrimage of Grace, had been appointed as one of the commissioners to investigate the monasteries by Thomas Cromwell. In January 1536, he advised Cromwell that he and his colleagues had found great corruption among the religious persons in Yorkshire – just as they had done in the south.[2] In the same month, Archbishop Lee of York confirmed to Cromwell that he had received his instructions to avoid 'contrariety' in preaching against the new 'novelties' and that he was to repress the temerity of the adherents of the Bishop of Rome.[3] In the spring, Lee reiterated the fact that he was 'on-message' and confirmed that he had given orders that preachers would not be tolerated who might use 'novelties' in order to sow dissension, in accordance with the king's commandment. He also requested that Cromwell prevent the suppression of the two monasteries of St Oswald's and Hexham.[4]

Opinion during these embryonic stages of the Henrician experiment was in a state of flux, and theological conceptions were not clearly demarcated. As Steven Ellis has pointed out, there were 'rapid shifts and ambiguities in the government's religious policy'.[5] The king himself had written to Gardiner and Wallop, his diplomats at the French court, in the spring, a few weeks before the fall of Anne Boleyn. Henry stated that he had undertaken nothing lightly regarding the Bishop of Rome, but on the foundations of God, nature, honesty and – tellingly – with the assent of Parliament.[6]

The Humanist scholar Thomas Starkey expressed concerns about the control of preachers who, under the colour of driving away tradition, he stated, had almost driven away virtue and holiness.[7] Starkey's most famous work, *The Dialogue*, published in the late 1520s, was a heavy rhetorical work. It provided a description of the ideal commonwealth, identified the general causes of its decay and specified remedies. Drawing on St Paul, this work emphasised the need for a multiplicity of function or parts in society. For Starkey, the diseased body was characterised by a state of imbalance.[8] He was licensed as a preacher, and in December 1536, he began a tract against the Pilgrimage of Grace but only completed a few lines. Thomas Mayer has suggested that this reflected his ambivalence.[9] Starkey, who had been friends with Reginald Pole in Italy, was in favour of the Royal Supremacy and asserted that More and Fisher had suffered because of their own folly – they died, he said, for a superstition.[10] It is revealing that even a pro-Henrician polemicist had highlighted the pitfalls of religious innovation and was concerned with the effect on spiritual virtue.

Similarly, the Bishop of Lincoln, John Longland, much detested in the Lincolnshire Rising was, in reality, doctrinally orthodox. He did not endure qualms about reconciling his conservative position with acceptance of the Royal Supremacy and is an example of the acquiescent clergy, for whom expedience was the primary motivator. In August, 1536, Longland requested authorisation for the king's writ, so that *De Haeretico Comburendo* might be applied to heretics in his diocese.[11] *De Haeretico Comburendo* (Latin for 'of burning a heretic') was a law passed by Henry IV in 1401, enabling the punishment of heretics by burning at the stake.

After the rising was underway in Lincolnshire in October, the king informed Gardiner and Wallop that 'injurious rumours have been blown abroad lately that the king intends to confiscate all the ornaments, plate and jewels of all parish churches'. He attributed these rumours to the work of traitors.[12] The king evidently wished it to be known abroad that the risings were the result of false rumours which had been exploited by the ringleaders. After the First Appointment and truce at Doncaster on 27 October, Henry was still perplexed by the behaviour of his subjects. He sent instructions to ascertain that the commons had indeed dispersed or whether they remained in their madness. He reiterated the fact that the rumours which had been circulating were false, such as charges for baptisms, and advised that the dissolution of the monasteries did not concern the commonalty. The king urged his subjects to submit and promise their obedience.[13] On the same day, one John Williams furnished Cromwell with a derogatory appraisal of the Lincolnshire men – they were, according to him, asses with dull wits.[14]

Lancaster Herald, as previously noted, had been intercepted by the commons en route to Pontefract in late October – his intended proclamation spoke of the king's *lawful* occasion to advance with fire and sword against the rebels.[15] Writing to the Earl of Derby on 28 October, Henry described Aske as a villainous traitor.[16] It is clear that the king was angry at the disobedience and temerity shown by his subjects and judged them as traitors against his lawful religious changes. At this stage the king's correspondence was quite frequent, which suggests just how affronted and perhaps anxious he was with regard to the insurrection – this was a monarch who was notoriously inefficient in dealing with his own letters and tended to delegate affairs to his ministers.

Henry then set about providing an answer to the demands of the rebels. On 2 November, he addressed their points with his characteristic perception of the right of his position. The king wondered 'that ignorant people go about to instruct him what the right faith should be', and stated that 'we have done nothing that may not be defended by God's law and man's, and to our own Church, whereof we be supreme head, we have not done so much prejudice as many of our predecessors have done upon less grounds'. Henry sought to remind the people of the advantages which had come with his rule, 'What King has kept you his subjects so long in wealth and peace, ministering indifferent justice, and defending you from outward enemies? What king has been more ready to pardon or loath to punish?' Henry concluded by reminding them that they were fortunate in obtaining his pardon, 'to show our pity we are content, if we find you penitent, to grant you all letters of pardon on your delivering to us 10 such ringleaders of this rebellion as we shall assign to you. Now note the benignity of your Prince.'[17]

Henry himself cultivated the image of a 'strong' king and was convinced that his subjects owed him complete loyalty irrespective of any misgivings. Henry did, in fact, issue circulars himself and in one, dated 19 November 1536, he reiterated the 'obedience due by God's law to the Sovereign' and emphasised that his subjects had no right to resist his commandments, even if they perceived them as unjust. The same circular began with Henry pointing out that the king had advanced the bishops and endowed them with 'great revenues'. They were thus compelled to follow his instructions and plainly read his Articles on pain of deprivation of their bishoprics and further punishment.[18]

Henry forwarded quite detailed instructions to Norfolk and William Fitzwilliam prior to the Pontefract Appointment of 2–4 December. Discussing the tactics they should deploy, he stated that he thought that the rebels would be very obstinate, 'stiff', with regards to the issues of the free pardon and a parliament in the North. Henry was adamant that his honour as sovereign should not be diminished by granting the rebels' desires; he did not wish Norfolk and Fitzwilliam to enter into talks with the Pilgrims unless they had disbanded their forces. He wanted the message hammered home to the rebels that he was at a loss to understand their ingratitude and their attempts to achieve their objectives by violence instead of humility. Henry went on to state that his commanders must, however, with all dexterity, induce the Pilgrims to consider the 'infinite mischiefs' that might ensue as a consequence of the gravity of the situation.[19] Henry admitted that he only granted the free pardon at Pontefract reluctantly, upon the advice of his council.[20]

Henry was by no means alone in perceiving the Pilgrims' actions as worthy of condemnation. During the meeting at Pontefract, Lord Monteagle advised that he had apprehended a vicar who had spoken out against the king's acts and in favour of the insurrection.[21] Neither was criticism exclusively reserved for the Pilgrims: disobedience to the monarch was denounced by Tunstall and Stokesley in a letter to Reginald Pole. Pole had been created a cardinal by the consistory at Rome[22] and was urged to surrender his red hat to the Bishop of Rome. The pope, they argued, had seduced Pole from his duty to his sovereign.[23] Meanwhile, Cromwell was busy putting a positive spin on the rebellion to Gardiner and Wallop. He stated that the king had healed the corrupt members instead of cutting them off. Here, we see a continuation of Henry's physician's analogy with regard to the body politic[24] – hardly surprising, for early modern, organic, political analogy was fixated with illness.[25]

Henry's personal involvement was one feature of the Crown response to the Pilgrimage – the control and supervision of sermons and preaching were another important method by which the Crown sought to justify its position. Cromwell was acutely aware of the power of the pulpit in securing support for the Royal Supremacy and exerted his power as patron in order to strengthen the voice of the government. Cromwellian patronage of preachers became a strategy of ecclesiastical reform and the Lord Privy Seal appreciated the importance of those selected to preach. Cromwell granted substantial benefices to those who would further the cause of reform and the Crown.[26]

Bishop Hugh Latimer delivered a sermon against the Pilgrimage of Grace on 5 November 1536 and another sermon began by attacking the unnatural rebellions of the people, who:

> … are so abhominable in the sight of God and so evill of their own nature that no cause canne make them goode and iuste, no not if the people shulde rise against the king for the defense of the gospel, for God woll not have his trowth of holye scripture promoted and set forwards [by treason]

and murders, but onlye by such leefull and good meanes [as] he hath pre-
scribed in his holye scripture that is by preaching and hearing the worde
of God, by obedience unto princes, by patience, and honest lyving.[27]

Early in 1537, the king's council was seeking to portray Pole as having a role
in propagating dissent and, by implication, the recent rebellion. They wrote
to the cardinal on 18 January stating that his purpose was to slander the king,
bring his honour into contempt, set forth untruths and provoke Henry's
subjects.[28] Around the same time, in mid-January, Starkey was again admon-
ishing his former friend. Discussing the 'rumours' of Pole's appointment as
a cardinal, Starkey implored him not to accept as to do so would draw the
king's displeasure upon him and other members of his family. Prophetic
words indeed. Starkey continued, stating that he was sure that Pole's love of
his country and desire to serve his prince would prevent him from accepting that 'dignity' without first considering the state of the Church and
Henry's wishes.[29] In March, Cromwell called the bishops together to listen
to Starkey's directives on preaching.[30]

At the outset of this chapter, an example of Richard Morison's rhetoric
against the monasteries was given. It is now time to examine the role of
propaganda in shaping perceptions and public opinion in a volatile and fearful climate. Morison was one of a small number of English Humanists active
on the Continent in the early 1530s. There, he was in contact with Thomas
Starkey and actually stayed in Reginald Pole's household at Padua, northern
Italy, between the spring of 1535 and May 1536. He returned to England
at this point, after Starkey had intervened on his behalf, to obtain a post in
Thomas Cromwell's service.[31] Here again we see an illustration of clientage
and patronage at work. Morison's career in central government was barely
five months old when the Lincolnshire Rising broke out. As he was the
most junior member of Cromwell's staff and had demonstrated a talent for
polemic, this presented him with the opportunity for self-aggrandisement.
As Berkowitz has pointed out, the battle for men's minds was as important
to Henry as military campaigns.

Morison was to write, anonymously, as the voice of loyal England, and his
first tract, *A Lamentation in Which is Showed What Ruin and Destruction Cometh
of Seditious Rebellion*, was composed between 5 and 15 October. The tract
must have pleased the king and Cromwell, for Morison was soon given an

instruction to compose another, *A Remedy for Sedition Where Are Contained Many Things Concerning the True and Loyal Obeisance That Commons owe Unto Their Prince and Soverign Lord the king.*[32] Both tracts share similar themes and a heavy emphasis on classical references. They are based upon the themes of obedience, the body politic and the society of orders. *A Lamentation …* also equates the love of God with the love of the prince, whilst *A Remedy …*, written because of the outbreak of the Pilgrimage, takes the opportunity to specifically attack one of the Pontefract Articles. Let us now turn to examine the themes in each tract.

A Lamentation … is quite a passionate and persuasive piece and resonates emotionally, despite the usual inclusion of classical and Old Testament references. Morison opens the tract by stating that those guilty of sedition are worthy of punishment, not least because they 'traitorously make of one nation two'.[33] This would, perhaps, stir instinctive responses from a people whose families had borne the scars from the ravages of the Wars of the Roses, and it was, after all, just over fifty years since Henry Tudor had ended this conflict at Bosworth Field. Morison then declared his objective of making 'all honest stomachs … detest and abhor seditious traitors'.

The theme of obedience, of crucial importance to Henry, is discussed throughout the tract: 'Who is he that very nature hath not taught to be obedient to his sovereign lord the king? Peter, Paul, Christ finally, all say that well; "Obey thy prince".' Morison was concise and explicit: 'Obedience is the badge of a true Christian man.' He then turned specifically to the Lincolnshire Rising: 'It far passeth cobblers' crafts to discuss what lords, what bishops, what counsellors, what acts, statutes and laws are most meet for a commonwealth and whose judgement should be best or worst concerning matters of religion.'[34] Here is a direct rebuke to the Articles of the Lincolnshire rebels and their attack on the king's advisors. The shoemaker, Nicholas Melton, is ridiculed for having the temerity to lead the rebels and was known, colloquially, as 'Captain Cobbler'.

We see the accepted perception of the body politic as a society of orders. In Tudor England, the body politic was imbued with cosmic significance: an emphasis on the hierarchical order placed by God in the human body and all creation.[35] Melton had no right to interfere with or presume to advise his social and political superiors. Morison was to develop this theme further in *A Remedy …*.

Morison then played a somewhat emotive card – an appeal to patriotism:

If England could speak might it not say thus? 'I am one; why do you make
me twain? Ye are all mine; how can any of you, where none ought to do
so, seek the destruction of me, my most noble and prudent prince, King
Henry VIII, and his true subjects?

'Lincolnshire! thou art a member of mine. I thought if need had been, if
mine enemies had infested me, to have found help and succor at thy hand:
and thou thus traitorously settest upon me?'

The trend continued with, 'If Lincolnshire seek to destroy England, what
wonder is it if France and Scotland sometime have sought to offend me?'
Morison proceeded to cite examples from the Greco-Roman world
before declaring, 'I would have men believe that there was never none so
unnatural as to rise against his prince and country', and 'What folly, what
madness is this to make an hole in the ship that thou sailest in?' The argument is then more specific: 'Their pope, their puppet, their idol, their
Roman god, will not out of their hearts. … He is gone, but too many of
his livery tarrieth still.'[36] Here is an early manifestation of what will become
the enduring claim that dual loyalty to the king and the pope is not possible. Catholic self-identity came to be fraught with the inherent tension
between reconciling Catholic belief and allegiance to the English Crown.[37]

Early modern England, like its European counterparts, was a society
of orders and Morison drove home the point when discussing the sanction given to the dissolution of the monasteries. It was done, he said, 'by
the whole counsel and consent of the three estates of England' and to the
honour of God. The king, in this view, should be loved by his subjects next
to God. Morison maintained that the king should not hear 'suitors that
come in harness and, being heard, apply to their requests that seek nothing
but dissension, shedding of blood and the ruin of the whole realm'.[38] This
perception of the act of petitioning is clearly compatible with the contention put forward by Hoyle, that it may be regarded as a conservative form
of behaviour and a public activity which accepted the existing political
structures.[39] Clearly, Morison was particularly irked that existing political
structures – rites of negotiation, rituals and gestures – were not respected in
this case, as is shown in his contempt for Nicholas Melton.

Morison then went on to compare Lincolnshire unfavourably to London and 'other civil places of England'. Here Morison was echoing Henry's own reproach to the Lincolnshire rebels of 19 October. The king was characteristically indignant and sharp in his rebuttal of their grievances:

> How presumptuous then are ye, the rude commons of one shire, and that one of the most brute and beastly of the whole realm and of least experience, to find fault with your prince for the electing of his counsellors and prelates? Thus you take upon yourself to rule your prince.[40]

Morison continued with praise for Henry 'that taketh such care to see religion restored, his people now well taught who so long hath been deluded' and condemned the rebels: 'Let not this, the pernicious example of these rebels, anything alienate our minds from the fear of God, the love of our prince. Let us recognize our duty unto both.'[41]

Here, Morison is justifying Henry's Caesaropapism: the people had been deluded and ill-taught whilst Rome was in control of the Church. The fear of God and the love of the prince were one and the same. The tract concludes with the somewhat rousing 'all traitors, God willing, shall learn by Lincolnshire nothing to be more odious to God and man than treason'.[42]

By the time *A Lamentation ...* was published, the Lincolnshire Rising was at an end but the eruption of the Pilgrimage of Grace, hot on its heels, gave Morison another project to work on. He produced *A Remedy* .... Again, there was a heavy emphasis on classical references from Greece and Rome and, as Berkowitz has stated, the 'concrete experience of the past'. Morison set out to pointedly attack one of the Pontefract Articles – the demand to expel villain blood from the King's Council. This demand would have irritated Cromwell and angered Henry as an invasion of his royal prerogative.[43] Morison maintained that men must 'be esteemed that have most gifts of the mind'. This would appear to refer to his master, Cromwell, and perhaps, indeed, himself. It is, of course, indicative of the patron–client bond discussed in the previous chapter. Morison is here using effusive and flattering language – it is sycophantic praise for his patron who had been scathingly disrespected by such rebels. He hammered home the point: 'His Grace govern us by such officers as he shall know to be best for us.'[44]

'God maketh kings, especially when they reign by succession.' Morison went on to emphasise the point that God made Henry VIII king, 'and also made this law, Obey your king'.[45] Perhaps Morison would have been more astute if he had avoided the mention of succession, given the fact that Henry VII had not reigned by succession, and had possessed an extremely flimsy claim to the throne. Morison, as in *A Lamentation ...*, went on to emphasise the accepted wisdom of the time, the belief in a society of orders. As Fletcher and MacCulloch has stated, the different groups in the social order were fixed for all time. Early modern England glorified and embraced the fact that it was an unequal society[46] and would have had no concept of any alternative. Morison put this succinctly to his purpose: 'Lords must be lords, commons must be commons, every man accepting his degree.'[47] Morison allied this with the prevailing belief that the commonwealth was like a body[48] and he used the analogy of a physician, as did both the king and Cromwell during the Pilgrimage.

Morison attributed the malfunction in the body politic and the malaise of sedition in England to a number of factors; lack of education, idleness, gluttony and division. 'Education, evil education, is a great cause of these and all other mischiefs.' Morison felt compelled to elaborate on this contention: 'If the nobles be evil taught in points concerning religion, as if they be popish', 'how can their servants choose but be so too?' Morison then questioned how neighbours could agree and live harmoniously if they were not of the same faith and belief, before declaring, 'The king's Grace shall never have true subjects that do not believe as His Grace doth. For how can they love him (as they should do) who, being in errors themselves, in darkness and ignorancy, suppose His Grace to be in a wrong faith.'[49] Again, we see the advocacy of Henry's Caesaropapism and a principle which would come to be known in Europe as *cuius regio, eius religio* ('whose realm, his religion').[50] The pope is then criticised as the 'foreign head' in Rome, whilst the body was in England. This foreign head had 'brought the silly brains of many a poor man into deep errors'.[51] Morison declared that, 'We must agree in religion, we must serve but one master; one body will have but one head', and the nobles 'must be of one belief, of one faith, of one religion; they must all agree on one head'.[52]

A Remedy ... laments the fact that England is so divided and compares Christians unfavourably to Jews and the Turks – 'Turks go not again Turks, nor Jews against Jews, because they agree in their faith.'[53] The English are criticised for being idle and Morison believed that they were only too ready to believe the rumours about bread, pork, geese and capon prior to the Lincolnshire Rising because 'all the senses be drowned with drink' and 'too much feeding'.[54] Morison then used a quotation from Erasmus in 1519 to present the king in a good light – 'He hath set up good laws.'[55] After heaping such selective praise from the leading Humanist of the day upon Henry, Morison maintained that the king, by his long experience 'well perceiveth that the chief honour that a Christian prince should seek is the saving of his people'. The tract concludes with the assertion that concord 'maketh us the friends of God, the inheritors of heaven and prevents England's enemies from laughing at its destruction'.[56]

Having produced his royal propaganda in the autumn and winter of 1536, Richard Morison was at work on the king's response to the suggestion of a council of the church in Mantua in the spring of 1537. Pope Paul III was concerned about the spread of Protestantism, particularly in Germany, and he sent nuncios throughout Europe to propose the idea of a council. The pope issued a decree for a general ecumenical council to be held in Mantua, Italy, to begin on 23 May 1537. While Morison was busy setting out Henry VIII's position, Martin Luther wrote the Schmalkald Articles in preparation for the general council. These sharply defined where the Lutherans could and could not compromise. The council failed to convene after another war broke out between France and Charles V and a general council eventually covened as the Council of Trent in 1545.

True to form, Morison suggested to his patron, Cromwell, that he include content to demonstrate that England had nothing to fear from those who attempted to put down God's word and restore the papacy.[57] Henry, at this time, was eager for rapprochement with his nephew, King James of Scotland, and dispatched Ralph Sadler north with a gift and instructions for an audience. Sadler was to proceed as follows: he was to acknowledge that although James continued to regard the pope as the Vicar of Christ on earth, he was nonetheless eager for him to listen to Henry's point of view; the king was to request his good nephew not to be biased by the false reports they had spread of him throughout Christendom, nor to think of him otherwise than as a Christian Catholic prince; the king was slandered only because he had removed Roman abuses and superstitions, and had ventured to exercise the power long usurped by the Bishop of Rome.[58]

In the aftermath of the Pilgrimage and the resumption of revolts, there exists evidence of perceptions of both pro-regime and anti-regime standpoints. In March 1537, the Earl of Sussex advised Cromwell that he had kept his promise to punish the traitorous monks of Whalley. The accomplishment of the matter was, he thought, God's ordinance.[59] Sir Marmaduke Tunstall was clearly instructed by Cromwell as to how to conduct himself in Yorkshire with regard to the Royal Supremacy and sedition.[60] Sir Arthur Darcy advised the king that the recent commotions had disclosed the papist errors and it was adherence to these which had induced the commons to rise.[61] This, from the son of the conservative and orthodox Lord Darcy who, at the time, was incarcerated in the Tower.

After the Lincolnshire Rising and the Pilgrimage of Grace were consigned to memory, Cromwell was anxious to ensure that the task of promoting the Henrician Reformation in the North was set to with renewed vigour. In October 1537, the Bishop of Carlisle advised the vicegerent of the dissemination of the injunctions in his diocese and stated that he would ensure that Cromwell's injunctions were performed as directed: he would apply himself to the reformation of all such negligence as he could detect, either in himself or in those who were at his direction.[62] Reports of seditious words were also treated with diligence and reported to the Council of the North for investigation, as is illustrated by the following example.

In December, the Prior of Newburgh was reported by one Brian Boye for words he had spoken the previous August. A Mrs Fulthorp had apparently praised the Duke of Norfolk for his handling of the rebellions and the prior said, 'It maketh no matter if one of them were hanged against the other' (meaning the king and the duke).[63] The prior, Mrs Fulthorp and Mr Boye were sent for and commanded to attend at York the following day. The prior denied the charges completely and other witnesses said that they did not hear him utter those words. Sir George Lawson settled the matter and said to say no more about it.

Cromwell continued to issue instructions for the setting forth of the Royal Supremacy in the North. In December, he instructed John Lamplieu of Furness Abbey that he should have a vigilant eye that all curates do their duty in setting forth the king's Supremacy, and if he were to hear of any seditious person provoking diversity of opinion, either by open preaching or in secret, he should put him in prison until further instructed.[64]

The Bishop of Lincoln instructed his clergy to preach sermons at least four times a year – either in Latin or English – in order to clearly set forth the injunctions sanctioned by the king. It is worth highlighting that the Diocese of Lincoln was the second largest in England and stretched across ten counties[65] so Bishop Longland was attempting to ensure that the official message was being driven home across the North in the aftermath of rebellion.

Cromwell issued a second set of injunctions in September 1538 and these reiterated the requirement of obedience. Item eleven is clear:

> If you … know any man within your parish or elsewhere who does not comply [with the injunctions] … now by the law of this realm … you shall detect and present the same to the King's Highness or his honourable council or to his vicegerent aforesaid or the justice of the peace.[66]

The punishments for non-compliance were listed in Item 17 as 'deprivation', 'sequestration' and 'other coercion'.[67] It is apparent that the policing of the Reformation was the responsibility of a layman, Thomas Cromwell, and was enforced according to the secular law. The upper echelons of the clergy were, as such, noticeably confined to the peripheries of enforcement.

In December, the king followed this up by issuing a circular to the Justices of the Peace. It is apparent from this that Henry was still feeling a little vulnerable in the wake of the Pilgrimage of Grace. The king expressed his opinion that the people who had been involved in the Pilgrimage might have destroyed the country and it was his own clemency which had prevented this. Henry stated that he could have destroyed the rebels, their wives and children 'by the sword'. He also described the Pilgrims as miserable, papistical and superstitious wretches. The king thanked the Justices of the Peace for their previous efforts and instructed them to 'try out and hand over to … punishment maintainers of the bishop of Rome's usurped authority and … punish spreaders of seditious rumours'.[68] This circular also commanded them to use their utmost indulgence to find parsons, vicars and curates, who did not substantially declare the injunctions, instructing them that they were compelled to read them. King Henry VIII's circular succinctly summarises his views on the enforcement of his Reformation.

This sense of unease and suspicion can also be illustrated by the example of a preacher, who was recorded as having to preach a sermon 'by command', as a result of having being reported to the king and Cromwell. This particular preacher was reported for having criticised the translation of the Bible into English and of having said that the peers who had agreed to it would also put Christ to death, if He were alive at the time. To make amends, and for self-preservation no doubt, he insisted that he had shown his loyalty through his preaching at the time of the insurrection. He had, he said, preached that in his prince's quarrel, he would have killed his own father if he had been a rebel. Further, he argued that the uprising was only to maintain superstition, hypocrisy and the abominable lifestyles of canons, friars and monks.[69]

The 'fear factor' was undoubtedly an important tool in achieving obedience to the king and compliance with his religious changes. Rory, Bishop of Derry wrote to Pope Paul III on New Year's Eve 1538 that:

The king of England's deputy in Ireland and his adherents, refusing to recognise the Pope, burn houses, destroy churches, ravish maids, spoil and kill the innocent. They kill all priests who pray for the Pope or compel them to erase his name from the canon, and torture preachers who do not repudiate his authority.[70]

These are obviously the words of a disaffected clergyman and no doubt are prone to exaggeration, but again one can see fear and violence associated with the king and his regime. It also illustrates that dissent and disaffection were not confined to the North of England.

Richard Morison produced a new treatise against treason in February 1539, *An invective against the great and detestable vice, treason, wherein the secrete practises and traitorous workinges of theym that suffrid of late are disclosed. Made by Rycharde Morisyne,*[71] and Henry thanked his nephew, James V, for prohibiting slanderous rhymes against him by proclamation in Scotland.[72] Bishop Cuthbert Tunstall of Durham delivered a pro-regime sermon the following month on Palm Sunday. Preaching in the presence of the king, Tunstall denounced the worldliness and ambition of the papacy and criticised the Bishop of Rome's encouragement of war against England.[73]

It seems clear, as G.W. Bernard has stated, that Henry came to view himself as an Old Testament king, a Josiah, with responsibility before God to implement the laws of God. In this respect, he was aided and abetted by

Thomas Cromwell in attempting to promote this perception to his subjects. In the aftermath of the Pilgrimage of Grace, Cromwell insisted that pamphlets and sermons published by his scholarly clients, such as Morison and Starkey, should reiterate the message of due obedience to the king.[74]

Royal propaganda increased in the aftermath of the Pilgrimage and one famous and unashamedly biased account of the events in the North was written by the Tudor chronicler Edward Hall. This document is commonly referred to as *Hall's Chronicle*, but its full title is *The Union of the Two Noble and Illustre Familes of Lancastre and York*, and was first published in 1542. Hall was a lawyer by profession and sat in Parliament on four occasions – 1529, 1539, 1542 and 1545. Hall's account of the rising is relatively brief (compared to Morison) and is worth highlighting as it reveals a deep-seated enmity towards the Pilgrims, the North and Roman Catholic doctrine. As C.H. Williams has argued, Hall's objective was to provide an account which was a deliberate, unqualified praise of the achievements of the Tudor dynasty.[75]

Hall's description of events is a blatant piece of propaganda and reveals more about his deep-rooted prejudices than actual detailed, historical fact. His account will be examined below. He described the Lincolnshire Rising in quite scathing terms: 'The inhabitants of the North parts being at that time very ignorant and rude, knowing not what true religion meant but altogether noseled in superstition and popery had risen as a result of rumours and prompting by priests.'[76]

Having dealt with the demise of the Lincolnshire Rising, he turned his attention to the Pilgrimage in Yorkshire. He began his narrative of the Pilgrimage with:

> The king was truly informed that there was a new insurrection made by the northern men, who had assembled themselves into a huge and great army of *warlike* men, well appointed with captains, horse, armour and artillery, to the number of 40,000 men, who had encamped themselves in Yorkshire. And these men had bound themselves to each other by their oath to be faithful and obedient to their captain.[77]

Hall's description of the Pilgrims as 'warlike' is pejorative and actually at odds with the restraint with which the Pilgrim host conducted itself. He is broadly correct with his estimation of the amount of men involved – 40,000 – and the Duke of Norfolk did indeed describe the Pilgrims as the 'flower of the north'.[78] Hall then stated that the Pilgrims believed their action as being for 'the maintenance and defence of the faith of Christ and the deliverance of Holy Church, sore decayed and oppressed'. In Hall's eyes, the rebels had embarked upon 'their seditious and traitorous voyage and called this a holy and blessed pilgrimage'.[79] Revealingly, he treated the Pilgrims' use of imagery with complete contempt. He described the Pilgrims' banners as depicting Christ on the cross on one side and a chalice with 'a painted cake' on the other.[80] The 'painted cake' – the Eucharist – is scathingly dismissed. That King Henry upheld his belief in the doctrine of Transubstantiation (that bread and wine is literally the body and blood of Christ) is conveniently ignored. Transubstantiation had been confirmed as an essential tenet of doctrine in the Church of England by the Act of Six Articles in 1539.[81]

The banners were, according to Hall, hypocritical and they 'feigned sanctity'. The Pilgrims' badges of the Five Wounds of Christ appear to have particularly irked Hall, thus 'the rebellious garrison of Satan set forth and decked themselves with his false and counterfeited signs of holiness'. This, in Hall's opinion, was done 'only to delude and deceive the simple and ignorant people'.[82] It has been noted how the king and others perceived the people of the North as rude – Hall was a little more gracious in his use of the word 'ignorant'.

Hall then described how the dukes of Norfolk and Suffolk, with the Earl of Shrewsbury and others, 'led a mighty royal army of great power and strength to set upon the rebels'.[83] The contemporary sources do not lead one to believe that the army royal was either mighty or possessed of great strength and power. According to Hall, the nobles encountered the rebels and saw 'how determined they were on battle' and the noble captains then 'worked with great prudence to pacify all without shedding blood'.[84] Hall then drew upon previous descriptions of the northern men as being obstinate,[85] 'But the northern men were so stiff necked that they would in no way stoop, but stoutly stood and maintained their wicked enterprise'.[86] The nobles then, 'perceiving and seeing no other way to pacify these wretched rebels, agreed upon a battle'.[87]

Hall continued by painting a picture whereby the superior royal army would have routed the rebels but for divine intervention. The night before the battle:

> ... a little rain fell, nothing to speak of, but yet, as if by a great miracle of
> God, the water ... suddenly rose to such a height, depth and breadth that
> ... when the hour of battle should have come, it was impossible for one
> army to get at the other.

God had intervened, according to Hall, because of his 'compassion on the
great number of innocent persons who in the deadly slaughter would likely
to have been murdered' and the battle could not take place. This is not mentioned as being a significant event in any of the contemporary sources and
one wonders if Hall was drawing upon some of the accounts of the battles
during the Wars of the Roses for inspiration and embellishment.[88] In Hall's
portrayal, the Pilgrims were belligerent, traitorous, superstitious, ignorant
and obstinate. That their annihilation was prevented was only attributable
to divine providence and the king's promise of a pardon and assurance that
the grievances they had would be 'gently heard and their reasonable petitions granted'.[89]

Another valuable source for the Pilgrimage is *Thomas Master's Narrative*,
written between 1635 and 1638.[90] Master (1603–43) was a fellow of New
College, Oxford, and Richard Hoyle has arranged his documents into a
narrative account of the rebellion. Most of the documents in Master's col-
lection are familiar from the State Papers, but as Hoyle has pointed out, five
were previously unknown and are thus important in filling in some of the
gaps in the understanding available to the Dodds some seventy years before
Hoyle's research.

One such illuminating document highlights a description of the military
situation at Doncaster prior to the first meeting there.[91] This account can
be compared with Edward Hall's description and perhaps drew upon it.
It also refers to the weather as being instrumental in the outcome of proceedings at Doncaster. The account mentions a 'Foorde not [more] than
2 foote deep' that separated the rebels and the Duke of Norfolk's forces. The
'Enemyes' forces were estimated at being at least 30,000 and contained all
the lords from Doncaster to Scotland, apart from the earls of Westmorland
and Cumberland and Lord Dacre. However, 'God of his infinite goodness
sent, that night, such a Raine that it was not possible without swimming to
passe the water'.[92] This account goes on to state that the country was in the
hands of the rebels and they 'have made it desolate'. There was pestilence in

the Crown's army and they were in need of 'vittayles and Money'. Of the rebels, it was said, 'we cannot force them to a Battayle', but they 'have made us condescend to a Treaty with them'.[93]

Master's account continues on 28 October and confirms that Sir Ralph Ellerker and Robert Bowes were sent with the Duke of Norfolk following the rebels' dispersal. It makes the highly dubious claim that Ellerker and Bowes had 'manfully' defended Hull 'against the Rebells, yet were forced to yield it to them, and ioyne with them', but acknowledges the fact that Ellerker and Bowes presented the Pilgrims' petition to the king.[94] On 22 November, it was recorded that the 'Rebells' were at York to hold their council and hear the reports of Ellerker and Bowes from the king. By 26 November, the commons are described as being of great number 'and so well provided and so stubbornely minded'. They were, in this account, of the mindset that 'they will all dy, in case theyr Articles sent to the king be refused, and they will rather dy than deliver up Ask'. Norfolk's council is described as thinking 'it necessary for the present to grant a generall Pardon, and Parlement, and afterwards time may be to rectify all'. It is revealing that here again, the 'rebels' are portrayed as stubborn (see Hall's term, 'stiffnecked') and it is quite obvious that the pardon and promise of a parliament was a delaying tactic to buy the Crown time. The time to 'rectify' this condescension would come.

By 30 November, this account tells us that 'the Rebells increase in number and malice', and that they 'are so strong, and our forces so small, that, if this meeting take no effect, and warre follow, we are in ill case'.[95] This is in marked contrast to Hall's contention that a far superior royal army would have routed the commons but for divine intervention.

Master's description of the Pontefract Articles on 4 December is highly illuminating – the Articles, he stated, were, 'far from all reason'.[96] Master also confirmed a letter written by Edward Lee to the king on 3 December, although he dates it as tenth of that month. This account records that the Archbishop of York noted the mindset of the 'Rebells' at the start of the rising and stated that they 'took it ill that mention was made but of 3 sacraments, and no Purgatory. He told the king how he preached to them and shewed them how *theyr Pilgrimage (with the sword in the hand) was not lawfull*'.[97]

Master continued his account with a description of Bigod's rebellion in January 1537. By 4 February, Master described how the 'Duke of Norfolk's

coming into the North terrified the Comons and indeed he took punishment of many through hanging them up in chains in divers places'.
However, he emphasised that 'they were such as had attempted New
Rebellion, since the king's generall pardon granted'. Master then referred
to the letter from Darcy to Cromwell of 18 March 1537, in which Darcy
stated that 'I have served above 50 years the king's Majesty and his Father,
and should not willingly in my ould age enter Rebellion'. Master, however,
confirmed that Darcy was sent to London shortly afterwards and 'impri-
sioned'. By July, it is confirmed that Robert Constable and Aske had been
executed but no mention is made of Darcy's fate. The king, meanwhile, had
sent his 'Pardon to the North: which was received with great joy for they
were in a great feare'.[98]

The demise of the Pilgrimage of Grace was swift and the Henrician
regime seized the opportunity that Bigod's futile uprisings presented in
order to deal harshly with those it believed had been instrumental in the
initial rising. In the period during and after the rising, the Crown defended
and justified its position through the medium of propaganda, preaching,
punishment and the personal involvement of King Henry. The works of
Richard Morison, the foremost propagandist of the time, and those of
Edward Hall and Thomas Master, have been useful in illuminating the perceptions of those in agreement with the king's stance and hostile to the
Pilgrimage and all it represented. These ideas of loyalty and obedience to
the prince were recurring features of the late 1530s in England, specifically
with regard to religious changes. Obedience to God, the king, one's lord
or husband was expected and should not be questioned. Such obedience
was reinforced by biblical evidence and created the deference which held
the system together.[99] These constructs were to influence thinking about
religion, obedience and national identity far into the future.

Of course, propaganda in the form of treatises was not the only weapon
the Crown had at its disposal. Henry and his council justified and defended
both his religious innovations and response to the Pilgrimage using the
other methods mentioned. The use of uniform and consistent preaching
and sermons in tandem with written propaganda was meant to ensure that
the king's religious policies were disseminated and reinforced. This was carried out in conjunction with the promulgation of both the First (1536) and
Second Henrician Injunctions (1538) and the setting forth of the Royal

Supremacy. The theme and duty of obedience was of paramount importance and was reiterated at every opportunity.

Henry also justified his actions in writing: he responded with characteristic righteousness to the demands of the rebels and defended his position in correspondence with other monarchs and diplomats abroad. He based his position and justified his actions citing God, nature and, revealingly, Parliament. Henry also gave explicit instructions to his commanders in the field and issued circulars to the Justices of the Peace.

These tactics were allied with the use of punishment and retribution. Reports of sedition were followed up and individuals were apprehended. In addition to the retribution following the collapse of the Pilgrimage, suspected sedition was investigated by the Council of the North. The Crown sought to win the hearts and minds of its northern subjects by consistent persuasion, allied with fear and the use of force. To this end, it ostensibly achieved its goals – the result was that another uprising in the North was not attempted for more than thirty years.

Let us now turn to consider how the prevailing, 'official', domestic paradigm was contested and examine the instances of dissent and sympathy for the Pilgrims and the ideas they stood for.

7

The Rhetoric of Resistance and Religiosity

In the previous chapter the Crown's responses to the Pilgrimage in terms of the justification and defence of its position were analysed. The role of preaching and, especially, propaganda in disseminating the official Henrician position was examined. The construct of loyalty to the king as opposed to a foreign bishop (the pope) in Rome, which underpinned the Crown's response, was to become an enduring characteristic of English national identity. It was exceedingly difficult to retain dual loyalty during the Pilgrimage and the Henrician phase of the Reformation: it was to become virtually impossible and treasonous in the future.

However, opposition to the king's laws and reformation undoubtedly existed and Professor Jack Scarisbrick was of the view that those 'who were enthusiastically behind the Henrician Reformation were probably a small minority'.[1] Michael Graves went further when he stated that, during the turbulent years of the 1530s, public discontent with Henrician policies and hostility to the king were 'frequently voiced and publicly expressed in many parts of the country'.[2]

What, then, of the perceptions of those opposed to the course that the king was taking? Our main sources with regard to the Pilgrimage are the views of the rebels as expressed in the York and Pontefract Articles. However, as Fletcher and MacCulloch have pointed out, the precise views of the rebels are much thinner on the ground because they did not have the resources that were available to the government to publish them.[3] The York and Pontefract Articles, together with the evidence of those interrogated for their part of the rising and examples of dissent from outside of Yorkshire and Lincolnshire, illustrate that the grievances of the northerners and opposition to Henrician policy was far from being confined to one geographical region. This chapter will consider further examples from other parts of the realm, as the North cannot be viewed in complete isolation. An insurrection of this magnitude cannot be treated as idiosyncratic and viewed as an insular phenomenon. This analysis will also include a brief exploration of the perceptions of the Pilgrimage in a wider, European context. How, for instance, did the Spanish and the papacy view and monitor events? Did they view the uprisings as an opportunity to coerce Henry into compliance or were they merely interested spectators?

Once the risings were underway, the Earl of Derby wrote to Lord Darcy with regard to the situation in Lancashire. On 20 October, he stated that the people there were 'wholly' with the commons, although he remained very 'stiff'.[4] On 24 October, dissent from within the king's own household is recorded. Queen Jane Seymour, it was reported, threw herself on her knees before the king and begged him to restore the abbeys.[5] This plea was given short shrift as the king told her to get up and not to meddle in his affairs; he referred to Anne Boleyn and this, unsurprisingly, frightened the timid and insecure queen. By 30 October, sympathy with the northern insurgents was reported by the Sheriff of Sussex.[6] There is evidence of the pope being prayed for in the North at the outset of the Pilgrimage and reports suggested that the people of Dent were apportioning blame to Cromwell, as opposed to the king.[7] On 2 December 1536, it was reported that copies of Aske's manifestos were in circulation in Berkshire. The Pilgrims' Oath and recruiting letters were also being circulated in London in 1536, where magistrates confiscated copies which came to light.[8]

Further evidence of clerical opposition is visible in December when Lord Wentworth described the behaviour of the parson of Wittillisham, stating that he had advised his parishioners within a month of the injunctions to beware of the English books. The parson also told one of his parishioners, Thomas Busshope, that by the authority God gave to Peter, the Bishop of Rome ought to be Supreme Head of the Church.[9] In the same month, we are also told that twenty-two people in the parish of St Michael's in Wood Street heard the curate speak contemptuously of the king's injunctions.[10] The northern clergy also gave their verdict on the Ten Articles and the First Injunctions in December 1536: they condemned all ten articles, denied the Royal Supremacy and called for the restoration of all clergy who had opposed the king's position.[11] Christopher Bradeley, discussing Aske's rebellion in the company of his parish priest in Bromsgrove, Worcestershire, commented, 'I trust to God we shall have the old world again'.[12]

The Pilgrims did not perceive themselves as traitors, as is indicated from the reports of a conversation which took place in Colchester, Essex, in December 1537. During a dinner with the abbot of St John's, Marmaduke Nevell and others were asked how the 'traitors' in the North were. They responded that they were not traitors and if this charge were levelled at them, they would retaliate by calling the accusers heretics. They then argued that all the abbeys in England were beholden to the Pilgrims, as they had re-established the abbeys in the North. Further, they stated, the malice of the commons was chiefly directed against Cromwell and Cranmer.[13] This stance reiterated the position of the Pilgrims. They had criticised policies which appeared to undermine the prince's duty to the commonwealth and displayed a willingness to assert constitutional propriety when the king appeared to have broken trust by imposing religious changes.[14] Perhaps Richard Marshall encapsulated the reality of the time when, in a letter to the Convent of Blackfriars in Newcastle, he confessed to repeatedly denying the Royal Supremacy and, as such, had decided that he ought to flee. He would, he stated, willingly tarry and suffer death for his opinions but his flesh was weak.[15] From this brief snapshot, it is apparent that dissent existed in both the West Country and the South, and 'conservative' opinions were by no means confined to the North.

The perception of Cromwell as the architect of the malaise afflicting the spiritual health of the country was recurring. The list of the rebel grievances produced for the meeting at Pontefract in early December (a forerunner of the Pontefract Articles), had this to say of the Lord Privy Seal: 'traitur Thomas Crumwell, hys dyscypyles and adherents at leste exile hym and theym further of the relm'.[16] Here, it is Cromwell who is portrayed as the traitor, and the use of the biblical term 'disciples' is quite revealing. Cromwell's evangelical tendencies were well known and the usage of a descriptive term from the Gospels in relation to his adherents casts him in the role of leader. It also suggests that his status was so exalted that he had taken it upon himself to determine theology and doctrine. His position as vicegerent was clearly not welcomed. He is also described as the 'false flatterer' who said that he would make Henry the richest prince in Christendom and is repeatedly referred to as the 'traitor'.

At this juncture, the northern clergy also condemned the Ten Articles. The clergy denied the Royal Supremacy and denounced the punishment of the clergy by temporal powers. The violation of sanctuary was also condemned. The clergy upheld papal dispensations and stated that all clergy who had opposed the Royal Supremacy should be restored.[17]

The twenty-four Pontefract Articles have been discussed but it is worth reiterating that the Pilgrims were explicit in who they would negotiate with. In the preamble to the articles it was specified that 'Richard Cromwell nor none of his kind nor sort be at our meeting at Doncaster'.[18] Richard was Cromwell's nephew. After the resumption of revolts in January 1537, some in the North believed that they had been duped and the perception of Cromwell as the author of their misfortune continued. A bill sent to Richmond on 19 January illustrates this point:

> That the commons in every township should rise on pain of death and make all lords and gentlemen swear on the mass book to these articles. (1) To mainten the profet of Holye Churche, which was the upholding of the Christian faith. (2) That no lord nor gentlyllman take nothing of their tenants but their rents. (3) To put downe the lord Cromwell, that hereyke, and all his sect, the whyche has mayde the kyng put downe prayinge and fastyng. (4) That no lorde nor gentleman shall not go to London.[19]

It is revealing that the instigators of this bill believed that the Holy Church (i.e. the Church of Rome) upheld the Christian faith and that Cromwell and his heretical sect induced the king to prevent praying and fasting. The oath was to be sworn on a Mass book. Tellingly, the proviso that no lord or gentleman should go to London was included. Clearly, the commons felt that they had been deceived by Ellerker, Bowes and Aske during their trips to Court.

During his examination in early 1537, Dr Pickering stated that he did not consider the Pilgrims as traitors and named the bishops of Canterbury,

Worcester and Salisbury as heretics.[20] Archbishop Lee of York gave evidence that Aske, Darcy, Sir Robert Constable and others told him at Pontefract that they were organising the holy Pilgrimage for the redress of certain grievances and required others to join them. In mitigation, he said that he was deceived, as others were, by the belief that they did sacrifice to God and no injury to the king.[21]

The ongoing rhetoric of the period requires closer examination. Opposition to the Royal Supremacy was a significant factor in anti-Henrician thinking: in March 1537, a monk named Henry Salley was reported for stating that there should be no lay knave head of the Church. One Barnarde Townley, a clerk in Cumberland, confessed that the cause of the insurrection there was that the vicar of Burgh read a letter from Richmondshire which stated that the people there, their brethren in Christ, had assembled and were ready for the maintenance of the faith of God, His laws and His Church. They confirmed that abbeys which had been suppressed had been restored again.

John Rochester was a very brave, or foolhardy, man when he wrote to the Duke of Norfolk that he had offered to prove before the council that the king had been deluded by those who enticed him to assume the authority of Supreme Head of the Church of England. He said that he was ready to do so and begged Norfolk to help the matter to come before the king, as he would rather die than have the truth cloaked and hidden as it had been.[22]

The resentment and opposition towards the Crown's religious innovations continued unabated in the period after the pardon and the resumption of revolt. On Sunday, 4 February, the parish priest of Kendal, Sir Walter Browne, prayed for the pope and in so doing, was supported by about 300 people. Also in February, one John Hogon was reported for singing seditious songs by four informants. Hogon explained the verses of his song to the listeners and it was to the effect that if the Duke of Suffolk had allowed the Lincolnshire men to join with the northern men, England would have been brought 'to a better place than it is now'.[23]

At the time of the examinations in April 1537, Lord Chancellor Audley reported words alleged to have been spoken by Lord Darcy to Cromwell. Whether they are true or not, they encapsulate the perceptions of the Pilgrims:

Cromwell it is thou that art the very original and chief causer of all this rebellion and mischief, and art likewise causer of the apprehension of us that be noble men and dost daily earnestly travail to bring us to our end and to strike off our heads, and I trust that or thou die, though thou wouldest procure all the noblemen's heads within the realm to be stricken off, yet shall there one head remain that shall strike off thy head.[24]

Prophetic words indeed.

In the following year, reports of sedition among the clergy were being forwarded to Cromwell. Sir John Markham prepared articles against a Master Lytherland, the vicar of Newark-upon-Trent, with regard to the Royal Supremacy, the use of English books, Purgatory and the worship of the Blessed Virgin Mary.[25] Henry Lytherland had preached a sermon when Markham had been present and neglected to mention the Bishop of Rome's 'usurped' authority or to emphasise the Royal Supremacy. He had also denounced translations of scripture into English and had instructed the congregation to pray for souls in Purgatory.

In April 1538, the abbot of Pershore, John Stonywell, sailed very close to the wind in his hostile opinion of the Henrician changes and favourable perception of the action of the Pilgrims. William Harrison, a groom of the king's chamber, gave Cromwell information regarding a conversation which had taken place at Pershore in Worcester. The abbot had allegedly said that he trusted that he would die as one of the children of Rome. This was risky enough, but then Stonywell stated that the people in the North had died 'fast enough' the previous year, not only for themselves but for those in his own area as well. This reference to the executions in the aftermath of the Pilgrimage enraged Harrison, who argued that the king had been more than merciful to the rebels: 'His grace might justly have put 4,000 more to death.'[26]

A few months later, in June 1538, another parish priest, of Kirkby Moorside, was reported for speaking evil of the king. The priest stated that the king deserved to be punished: 'that vengeance must need light upon hym' because he had put 'soo many … wrongfully to dethe'. The cleric was also reported for saying that if Cromwell were also dead, it would not be a halfpenny loss.[27]

This anti-Cromwellian feeling continued unabated in the North throughout the summer, and seditious songs about the Lord Privy Seal were circulating in Lancashire in July.[28] The Council of the North was also busy during this period. One James Prestwich confessed in July that he never thought the king could be Supreme Head of the Church of England.[29]

There are other examples of resistance to the Henrician Reformation and injunctions throughout the realm. On 8 October 1538, Cranmer wrote at length to Cromwell regarding the situation at Oxford University. There was a catalogue of complaints 'against the Oxford men'. They were not, he stated, fulfilling the king's injunctions with regard to preaching and would not allow the Bible to be read openly in the halls at dinner. A dean named Mr Chedsay had stated that if he saw a scholar with a New Testament, he would burn it. In addition, a Mr Slater was reported for saying that there were some present who could prove the Bishop of Rome's authority. Those masters and fellows who were deemed to be advocates of the new learning were not admitted to any office of the college.[30] These are examples of the mood which existed in various parts of the country during and after the northern uprisings. As Richard Hoyle has stated, the North in the 1530s 'was not especially conservative so much as typically conservative'.[31]

What of the perception of Henry, his actions and the Pilgrimage outside of England?

After the start of the rising in Lincolnshire, Chapuys reported to the emperor that a great number had risen there against the king's commissioners. He stated that the people swore fidelity first to God, secondly to the Church and thirdly to the king. Chapuys also mentioned the Duke of Norfolk as a potential supporter of any rebellion as a means of ruining his rival, Cromwell, and preventing further religious innovations, which were not to his mind.[32] It is evident that Chapuys was alert to the opportunity presented by the rising in terms of arresting any further religious innovation and removing the arch-evangelical in the Privy Council. Norfolk, however, was not so foolhardy, and his desire for self-preservation was probably enhanced by the fall of his niece, Anne Boleyn, only four months before. He had also witnessed the examples of Fisher and More. Indeed, Norfolk was to write to Cromwell from Stoke-on-Trent on 8 October and describe how many of the people of the town rejoiced at the situation in Lincolnshire. He stated that if he had not gone there, a rising might have occurred.[33]

Once the Lincolnshire Rising was over and the Pilgrimage of Grace was underway, Pope Paul III wrote to Francis I and exhorted him not to help the

King of England. Dr Ortiz advised the Empress Isabella in late November that the pope had ordered the Bull of Privation to be printed but had yet to publish it. A few days later, he wrote to her again and reported that the rebels numbered 70,000–80,000 and were quite capable of defeating the king's troops. No doubt the numbers were exaggerated – most estimates were nearer 40,000 – but the force was, indeed, far larger than any the Crown could field.[34] Ortiz said that the rebels wanted the king and pope to be as they used to be before, that Katherine's marriage should be declared valid, and hence Mary legitimate, and for the dissolution of the monasteries to cease.

Shortly afterwards, the Bishop of Faenza, the papal nuncio in France, was of the opinion that the pope could easily publish the censures against Henry in England by deploying Reginald Pole. Pole, he stated, had great influence in the country and Faenza believed that the people would ultimately murder the king if he persisted in his errors.[35] However, in December 1536, the negotiations between the emperor's Privy Council and Rome shed a revealing light on the pope's true assessment of the situation in England. It was reported that the pope could not help effectually and had no real interest in the matter. Still more surprising was the revelation that:

> ... it might be that he himself would not be so sorry for the death of the Princess now as he might be after her father's deprivation, by which he might be enabled to dispose of England at will in virtue of the Papal sentence, whereas, once in England, the Princess might easily defend her rights.[36]

One wonders about the accuracy of this report and how the staunchly Catholic Princess Mary would have felt had she known.

By mid-February 1537, both the Pilgrimage and the renewed revolts of Bigod and Hallam were also over. At this juncture, Faenza asserted that the Scots abhorred the ways of the King of England and also that the pope should use every opportunity to show himself against Henry.[37] The commons involved in the post-pardon uprisings were not alone in their distrust of the king's motives. Cardinal Reginald Pole was not, perhaps, the most objective of commentators on the Henrician Reformation but he seems to have been shrewd in his assessment of the situation in England in early 1537. In a letter to Pope Paul III on 7 February, Pole stated:

It may be that the king has sought, by asking for the people's petitions, and pretending to approve them, and promising to accept them, to escape their fury, with the intention of not observing anything when he is out of danger, and of getting rid of the authors of the sedition upon one pretext or another.[38]

Pole was obviously of the opinion that Henry had played the Pilgrims false with his promise to hear their petitions. Pole also spoke of the necessity of an expedition to show support for the 'manly and Christian demonstration those people are making'. He argued that what was desired in England was for the king to turn back and for the accustomed obedience and authority to be restored. He also suggested that the people needed someone to exhort them in the pope's name to stand firm, and requested money.[39] Obviously, by the time Pole wrote this, it was too late to harness the initial enthusiastic zeal of the Pilgrimage and this lends further support to the contention that the Pilgrimage was not the result of some Aragonese conspiracy.[40]

In March 1537, Faenza reported that Henry allegedly said that he knew the pope would revoke his title of Defender of the Faith and give it instead to his nephew, James V of Scotland. There is no indication as to how a papal nuncio in the French court should know such information. However, Faenza went on to say that, according to his sources, the people were enraged with a treacherous king, who daily put them to death.[41] Faenza's rhetoric is openly and consistently hostile to Henry, as might be expected, but he is a prejudiced source and as such, his evidence needs to be treated accordingly.

The pope's rhetoric was succinct and somewhat chilling in a Bull that appointed Cardinal Pole *legate de latere* (temporary Papal representative) to the King of England on 31 March. Pole's remit was to exhort Henry to return to the faith and Paul III's summary of Henry's behaviour was that it was, perhaps, driven by Satan:

It may be that the enemy of mankind has such a hold upon the king that he will not be brought to reason except by force of arms. It is better, however, that he and his adherents should perish than be the cause of perdition to so many.[42]

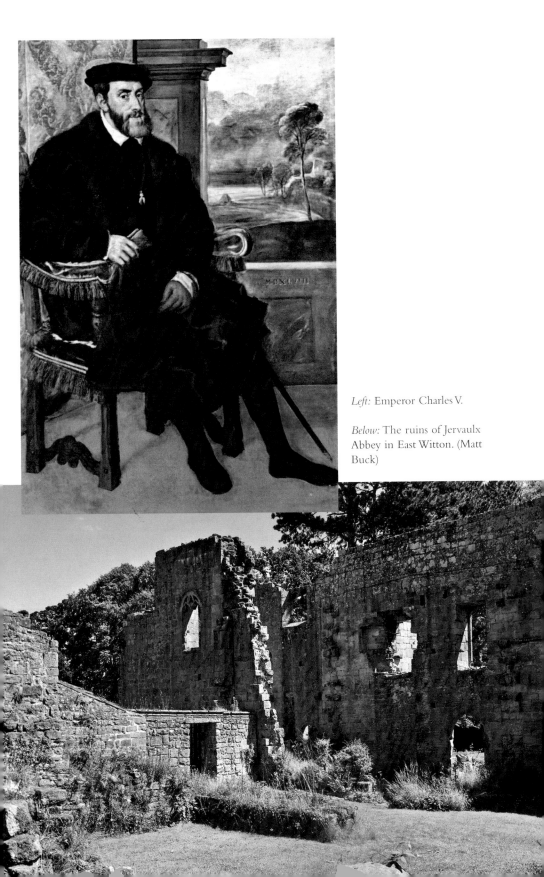

Left: Emperor Charles V.

Below: The ruins of Jervaulx Abbey in East Witton. (Matt Buck)

Right: Charles Brandon, Duke of Suffolk.

Below: The ruins of Barnard Castle in Teesside. (alljengi)

The ruins of Scarborough Castle. (Steve)

An execution plaque at the Tower of London bearing, among others, the name of Thomas Darcy.

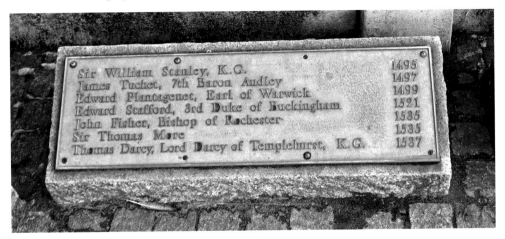

Sir William Stanley, K.G. 1495
James Tuchet, 7th Baron Audley 1497
Edward Plantagenet, Earl of Warwick 1499
Edward Stafford, 3rd Duke of Buckingham 1521
John Fisher, Bishop of Rochester 1535
Sir Thomas More 1535
Thomas Darcy, Lord Darcy of Templehurst, K.G. 1537

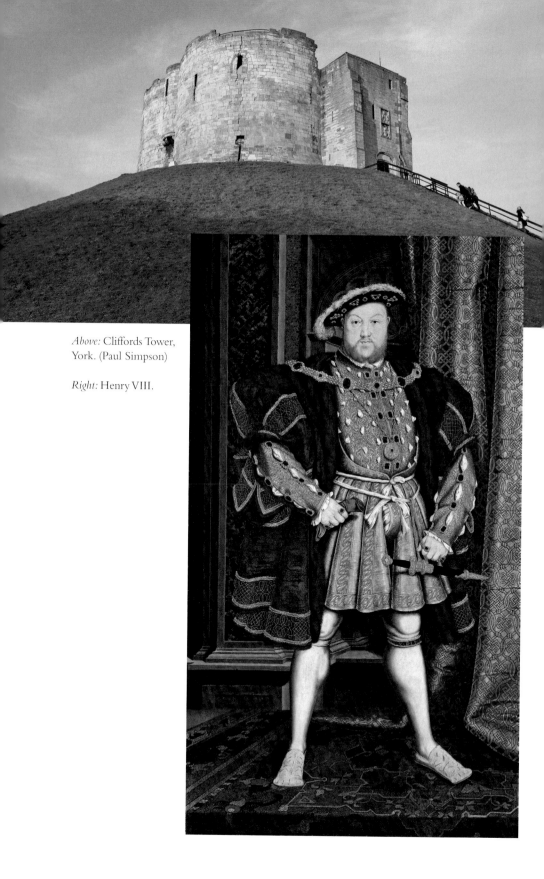

Above: Cliffords Tower, York. (Paul Simpson)

Right: Henry VIII.

ANNO DNI · 1 · 5 · 4 · 4 ·

LADI MARI DOGHTER TO
THE MOST VERTVOVS PRINCE
KING HENRI THE EIGHT

THE AGE OF XXVIII YERES

Above: Princess Mary Tudor.

Left: Pilgrimage of Grace Banner of the Five Wounds
of Christ.

Left: Pontefract Castle.
(Tim Green)

Below: Skipton Castle.
(Tim Green)

HERE LIETH THOMAS LORDE DARCY OF THE NORTHE AND SVMTYME OF THE ORDER OF THE GARTER SIR NICHOLAS CARREW KNIGHT SVMTYME OF THE GARTER, AND LADY ELIZABETH CARREW DAVGHTER TO SIR THOMAS BRIAN KNIGHT, AND SIR ARTHVR DARCY KNIGHT YONGER SONNE TO THE ABOVE NAMED LORDE DARCY AND LADY MARY DARCY HIS DERE WIF, DAVGHTER TO SIR NICHOLAS CARREW ~ WHO HAD TENNE SONNES AND FIVE DAVGHTERS HERE LIETH CHARLES WILLM AND PHILLIP, MARY AND VRSVLY SONNES AND DAVGHTERS TO THE SAIDE SIR ARTHVR AND MARY HIS WIF, WHOSE SOWLES GOD TAKE TO HIS INFINIT MERCY AMEN

Above: The monument to Thomas Darcy at St Botolph, Aldgate.

Left: Thomas Howard, Duke of Norfolk.

Left: York Minster.
(Richard Penn)

Below: A plaque commemorating where the Lincolnshire Rising began in 1536.

THE
LINCOLNSHIRE
RISING
began in this church
1st October 1536.
For his part in it, the
Vicar was hanged,
drawn and quartered
at Tyburn
25th March 1537.

The pope went on to explain that he hoped that those people who had lately taken up arms against the king would 'do so again' if they saw that the hope that he gave of returning to his right mind was illusory. Further, he prayed that God would be a shield to them in that war, and promised full remission of sins to those who fought in it. Fine, stirring words, it can be said, but also an example of empty rhetoric because the papacy gave very little practical support in waging a 'Holy War' in England. Pole lamented the scarcity of money to Cardinal Contarini in March and Contarini approached the pope, 'who was sorry for Pole's difficulty … but was unwilling to increase the sum of 500 pieces of gold a month usually given to ultramontane legates lest it should be taken as a precedent'.[43] Pole lacked the money, men and arms that would have given disaffected conservatives a fighting chance of success. Charles V commented that there was little appearance that Pole was provided with money or men and that he might arrive too late.[44] In any event, it was too little, too late.[45] The Post-pardon Revolts had been crushed by 31 March 1537 and the initial euphoria and impetus of the Pilgrimage of Grace had not been capitalised on.

However, in April, Pole advised the Cardinal of Carpi of the state of affairs in England and spoke about his mission to:

> … bring an island fluctuating in dogmas and tumultuous with all kinds of sedition back to its ancient stability? When, therefore this disease had from the head overflowed the whole body of the island, to remedy which there were two methods, one by surgery (to speak medically) and the other by diet, and when many advised the first method for so inveterate a disease – indeed, many in the island showed this was their opinion by taking up arms.[46]

Pole here uses a physician's analogy in the same way that the king and Cromwell did, from vastly different perspectives. Here, the Pilgrims are not traitors or corrupt members of the body politic. Instead, they took up arms in an attempt to surgically heal the diseased head (i.e. Henry) in order to prevent the infection from spreading all over the rest of the body (the island). Pole then went on to assert that Henry, by nature religious, observant, benign and liberal, had been persuaded to 'alter dogmas, rob churches, overthrow monasteries, vex the ministers of the church' and to 'slay those who were the greatest ornaments of the island (not Rochester and More only but all the rest who have been murdered)'.[47]

Writing to Cardinal Contarini in June 1537, Pole again succinctly summarised the perception of the Henrician innovations in conservative opinion in the aftermath of the northern uprisings. Pole despaired of the state of the English Church and suggested a four-day fast to pray for its conversion and return to the fold. He then wrote revealingly of the leadership being shown within the Church: 'What health is to be expected there where Lee and Tunstall, otherwise most grave and learned men, take the lead in vomiting lies from the pulpit and impugn the decrees of the holiest fathers?' The king and Cromwell were described as wilful and selfish men and the country as 'a branch broken off from the true vine'.[48]

Despite the pope having made Cardinal Pole *legate de latere* in March 1537 and Paul III's damning assessment of Henry's character, Pole was provided with little in terms of practical support. The emperor was of the opinion that no declaration should be made against Henry without the strong appearance that it could be backed up by force. Charles was of the view that popular movements rarely lasted long, especially in the case of England. The risings in the North, however, had taken a period of five months, all told, and Charles' assessment was made almost six months after the initial outbreak in Lincolnshire. It was too little, too late.

This reinforces the argument that the Pilgrimage of Grace was absolutely not the result of some conspiracy hatched by an Aragonese faction, aided and abetted by Chapuys. Charles justified his own inertia by stating that he was preoccupied with the 'important' affairs of Christendom. His priorities were the King of France, the Turks and 'other infidels' (by which he probably meant the Lutheran German princes). He felt that he could not provide the assistance which would be necessary for a successful enterprise against Henry.[49]

Reginald Pole attributed the Kildare Rebellion in Ireland (1534) to the cause of religion and, as Professor Steven Ellis has argued, the rebellion was couched in religious terms in order to obtain foreign support, most notably from Charles V, Paul III and James V of Scotland. However, although Charles was initially enthusiastic about the prospect of intervention in Ireland, his support, as in the case of the Pilgrimage, was ultimately insubstantial. Ellis has stated that it appears that Kildare received 'very little more than prayers and promises from Charles V and Paul III' and that this was also the case with James V.[50]

There is some evidence to suggest that the Irish later viewed the precedent of the Pilgrimage of Grace as an opportunity for rebellion and acquiring foreign support. A document detailing the discussions of an Irish canon in Rome referred to England as a land divided because of the Royal Supremacy, and described the Pilgrimage (though not by name) as 50,000 against the change. The canon's opinion was that very few of the king's subjects of England would be quiet until they made peace with His Holiness. The canon had, according to the document, been received with compassion by the pope and had stated that he believed the Irish were all ready to rise against the King of England at the bidding of the Apostolic See, because they would not be governed after the order of the Church of England against that of the Apostolic See.[51] (An Apostolic See is any episcopal see which can attribute its foundation to one or more apostles of Jesus. In this case, the canon was referring to the see of Rome which was founded by Saints Peter and Paul. Henry, of course, persisted in referring to the pope as the Bishop of Rome.)

However, the correspondence of Cardinal Farnese sheds further light on the papal position. A letter from him to the Cardinal of Brindisi on 8 January 1539 is illuminating.[52] The letter speaks of the new and great impieties and heinous offences of the King of England which had disgusted the Christian princes, especially the emperor and the French king. According to Farnese, His Holiness hoped that God would work some good effect for the reduction of that realm. He confirmed that the Bull had been expedited, which, however, was to be kept private or only shown to such as were prudent and trustworthy. Farnese maintained that the pope would do everything possible. Cardinal Pole had been sent to the emperor, and would proceed afterwards to the French king to rouse them to the punishment of 'wicked' King Henry. It can be argued that the new, heinous offence that Henry had committed was the spoliation of the shrine of St Thomas Becket at Canterbury. This is an example of the late Henrician attack on shrines and relics which was part of the power struggle between the State and the papacy. To this day, there is a space in Canterbury Cathedral where the shrine of Becket was once placed.[53]

In April, the Bishop of Verona wrote a warm letter to King Henry and assured him that 'His Holiness desires as much good for the king as for himself, and sends on this account Cardinal Pole, who I know, loves the king's salvation as his own'. The bishop went on to say that if the king meant to be the pope's adversary, His Holiness only desired to cure him of error, and could have no greater consolation in the world than that the king should accept his holy mind to his own salvation. The bishop referred to the 'tumults' in the North, but only in so far as to confirm that Cardinal Pole's brother, Lord Montague, had played no part in them.[54]

Pole was sent on his mission to rally the Catholic powers, and in early 1539 England was on a war footing. Around this time, Chapuys reported to his master that Henry had been allegedly named as a tyrant in Francis I's council. The result of this was that Cromwell had informed the French ambassador that there had been no innovation in religion except that which concerned the pope's authority. Cromwell added that one who legally punished traitors did not deserve the label 'tyrant'.[55] The pope, meanwhile, was in discussions about the English 'mission' with the Emperor Charles and was concerned with the possibility that Henry might assist the Lutherans 'with the money he robs from the churches and monasteries'.[56]

The following month, Aguilar, the emperor's man in Rome, wrote regarding the remedy and punishment of the King of England. He stated that Francis I was very content to forbid commerce with England. He also was of the opinion that it was 'easy to conquer' that kingdom with three armies – the emperor's, the King of Scots and his own – it could then be divided into three parts. If the enterprise was potentially so easy, one wonders why it was not undertaken previously, when approximately 30,000 Englishmen had been roused to revolt as a result of the king's actions. However, Charles V was quite unwilling to take any action against Henry[57] – for all his posturing and empty rhetoric, the fact of the matter was that England was a low priority for the emperor. Henry's matrimonial entanglements and resultant religious machinations were not enough to rouse this Habsburg into action. Charles, quite simply, had bigger fish to fry.

Richard Morison's official government propaganda and the unashamedly biased later account of the Tudor chronicler Edward Hall have been examined. It is now time to consider the perceptions of another individual whose view is somewhat at odds with the 'official' line. Robert Parkyn's *Narrative of the Reformation* was first published by A.G. Dickens in 1947 and Dickens, tellingly, described it as a work affording 'a fairly satisfying picture of the conservative opinions and archaic culture of this curious writer'.[58] Parkyn was the curate of Aldwick-le-Street, near Doncaster, and composed his work at various dates during the middle of the sixteenth century.[59] What did this priest record?:

> Be itt knowne to all men to whome this present writttingge schall cum, se, heare or reade, that in the yeare of our Lorde God 1532 and in the 24 yeare of the reigne of Kynge Henrie the 8 thes grevus matters enewynge first began to tayke roote: and after by processe of tym was accomplisshide and browghtt to passé in veray decade within this realme of Englande, to the *grett discomfort of all suche as was trew Christians.*

The last sentence is unambiguous and Parkyn makes his position clear with regard to the grievous matters which took place in the 1530s; they were of great discomfort to all who were true Christians. Parkyn continued:

> Fyrst the Kyngs Maiestie was wrongusly devorcide from his lawfull wyffe gratius Qweane Katheryn and mariede Ladye An Bullan, wich was crownyde Qweyne of Englande on Whitsonday. ... The Pope of Rome with all his authoritie & power was abolischide qwytte owtt of this realme, & then the Kyngs Majestie was proclamyde Supreme Heade next & immediately under God of the churche of Englande & Irelande thrughe authoritie wherof he began to depose religious howsses.

Parkyn is unequivocal. Henry wrongly divorced the gracious Queen Katherine in order to marry Lady Anne Boleyn. This was followed by the abolition of the pope and his powers and authority. Henry then took the title of Supreme Head and one of his first acts, in this account, was the dissolution of the monasteries:

> Then in the yeare ... 1534 ... the good bischoppe of Rochester and Sir Thomas Moore two verteus men & great clerkes wolde nott consent to the Kynge that he scholde be Supreme Heade of holly churche, therfor thay were both headyde in the monethe of Junii at London with thre monks of the Charterrerhowsse

Unsurprisingly, Parkyn is sympathetic to opponents of the Royal Supremacy. The Bishop of Rochester, John Fisher, and Sir Thomas More are lauded as virtuous men and great clerks. They, together with the monks of the Charterhouse, were beheaded because they did not agree that Henry should be Supreme Head of the Church. Parkyn then continued:

> The abovesaide Queyne Anne beheadyde for hir wretchide carnall lyffinge and in Septembre & Octobre was great commotions (for maintenance of holly churche) both in Lincolneshire and Yorke shyre, butt disceattfully that were browghtt downe with treattie, withowtt bloode sheddynge, specially att a grownde namyde Scawsbie leas nott farre from Doncaster.

Here Parkyn deals specifically with the Lincolnshire Rising and the Pilgrimage of Grace. The risings were, in this version, solely for the maintenance of the Holy Church. Parkyn is clear in his interpretation of events: the movement was defeated by the deceitful treaty at Doncaster. It is also interesting to note Parkyn's unashamedly biased view of Anne Boleyn's demise – it was due to her wretched and carnal living.

Parkyn returns to the subject of the dissolution. In this account all the monasteries were suppressed by 1539. The abbots and virtuous religious people were 'shamefully' put to death. There was blame attached to one person, Thomas Cromwell: 'And all this ungratiusnes cam thrugh cowncell of one wreatche and heretike Thomas Crumwell, and such other of his affinitie, [all of the ungraciousness was the fault of this wretch and heretic; aided and abetted by others of his affinity] wich Crumwell was headyde for highe treason in the yeare after.'[60] Parkyn then takes the trouble to record that Cromwell was beheaded in the following year, 1540, but does not expand on this.

Parkyn's narrative continued until the death of Queen Mary in 1558, but we need not concern ourselves with the remainder for our purposes here. Dickens has derided Parkyn's version of events between 1532 and 1547 and stated that as 'such numerous inaccuracies' are present, it must have been compiled from distant memory or hearsay.[61] This is to miss the point. The account is a northern clergyman's perception of the Henrician religious changes and the Pilgrimage of Grace. So Parkyn admittedly recorded some dates incorrectly and tended to date important events to the year prior to their happening (e.g. the fall of Anne Boleyn and the Pilgrimage being in 1535), but the essential facts and developments are true. It is the perception of these events which is crucial to our understanding. After all, Parkyn was a minor clergyman based in the periphery – he hardly had access to details and documents from the core, i.e. the Court.

Numerous examples of the way in which the Pilgrimage and the Henrician religious innovations were perceived by Catholic Europe, most notably the papacy, the emperor and Cardinal Pole, have been given. However, one has to conclude that the vast majority of this was empty rhetoric. Examples of contemporary domestic dissent have been highlighted and such examples were not exclusive to the North of England. Lucy Wooding has described the rhetoric which followed the Royal Supremacy as 'exalted, inspirational and menacing', and maintains that the overriding perception of King Henry was as that of a bully. Indeed, it would be difficult to deviate from Wooding's view that the rhetoric of the 1530s was grand but that it was a statement of intent rather than a reflection of reality. Wooding is also of the opinion that the religious rhetoric with which Henry justified his laws and proclamations was questionable in both its logic and sincerity.[62]

Given the fact that Henry continually changed his opinions on doctrine, this is a fair assessment. The only constant was the king's Erastian position and consequent obsession with the Royal Supremacy. The continual changing of doctrinal position should make it clear that the word 'reformation' should not properly be used in conjunction with the king's behaviour from the 1530s to the end of his reign. It was clearly subject to change, based upon the monarch's personal whims, and, as such, should properly be regarded as an experiment.

Exalted the rhetoric undoubtedly was. Propagandists like Morison underpinned the legitimacy of the official Henrician position and the regime placed a great emphasis on the theme of obedience. However, Henry's own theological ideas were erratic: the numbers of sacraments varied at times in the 1530s, as did the belief in the doctrine of Purgatory. Added to that the inconsistent teaching on Transubstantiation, it is small wonder that the king's subjects were confused and apprehensive. Henry's theology was chopped and changed to suit his own personal moods and desires. It was also altered when politically expedient: for instance, he flirted with Lutheran doctrine when an alliance with the German princes suited him. He then reversed his position in 1539 with the more conservative Act of the Six Articles, when he had felt it expedient in order to demonstrate his orthodoxy to the Catholic powers in Europe.

The monarch who had basked in the approval of the papacy for his treatise against Martin Luther in 1521 now regarded the pope as his arch-nemesis. Henry appears to have conveniently brushed his previously held orthodox beliefs to one side to justify his own actions. His subjects were understandably bewildered. That the king should have changed so dramatically must have been due to evil influence – be that Anne Boleyn or Thomas Cromwell. Both Starkey and Erasmus had emphasised the danger of royal reason succumbing to the passions, especially if it were tempted by evil flattery.[63] It would appear that both the former queen and the Lord Privy Seal fitted the bill. The Pilgrimage of Grace was an expression of this insecurity and the northern risings were not treasonous, in so far as they blamed the influence of Cromwell and his fellow heretics and not the monarch. The Pilgrims, as has been demonstrated here, were by no means alone in their hostility to the Henrician religious experiments. Dissent existed in all parts of England and disapproval of the king's proceedings continued (albeit covertly) well into subsequent reigns.

The Religiosity of the North in the wake of the Pilgrimage of Grace

The movement was religiously motivated, but what impact did it have on the North of England in religious terms and indeed what does the event and its aftermath reveal about the Henrician project? We know about the retribution taken by the king in the wake of the rising and another significant rising in the region was not attempted for more than thirty years – the Northern Rebellion in 1569. What can be ascertained about the religiosity of the region in the intervening period? Unfortunately, we are severely hampered in this regard due to the paucity of evidence. Churchwardens' accounts would be the most informative tool in this regard but the North of England is sorely bereft of such accounts.[64] Diana Newton has found that not a single account exists for the diocese of Durham before 1580.[65]

What sources are likely to reveal indications of religious sentiment, then? In the absence of churchwardens' accounts, wills have been used, as they can be a valuable signifier of religious change. However, as W. Sheils has pointed out, wills can be difficult to assess statistically. Traditional wills mentioned prayers for the dead, Masses for the soul, the Blessed Virgin and the saints. Such wills therefore would indicate an orthodox and Catholic religious belief of the testator. Richard Rex has, however, cautioned against the evidence of wills for religious belief and practice in Henry's reign and stated that it needs to be handled with great care.[66] This book has attempted a study of a cross-section sample of wills from across the North with a view to gauging religious sentiment: a sample of 355 wills have been studied.

The first sample is taken from the *Testamenta Eboracensia*[67] and covers wills from the registry at York between 1536 and 1551. A total of 192 wills were studied in this sample, of which 140 (73 per cent) contained traditional preambles. Such preambles mentioned that the soul of the testator was bequeathed to 'Almighty God, the Blessed Virgin, the saints and all the celestial company of heaven'. Unequivocally Protestant wills did not contain such preambles and number only thirty-five (18 per cent) in this batch. Of these, fifteen were drawn up in the reign of Edward VI, as might be expected. Wills that explicitly mentioned Mass for the testator's soul comprise thirty-three (17 per cent) over the period, and other stipulations for prayers for the dead number forty-two (22 per cent).

Given that the First Henrician Injunctions and the Ten Articles had refuted the doctrine of Purgatory, it is hardly surprising that testators erred on the side of caution in this respect. What is interesting are the wills which clearly demonstrate an individual's concern with complying with the law of the land and the monarch's personal whims to the detriment of committing to paper their own personal wishes and feelings on these matters. There are a fair proportion of wills (forty-two, or 22 per cent) where the testators appear to 'hedge their bets', and one gets the impression that they did not wish their families to fall foul of the authorities by not adhering to official doctrine.

This batch of wills includes those of the nobility and gentry and some individuals who featured in the Pilgrimage of Grace. Henry Clifford, Earl of Cumberland's will, dated 2 April 1541 and proved on 4 June 1543, was traditional and specified diriges and Masses for his soul. This clearly indicates conservative religious persuasions. He left money to pay for the singing of a requiem and dirge by every curate in Westmorland and Craven willing to do so.[68] Yet this northern magnate remained steadfastly loyal to the Crown and was evidently able to put his own religious scruples to one side during the risings.

Katherine, the Countess of Northumberland in her will in 1542 specified that an annual Mass should be said for her soul.[69] Similarly, Sir Ralph Eure, Sir Marmaduke Constable and Sir John Eland made traditional wills which are included in this sample. Ralph Eure's will was made on 6 May 1544 and was of the traditional type, and his offices passed to his father. It specified that a priest should pray and sing for his soul before Our Lady of Walsingham.[70] It was, thus, hardly indicative of firm Protestant leanings. Ralph's offices passed to his father, William. William made his own will on 25 February 1548 and it contained a traditional preamble. Unlike Ralph, but in common with many of his contemporaries, William erred on the side of caution and hedged his bets. He specified that 'such obsequies and funeral expenses as shall and ought to appertain to be done for a baron after the custom of Englande'.[71] His will was made, of course, during the reign of Edward VI and Baron Eure obviously wanted to ensure that his will did not compromise his position or betray his own religious persuasions, whatever they may have been.

Sir Marmaduke Constable made his will on 2 March 1541 and it was traditional. He specified Mass and dirige for his soul[72] and he divided his property between his sons.[73] John Eland, the Mayor of Hull during the Pilgrimage, died in 1542. His will, made shortly before his death on 29 April, was traditional in form and revealingly specified an annual dirige and that a priest should sing for his soul for six years.[74] Christopher Stapleton, the father of the rehabilitated rebel William, made his will shortly after the punishments of the rebellions were carried out. On 30 July 1537, his will was drafted and was very traditional: it specified Masses to be said for him, his mother and father for a period of seven years after his own death.[75] The father appears to have possessed a stronger courage of conviction than the son.

The second sample studied relates to wills covering York, Nottingham, Northumberland, Cumberland and Westmorland between 1535 and 1547.[76] These wills reveal that twenty-nine out of eighty-five (34 per cent) were traditional and Catholic – they included provisos for prayers for the dead and Masses. Included in this batch is the will of George Talbot, 4th Earl of Shrewsbury, which is very traditional, and Brian Higden, the Dean of York, whose will, dated 1539, specified that, 'I will that a prest shall synge for me for five years'.[77] Unsurprisingly, the number of traditional preambles drops off dramatically following the accession of Edward VI in 1547, with only one out of twenty-three being of this kind. More surprising is the fact that there is not a significant increase during the reign of Queen Mary, with only two out of thirteen displaying orthodox belief. One of the two was the Archbishop of York, Robert Holgate, in 1555 but revealingly, Michael Wentworth, Master of the Queen's Household, only specified that he wished 'to be buried in Christian man's burial'.[78]

Another sample examined is from the registry at Durham.[79] This sample covers the years 1538–58, during the reigns of Henry, Edward and Mary. This reveals that twenty of the forty-five wills (44 per cent) were traditional and Catholic, mentioning saints and, crucially, provision for Masses for the soul of the deceased. In 1538, one John Hedworth in Chester specified that he wanted Masses for three years and anniversary Masses 'for ever more'.[80] Similarly, in 1540 Sir Roger Gray, brother-in-law to Lord Darcy, specified that money be given to a priest to pray for his soul for a year.[81]

On the other hand, there are examples to the contrary. Robert Lord Ogle (1544) stated that, 'I give my sowle to God omnipotent', and Robert Gower of Berwick (1545) referred to Henry as Supreme Head of the Church of England and Ireland 'immediately under God'.[82]

Some testators were astute in the drafting of their wills and hedged their bets, and we see other examples in this batch. For instance, one Henry Anderson of Newcastle (1558) specified, 'as I maye be layd wth my dutie to the vicar as the lawe hathe ordeyned'.[83]

A further study sample concentrates on Durham wills between 1543 and 1558 and refers to minor gentry and tradesmen.[84] Of these, twelve out of thirty-three (36 per cent) are traditional. Again, we see examples of testators being shrewd and hedging their bets. One Henry Sanderson (1550) left his money to 'poore naked children', but also specified that 3 shillings be given to 'three old men to praye for my soull'. Ambrose Middleton (1555) specified 'such divine service to be songe or said in the very day of my burial as shall appertain to the order and custome of the churche' – and this was during Mary's reign. In a similar fashion, Ralph Hutton (1558) wished his burial to be in accordance with 'the laws of this realme'.[85]

These samples of wills were examined to try and ascertain any trends in religious belief and practice in the North in the aftermath of the Pilgrimage and into the subsequent reigns. These, at least, indicate that traditional piety still existed but only overtly in approximately a third of cases. This appears somewhat surprising to the present writer, who had expected it to be a higher proportion at the outset. The fact that a relatively high proportion of individuals sought to shield themselves and their heirs from suspicion by inserting provisos that their executors dispose of their goods, for the health of their souls, in accordance with statute is surely significant and reveals that they were wary of falling foul of the preferences of the monarch of the day. There are also numerous references to bequests for priests without stipulation – might it be possible that these priests were already aware of the testator's wishes but the individual had been reluctant to commit these wishes to writing?

However, it is only a relatively small sample and cannot really be used to extrapolate a figure for the North as a whole. As Richard Rex has stated, definitive statements 'about popular religious beliefs and allegiances in an age which had neither the census nor the opinion poll are always going to be beyond the scope of the historian'.[86] It is, however, worth highlighting the will of John Longland, the Bishop of Lincoln, who died in 1547. He left, according to Sheils, a diocese with priests and laity as conservative as he was. Longland's own will is quite illuminating. He left money to almsmen of Henley and required them to say five 'Our Fathers', five 'Hail Marys' and one creed each morning 'in the worship of the Five Wounds'.[87] The bishop's servant, John Joseph, had made his own will in 1537 and this was also traditional in form.[88]

So, what can be deduced with regard to the religiosity of the region and in which context should it be placed in terms of a national historiography? It is worth briefly noting the Wakefield Conspiracy in March 1541. With the exception of Geoffrey Dickens, most historians have tended to minimise its importance. Although the North appears to have settled in the four years after the Pilgrimage, by 1541 the king had acquired the lands of the convicted rebels and all the monasteries were now gone.[89] Fifteen people were indicted as a result of the discovery of a plot to assassinate the president of the Council of the North, Robert Holgate. The objective was to demonstrate discontent with religious policy and remove central government interference in local affairs. The period between the Pilgrimage of Grace and the Northern Rebellion was, though, a comparatively peaceful interlude. So why did the North rise again in rebellion in 1569? The only conclusion that can be drawn from this is that the North still harboured disaffected individuals and still retained Catholic sympathies, or else it would not have been fertile ground for recruitment for another revolt. As Bastow has stated, the 1569 rising is 'most usually viewed as a Catholic revolt'.[90]

Diana Newton has stated that the Pilgrimage itself more than compensates for the lack of churchwardens' accounts in the north-east, as thousands of people were willing to risk their lives to defend traditional belief and practices.[91] She has also argued that there is abundant evidence of efforts to restore the fabric of the Catholic Church and to revive its rites and practices, both during the Northern Rising of 1569 and in its immediate aftermath. The rebels again used the imagery of the Five Wounds of Christ. According to the many depositions taken after the rebellion, Masses and anthems were sung in Durham Cathedral.[92]

The traditional and Catholic persuasions of members of the gentry such as the Babthorpes and Danbys continued for decades. The samples of wills were studied in an attempt to gauge the religious sympathies of the testators from the time of the Pilgrimage and into the subsequent reigns. The Earl of Shrewsbury, the Earl of Cumberland and Sir Marmaduke Constable made traditional wills, despite having outwardly opposed the Pilgrimage.[93] These wills, however, can only provide us with a limited insight into the real consciences of private men and women and, as such, need to be treated with caution.

The 1569 rising can be attributed, like the Pilgrimage, to religion. The nobility, however, featured much more prominently in 1569 than they had in 1536 and the Earl of Northumberland was later beatified by the Catholic Church for his role in it. The Earl of Westmorland was to spend the remainder of his long life in exile, intriguing with Catholic continental powers. It is also worth mentioning that the Duke of Norfolk's heir, his grandson – another Thomas Howard – was implicated in the 1569 rising. The 4th Duke had become embroiled in intrigues with the imprisoned Catholic Mary, Queen of Scots and had even proposed marriage to her, without the consent of Queen Elizabeth. He was executed as a traitor for his part in the Ridolfi plot in 1572.[94] The Pilgrimage and the Northern Rising obviously support the contention that the region was still, on the whole, conservative in its religious belief.

Examples of opposition thus existed throughout the realm; from the overtly rebellious North of England to Essex, Suffolk, Oxford, the West Country, Middlesex, through to Wales and Ireland. Broadly speaking though, the evidence examined shows Yorkshire and Lincolnshire as the location of the fiercest opposition. The North may have been outwardly compliant in the period between the two rebellions, but dissent was still very much a feature of northern society and the region retained and harboured orthodox and conservative tendencies.

Conclusion

In the summer of 1536, the changes that the Pilgrims sought were not out of the question: with Katherine of Aragon and Anne Boleyn both dead and Protestantism a minority in England, there appeared to be an opportunity for a return to Rome. Instead the king, aided and abetted by Cromwell, continued down the road towards that which many perceived as heresy. The timing of the first risings in Lincolnshire, barely six weeks from the First Henrician Injunctions, was surely no coincidence. The insurrection was a reaction to a suddenly imposed Crown religious experiment. The Pilgrimage was indeed the most potentially dangerous of all the unsuccessful rebellions of the Tudor period.[1] For a monarch whom Felicity Heal has labelled ostentatious in his piety[2] – the 'Defender of the Faith' and one-time adversary of Luther – to go to such seemingly heretical lengths over the space of a few short years must have been regarded as shocking to his conservative subjects. The Pilgrims blamed one man, Thomas Cromwell.

In the introduction, the point was made about distinguishing between secular and religious motivations in the Pilgrimage and it is hoped that it has been demonstrated that the motivation was overwhelmingly religious. However, it should also be noted that the two do not have to be regarded as rigidly mutually exclusive. Church and Crown were closely interlinked and this relationship was now enshrined in statute. Ecclesiastics were also power holders and bishops, for instance, sat in the House of Lords. The Church possessed vast influence and wealth. Its religious teaching sanctioned secular authority and shaped mentalities. Instead of being an insular development, any change in religion 'could not fail to be full of political consequence for a world in which its significance was so pervasive'.[3]

If Henry deluded himself that his religious policies were sincere and motivated by a desire for the good of the commonwealth, others disagreed. The spontaneous reaction of religious conservatives is evidence of this, but it is also interesting to note the disillusion of genuine reformers in the period after the Henrician religious innovations. *The Complaynt of Roderyck Mors* by Henry Brinkelowe, written towards the end of Henry's reign, is illuminating in this regard.[4] Brinkelowe felt compelled to remind people how to 'employ the goods and lands of the bishops, deans, canons and chantries, to God's glory, to the common wealth and to the help of the poor'. He clearly felt his 'Godly advisement' was required when he saw so much bounty from the dissolutions fall into private and speculative hands. The wealth, he stated, should be used to provide houses for poor men, those unable to work due to ill health and the blind.[5]

In a similar fashion, Thomas Lever preached a sermon at St Paul's on 2 February 1550. Speaking about the dissolutions, which had been necessary because the monasteries were idle, superstitious and indulged in vain ceremonies, he lamented what had been done with the abundance of goods resulting from the closures: 'Howbeit covetous officers have so used this matter, that even those goods which did seem for the relief of the poor, the maintenance of learning, and to comfortable necessary hospitality in the common wealth, be now turned to maintain worldly, wicked, covetous ambition.'[6]

The evidence supports a contention that the English 'Reformation' was, to use Christopher Haigh's analytical matrix,[7] a reformation from above but slow in the localities. This would be in contrast to those who advocate a rapid reformation from above, such as Geoffrey Elton. It is also a different perspective to the 'reformation from below' school, including Geoffrey Dickens and Claire Cross. For Dickens, the Reformation was one of conversion as opposed to coercion – the evidence presented here does not support such a view. The research presented here concurs with Haigh's assessment that the early Reformation was ineffective in the northern counties.[8] The

Pilgrimage of Grace indicates that the English Reformation, far from being inevitable, was indeed a disturbing and long drawn-out process. The insurrection provoked a conservative reaction, and a genuine and sincere attempt to introduce Protestant theology and doctrine did not occur until the reign of Edward VI.

It is worth referring to the fact that small-scale resistance occurred early in the reign of Edward VI, indicative of latent Catholic sympathies in the North. In 1548, in Seamer, Yorkshire, some 3,000 people attacked the commissioners for the dissolution of the chantries with violence. Matthew White and four others were murdered. However, this was a rare example of resistance and the leaders of the mob were executed. Thus, resistance was futile. There was clearly no appetite for large-scale protests a decade or so after the Pilgrimage. Outward conformity appeared to be the order of the day, given all the changes and tumultuous events which had gone before.[9] As Norman Jones has observed, there was 'scarcely a peep heard in complaint' during the second round of monastic dissolutions in 1540, as many knew of the profits to be made. Jones went on to argue that even 'men who might have led resistance to the changes of the late 1530s, had been either cowed or convinced'. Self-interest 'more effectively converted the propertied classes than evangelization';[10] such men included Norfolk, Shrewsbury, Latimer, Babthorpe and Danby.

Sixteenth-century England was a society of orders and the ruling landed elite normally viewed the commons as beneath contempt. Yet, on this occasion, some of the nobility, the gentry and the commons combined for a common purpose. Their mission was to save the Holy Church and preserve the religion of their forebears. Unlike the gentry and the nobility, however, the commons had no political voice and their only avenue to making the king aware of their grievances was generally by riot. Deference in society was ingrained; the commons expected the gentry to lead. This is exactly what happened during the Pilgrimage, irrespective of tales of coercion and life-threatening potential violence. Some of the gentry were involved precisely because they wanted to be involved. As Ralph Sadler perceptively alleged, the gentlemen 'winked' at the rising.[11] They were not immune to the same concerns and anxieties in matters of religion or the succession.

Yet, this is not to concede that the contention that there was a conspiracy holds any weight. The Pilgrimage was a mass, popular and spontaneous rising. There is nothing in the evidence to support a theory of preplanning and preparation. If the Pilgrimage had been conceived and planned by a defeated faction, or indeed anyone else, one would expect to find evidence of a more co-ordinated approach. One would also, perhaps, find evidence of preplanning and, indeed, requests for foreign assistance and/or intervention. As has been shown, despite the best efforts of Reginald Pole, support from the papacy and the Holy Roman Emperor were, at best, lukewarm and hardly conducive to achieving the objective of reconciling England with Rome or deposing Henry. The prayers and 'support' of other Catholic princes and the pope were woefully inadequate and when Pole did eventually set off for England, the momentum and the Pilgrimage were over. It was, quite simply, far too little, too late.

The hypothesis that the Pilgrimage of Grace was a result of a religious reaction against the Henrician religious experiment has been borne out by the evidence. The Pilgrimage was undoubtedly overwhelmingly about religious grievances. Although the Pilgrims could be, and may very well have perceived themselves as, armed crusaders, no actual physical violence occurred. However, Zagorin has made an interesting point in relation to the use of 'symbolic violence'. This, he argued, incorporated speech, gesture and writing deployed to transgress and reverse prevailing social norms: the objective being to destroy the sanctity or prestige of ruling people or institutions.[12] Such symbolic violence was undoubtedly a feature of the Pilgrimage of Grace, if one accepts Zagorin's analysis.

The Pilgrims' gestures were at the same time sacred (i.e. the Badge of the Five Wounds and St Cuthbert's banner) and profane (for instance, their appearance in military harness). This is important in that it highlights the fact that symbols and rituals were under threat as a result of the Henrician experiment. The Pilgrims deployed symbols because they wished to retain aspects which were ingrained and sacred in their religious experience and were manifestations of piety. Although the Pilgrims were careful not to destroy the sanctity or prestige of the king, they attacked his chief minister. The perception of Cromwell as a heretical, malign influence was not exclusive to the North. A ballad, in circulation at Reading, Berkshire, rejoiced in Cromwell's fall when it came: 'Thou dyd not remember, false heretyke, One God, one faith, and once Kynge Catholyke, For thous hast bene so long a sysmatyke'.[13]

The events of the early months of 1537 were discussed, as it was important to try to ascertain the reasons for the resumption of revolts. No discussion of the Pilgrimage as a protest would be complete without analysing these events. This exploration was also necessary to identify and highlight the behaviour of certain individuals who featured in the subsequent discussions of rehabilitation and reward. It was argued that the king never intended to fulfil any of the undertakings given by the Duke of Norfolk. Henry, as has been seen, was severely affronted by the 'rude' and ignorant people having questioned his policies and choice of advisors. The Crown's duplicity is amply illustrated by Norfolk's self-proclaimed use of a 'defective' commission. The sources suggest that a vengeful monarch was simply biding his time until his opportunity for retribution arose. Bigod's futile uprising presented this and the executions of 178 people ensued, most notably, Lord Darcy, Lord Hussey and Robert Aske.

The fate of the rebels posed an interesting question. How did some individuals manage successfully to rehabilitate themselves and prosper, whilst others perished? Some nobles managed to extricate themselves, for instance, Lords Latimer and Scrope. Latimer recalled, however sincerely, that his being among the Pilgrims was a painful experience.[14] This appears to be a disingenuous statement from an elderly and conservative nobleman who had been in attendance at the York council. However, the need for suitable candidates for the efficient government of the North overrode the king's appetite for revenge. There was indeed a dearth of suitably qualified gentry in this peripheral region.

Sir Robert Bowes' career demonstrates that the Pilgrimage and its aftermath provided many of the gentry with the opportunity to rehabilitate themselves by pursuing a career in government service in the region. It was a mutually beneficial situation. Both the Crown and some of the northern gentry benefited from the repercussions of the Pilgrimage. This situation was also a propaganda coup for the Crown. Demonstrably penitent Pilgrims had realised the error of their ways and became loyal servants of the regime. Patronage and the opportunity for social advancement were pivotal in this transformation. The chief patron was Thomas Cromwell, until his fall in 1540. Perhaps Cromwell's character is best summarised by Sir Thomas Elyot in his letter to the king when he described the Lord Privy Seal as the 'chief patron of virtue and cunning'.[15]

The Crown was provided with an opportunity for a realignment of power structures in the North and exerted its authority in the region anew. This it did through the diligent service of both 'rehabilitated' and consistently loyal gentry. Indeed, the study of reward and grants has indicated that the gentry were by far the most spectacular beneficiaries of lucrative grants and offices. The traditional northern nobles appeared to have been side-lined. Perhaps this was a contributory factor in the 1569 rising. The potential latent resentment of the nobility and their long-suppressed religious misgivings gave vent to open rebellion – a rising that was led by the nobles themselves.

So what exactly can be deduced from this study about the link between loyalty to the Crown during the Pilgrimage and its aftermath and reward? It is obvious that deference to a lord could secure work, land, credit, gifts, charity and patronage.[16] The ultimate Lord was, of course, the king, so the prospect of patronage through loyalty would have been very enticing, especially given the new-found wealth with the dissolution of the monasteries. The men who were within the scope of the Crown's patronage were generally quick to realise the implications and capitalise on their loyalty. Individuals such as Ellerker, Bowes, Arthur Darcy and, indeed, John Dudley prospered in the aftermath. Fletcher and MacCulloch have also pointed out that it was necessary to preserve the idea of a static social structure. Those who were successful in the competition for social advancement made 'frenzied efforts to conceal their movement in society by inventing pedigrees or taking arms'.[17]

Some heirs embraced the new order and were loyal again in 1569, whilst others tended towards recusancy and were involved in the 1569 rising. It is illuminating that the gentry, on the whole, remained loyal to the Crown in 1569, whilst many of the traditional northern magnates became embroiled in intrigue. Shrewsbury's role was absolutely crucial in 1536 and his heir was loyal again in 1569 – but it is surely significant that the Talbots appeared to be atypical in 1536, in that they were materially well rewarded.

The commons had, in reality, nothing to gain materially from the Pilgrimage. Indeed, the dissolutions had removed the chief source of support of the very poorest. At the other end, though, the rising presented opportunities for the northern gentry who chose to use loyalty as a gateway to a share in the ecclesiastical wealth.[18] The idea of the Pilgrimage as being for the commonwealth was just using contemporary language to state that all social orders were involved. Sir Thomas More, in 'Utopia', hit the nail on the head when he said that in truth, 'euerye man procureth hys owne pryuate wealthe'.[19]

The king astutely sought to divide and rule and 'tried to split rebel support by a judicious mixture of threats and inducements'[20] – the threat of retribution and the promise of reward. It was this strategy which yielded the result the Crown desired, the seeds of distrust between the gentry and the commons were planted and the movement's defeat was then inevitable. We have seen how the commons involved began to distrust the gentlemen: the visits of Ellerker, Bowes and Aske to Court exacerbated their suspicions. They were thus susceptible to Bigod and Hallam's rhetoric in early 1537.

The link between loyalty and reward in the aftermath of the Pilgrimage is, then, present. Some gentry benefited spectacularly in terms of material gains – see, for instance, Sir Arthur Darcy. Darcy is an example which refutes Bastow's claims that the Tudors had an outright policy of inflicting financial ruin on all members of a family where one individual had been disloyal or rebellious. Perhaps Henry would have liked to deploy that tactic but realpolitik, expediency and the necessity of effective governance in a problematic and distant region dictated otherwise.[21] However, Darcy was not to be as prominent in royal administration as the likes of Ellerker and Bowes. Darcy and Uvedale's requests to relocate to the South were unsuccessful; the regime sought to foster a loyal and stable gentry class in the region. For others, loyalty in the autumn of 1536 proved rewarding and gained individuals such as William Parr and Ralph Eure (both of whom were created barons) an enhancement in prestige and standing. Fidelity to Henry was undoubtedly a springboard towards advancement and the most meteoric rise, which continued into the next reign, was that of Sir John Dudley.

Pro-Henrician rhetoric and propaganda was another important method by which the Crown sought to achieve an acquiescent populace. Richard Morison was the main polemicist of the time and both Thomas Master and Edward Hall wrote unashamedly biased accounts of the Henrician religious project. Propaganda was an important tool in a three-pronged attack in securing compliance – persuasion, punishment and patronage. The role of preaching and its importance in reaching the illiterate masses, as well as instances of punishment, were also highlighted.

The changes were not popular, not only in the North, but in other parts of the country as well: examples were given from the South – including

Oxford – and Ireland. Robert Parkyn's narrative stands in contrast to that of Thomas Master. Yes, Parkyn was a fairly obscure northern clergyman, but that surely is what makes his recollections interesting. Reginald Pole was undoubtedly a biased source but this is hardly surprising given his deep religious convictions, exile and perhaps even his Plantagenet blood. Pole's own family were victims of Henry's vengeance and his 70-year-old mother, the Countess of Salisbury, was beheaded on the flimsiest of charges.

However, Pole shed light on the views of the papacy and ortho-dox thought. The Pilgrimage was an undoubted missed opportunity for domestic conservatives (the likes of the Duke of Norfolk and the Earl of Shrewsbury) and foreign powers alike. For all his self-righteous indignation and Catholic faith, Charles V did not choose to become involved. England, one must conclude, was way down the list of the emperor's priorities, even for mischief making.

The impact of the Pilgrimage of Grace in religious terms in the North was examined and samples of wills were studied and analysed in the absence of churchwardens' accounts. Many wills contained traditional formats and a significant proportion also appeared to err on the side of caution by specifying burial rites in compliance with statute. However, it is worth reiterating the recusant tendencies of the heirs of the rehabilitated Pilgrims, the Babthorpes and the Danbys. The area around the Yorkshire Plain still contained many Catholic gentry in the 1620s, over eighty years after the Pilgrimage of Grace These included the Fairfax, Constable and Stapleton families.[22] One cannot, of course, attribute this fact as being directly linked to the Pilgrimage, but it is surely revealing that Catholic sympathies remained within these families despite their forebears having been reprieved.

In addition to the gentry, some of the nobility retained Catholic sympa-thies, even though they had been steadfastly loyal to the Crown in 1536 and again in 1569. The Talbot Earls of Shrewsbury continued in their Catholic beliefs, despite the fact that the 4th Earl, George, had been instrumental in the defeat of the Pilgrimage. Had he joined the rebellion, the outcome may have been very different. The wife of the 7th Earl, Gilbert (1552–1616), was openly Catholic and the 16th Earl, John (1791–1852) was also Catholic.[23]

The other notably Catholic noble family were the Howards. Again, this is somewhat ironic, given the 3rd Duke's pivotal role in the defeat of the Pilgrimage and his subsequent campaign of retribution in the North. It is, of course, difficult to speculate, but one might say that had Talbot and Howard been true to their religious convictions, the Pilgrimage may have succeeded in 1536 and the course of northern history would have been different. As it was, Norfolk's heir and grandson, the 4th Duke, was implicated in the Ridolfi plot and paid the price for his treason. The Neville Earl of Westmorland and the Percy Earl of Northumberland were involved in the 1569 Rebellion. The 4th Earl of Westmorland did not participate in the Pilgrimage but the 6th Earl was raised as a Catholic and was present in Durham Cathedral when the Mass was restored.

As we know, the 6th Earl of Northumberland (d. 1537) made the king his heir and did not participate in the Pilgrimage. His brothers did, and Thomas Percy was executed. His son became the 7th Earl, as the 6th Earl had died childless. This Percy earl, described as a 'rank papist' by Sir Ralph Sadler, was involved in 1569.[24] It is worth reiterating the loyalty of and the material benefits accrued by the Earl of Rutland following his stance in the Pilgrimage of Grace. He died a rich man, owing to the acquisition of much monastic property and his dynasty prospered in the following centuries.

Although Geoffrey Elton has decisively rejected the idea that Cromwell used spies, this study has attempted to shed some light on the way in which the Lord Privy Seal operated. Evidence from elsewhere in the realm, as well as the North, supports the contention that Cromwell presided over a spy network: his role as a patron facilitated this. As Andy Wood has argued, accounts of seditious speech enabled the authorities to investigate, codify and crush popular politics.[25] It is interesting to note, during the course of this study, that reports of sedition and sycophantic begging letters almost disappear from the State Papers after Cromwell's fall in 1540 and for the rest of the reign. This leads to a conclusion that he was most probably at the epicentre of an effective, efficient and rewarding spy network.

At the beginning of 1541, the French ambassador, Marillac, wrote to King Francis that some suspected that the people in the North were ready to rebel if they had a leader.[26] Sansom acknowledges that the information on the Wakefield Plot is fragmentary and it is not the place here to attempt to delve deeper into it. Suffice it to say that Sir John Neville was involved and subsequently executed at York. Twenty-six people were held in custody, of which five lay people and four priests were executed in May and June.[27] The conspirators had been betrayed by an unknown informant before the plot. On 30 June King Henry and most of his Court began his four-month progress to the North. This was over four and half years since he had 'promised' to have his queen, Jane Seymour (now deceased), crowned in York and to facilitate a parliament to be held in the city. Instead, when the king finally arrived in the region, after being on the throne for over thirty years, it was with Queen Katherine Howard in tow and he used this opportunity to demonstrate his majesty and demand public submission from those towns implicated in the Pilgrimage. In both Lincoln and York, the men fell on their knees in grovelling submission and the king confirmed the 1537 pardon in person and in public in 'carefully choreographed ceremonies'.[28]

Of Henry himself, it is difficult not to concur with Lucy Wooding's assessment that in the aftermath of the Pilgrimage, 'he had become more majestic, less plausible but undoubtedly a more terrifying proposition as a king'.[29] Henry undoubtedly possessed a cruel and vengeful nature – we have seen examples of this throughout. Henry's vindictive character and desire for retribution was, for instance, evident when he instructed the Duke of Suffolk to destroy, burn and kill man, woman and child if there was renewed rebellion in Lincolnshire in the autumn of 1536.[30] The French ambassador Marillac succinctly summarised King Henry's three prevalent character traits or 'vices' – avarice, suspicious nature and inconstancy.[31] An apt appraisal.

The lack of resistance in the period after the Pilgrimage can be attributed to political circumstances: the nobility and gentry were reluctant to become embroiled in further rebellion. This should not be mistaken for a lack of fervour among the commons or lower clergy, or a decisive rejection of the old Catholic order. The Crown purchased support of the Royal Supremacy by creating and guaranteeing a property interest in the former ecclesiastical lands. Resistance was indeed futile when money could be made and power attained. It is also highly revealing, when discussing religiosity, to emphasise the fact that the king himself specified Masses for his soul in his will.[32] He also ordered 1,000 Masses to be said for the soul of Queen Jane Seymour.

Cromwell's spectacular career was to come to an abrupt end when he was executed for treason on 28 July 1540, the day of King Henry's marriage to Katherine Howard. All of Cromwell's honours were forfeited and it was publicly proclaimed that he could only be called 'Thomas Cromwell, cloth carder'. In the end, the son of a blacksmith from Putney had overreached himself and had been a disturbing influence in the static society of orders. It is to be expected that conservatives and Catholics would have regarded this as his just desserts. Hall said of Cromwell's downfall:

Many lamented but more rejoiced, and specially such as either had been religious men, or favoured religious persons; for they banqueted and triumphed together that night, many wishing that that day had been seven years before; and some fearing lest he should escape, although he were imprisoned, could not be merry. Others who knew nothing but truth by him both lamented him and heartily prayed for him. But this is true that of certain of the clergy he was detestably hated, & specially of such as had borne swynge [beaten hard], and by his means was put from it; for in deed he was a man that in all his doings seemed not to favour any kind of Popery, nor could not abide the snoffyng pride of some prelates, which undoubtedly, whatsoever else was the cause of his death, did shorten his life and procured the end that he was brought unto.[33]

The Pilgrimage was most definitely a missed opportunity for the conservatives in the realm. The Duke of Norfolk's expedient and calculating decision to lead the royal army when he could have potentially raised East Anglia was undoubtedly of great benefit to the Crown and detrimental to the Pilgrimage's chances of success. For Bush and Bownes, the Pilgrimage was an event of outstanding importance – if the rebels had succeeded, 'the religious, political and social history of early modern England would have undoubtedly have followed a different course'. They go so far as to state, 'what is certain is that the Anglican Church would have returned to Roman Catholicism' and that the dissolution of the monasteries would not have occurred. One has to agree entirely with their contention that the 'Reformation would have had to evolve as a social movement rather than as something imposed upon society by the state'.[34]

The Pilgrimage of Grace could be interpreted as exhibiting potential strengths, weaknesses, opportunities and threats. The Pilgrimage's great strength was in its huge numbers and popular support. Thirty-thousand men in the field dwarfed the army Henry Tudor recruited in his successful campaign against Richard III which had allowed him to claim the throne by right of conquest.[35] The Pilgrimage had the tacit approval of Catholic

Europe and the papacy and its participants were galvanised by the belief that they were undertaking a holy enterprise.

The Pilgrimage's weakness was the inherent distrust between the social classes – the gentry and the commons. In such a situation, the divide-and-rule approach was bound to pay dividends and the commons inevitably came to believe that they had been sold out by the gentry. The Pilgrimage was undoubtedly an opportunity which could have been grasped, had the strengths been harnessed effectively and the weaknesses addressed. Of course, this would have involved effective and strategic planning, which was manifestly absent.

The Pilgrimage could, perhaps have succeeded if it had availed itself of Reginald Pole's leadership. The opportunity was there for the taking but senior nobles, such as the Duke of Norfolk, the Earl of Shrewsbury and Lord Dacre, were not willing to become involved, whilst the pope procrastinated and Charles V did not feel the enterprise worth becoming involved in. The threat to the Pilgrims is self-evident: their actions were bound to be viewed as tantamount to treason. They took a risk, carried along by the momentum of mass popular approval, but the threat of social friction within their ranks and the lack of decisive leadership rendered their movement vulnerable. The inherent distrust between the commons and the gentry is critical in understanding why the Pilgrimage was doomed as an enterprise and a missed opportunity.

It is hopefully clear from the evidence that has been presented here that the Reformation was deeply unpopular in the North of England. The Pilgrimage of Grace substantiates this only too well. The Henrician religious innovations – constantly subject to change – were not well received in other parts of the realm either. It would probably be fair to say that opposition was more deeply entrenched in the North and to contend that this was as a result of it being a peripheral region, far removed from the core – the Court. It also explains why it remained fertile ground for another religious rebellion in 1569.

By the time of the Northern Rising, the North was largely 'unreformed' but Catholics in the region had managed to survive and prosper in the aftermath of the Pilgrimage due to the expediency of pragmatism. The Catholics, however sincerely, retained overt loyalty to Elizabeth and what could appear as ambiguous or apathetic was, in reality, practical. They had to reconcile the inherent struggle between their hearts and their minds – in the end, the mind, as manifested by acquiescence and conformity, tended to prevail. Many Catholics attended Protestant services and came to be known as 'Church-papists'.[36] After the Northern Rebellion and Elizabeth's excommunication, large-scale uprisings were replaced by plots.[37] It was at this point that religion and national loyalty truly became embedded in the English political identity, but the seeds were firmly sown in Henry's reign and the Pilgrimage was a reaction to the planting.

In the aftermath of the Pilgrimage acquiescence prevailed (despite individuals' private and guarded consciences). By the end of the sixteenth-century England, it could be argued, had taken significant steps on its evolution as a nation-state. This aspect of Whig analysis appears to hold true. Centralisation, uniformity, language and now the state religion were features of this. To be a loyal Englishman, one had to adopt English norms and values – language, dress and religion. There is no doubt that the Henrician religious experiment was just that – an experiment, and not a popular one either, particularly in the North. However, the changes were built upon and enhanced in the following reign and resumed in the reign of Elizabeth. Subjects had a duty of obedience and loyalty in all areas of their lives, religion included. The Pilgrimage was a conservative, mass, popular outburst, but the way in which it was handled by the regime, with a dual carrot and stick approach, resulted in its demise. The promise of position, patronage and power was enough to tempt avaricious men to remain loyal to whatever was the order of the day. After the dissolutions, they had a vested interest in maintaining and enhancing their positions.

As Susan Wabuda has stated, the 'religious landscape of England was far more diverse at the end of the sixteenth century than it had been at the beginning'.[38] In the end, Catholic habits and sympathy did not die hard, and from 1536 to 1570, given the state of flux, many in the North must have felt that a return to the 'old' religion was not just preferable but also possible.

In the aftermath of the Pilgrimage of Grace the government's tactics of punishment, patronage and persuasion prevented the recurrence of fresh revolt and there was a relatively peaceful interlude until 1569. The religious experiment undertaken by Henry VIII was unprecedented and largely unpopular. The misgivings of large numbers of his subjects were manifested in the Pilgrimage of Grace. The king's force of personality, the promise of patronage and the fear of reprisals were enough to keep the dissenters in place for the remainder of his reign. However, Catholic sympathy and a longing for the 'old' days lay dormant until the fresh explosion in Elizabeth's reign in 1569.

The Pilgrimage was arguably a watershed. Henceforth, loyalty, power and religion became inextricably entwined. Edmund Bonner summarised the Henrician period and the dilemma for religious conservatives succinctly. Writing in the reign of Queen Mary, he stated: 'Fear compelled us to bear with the times, for otherwise there was no way but one.'[39]

Notes

Introduction

1 Lucy Wooding, *Rethinking Catholicism in Reformation England*, Oxford, 2000, p.50.
2 Felicity Heal, *The Reformation in Britain and Ireland*, Oxford, 2003, p.133.
3 Ibid. – Heal cites Diarmaid MacCulloch, *The Reign of Henry VII*, p.178.
4 Susan Wabuda, 'The Reformation Revised: The English Reformation Beyond Revisionism', *History Compass*, Vol. 1 (2003), p.3.
5 Alec Ryrie, *The Gospel and Henry VIII: Evangelicals in the Early English Reformation*, Cambridge, 2003, p.7.
6 As Peter Marshall has stated, the study of the Reformation is often a personal engagement or debate about the meaning of religion. See Peter Marshall, '(Re) defining the English Reformation', *Journal of British Studies*, Vol. 48 (2009), pp.564–86, particularly p.574.
7 Anthony Fletcher and Diarmaid MacCulloch, *Tudor Rebellions*, 5th edition, Harlow, 2004, p.45.
8 Ethan Shagan, *Popular Politics and the English Reformation*, Cambridge, 2003, p.89.
9 R.H. Hoyle, 'Thomas Master's Narrative of the Pilgrimage of Grace', *Northern History*, Vol. 21 (1985), p.53.
10 Peter Marshall, *The Reformation: A Very Short Introduction*, Oxford, 2009, pp.65–66.
11 Claire Cross, *Church and People: England 1450–1660*, Glasgow, 1976.
12 G.R. Elton, *Reform and Reformation: England 1509–1558*, London, 1977; A.G. Dickens, *The English Reformation*, London, 1964; Cross, *Church and People, 1450–1660*.
13 Christopher Haigh, *The English Reformation Revised*, Cambridge, 1987, pp.19, 20, 23, 30 & 32.
14 Eamon Duffy, 'The English Reformation after Revisionism', *Renaissance Quarterly*, Vol. 59, No. 3 (2006), p.3.
15 In this respect, this work would appear to fit the post-revisionist/post-confessional paradigm as discussed by Ethan Shagan in *Catholics and the 'Protestant Nation': Religious Policy and Identity in Early Modern England*, Manchester, 2005, p.1, and Marshall, '(Re)defining the English Reformation'. Marshall makes the point that both Haigh and Duffy have been willing to embrace the post-revisionist label in recent years (p.566) and also draws attention to Diarmaid MacCulloch's concerns with regard to 'ancestor worship' – the temptation to focus attention of the perceived progenitors of one's own denomination (p.571), of which I am mindful.
16 P. Marshall, '(Re)defining the English Reformation', p.584. For other proponents of this perspective, see Richard Rex, *Henry VIII and the English Reformation*, Basingstoke, 1993, pp.171–73. Rex discusses the 'idiosyncratic nature of Henry's religious settlement', a view shared by Paul O'Grady, who was of the opinion that Henry's

'Reformation' reflected a 'melange of incoherent prejudices'. Paul O'Grady, *Henry VIII and the Conforming Catholics*, Minn., 1990, p.10.

17 Gerald Bray (ed.), *Documents of the English Reformation*, Cambridge, 1994, pp.162–74.

18 Michael Bush and David Bownes, *The Defeat of the Pilgrimage of Grace*, Hull, 1999, p.406. This book aims to avoid the label 'Protestant' for, as Marshall has highlighted, this is somewhat anachronistic in this context. See 'Is the Pope Catholic? Henry VIII and the Semantics of Schism', in Shagan (ed.), *Catholics and the 'Protestant Nation*, p.23. For the purposes of this work, 'reformers' or 'evangelicals' will denote those in favour of a reformed theology.

19 Bray, *Documents of the English Reformation*, pp.175–78.

20 The National Archives (TNA), Kew – SP1/108, f.106; SP1/108, f.212; *Letters and Papers, Foreign and Domestic of the Reign of Henry VIII* (L&P), arranged and catalogued by Gairdner & Brodie, H.M. Stationery Office, London, 1905; (L&P, Vol. XI: 739, 807, 698 and 848). All provide evidence of the numbers involved.

21 G.R. Elton, 'Politics & the Pilgrimage of Grace' in *After the Reformation*, B.C. Malament (ed.), Manchester, 1980, p.30.

22 See, for example, TNA, SP1/107, f.154; TNA, SP1/108, f.3; L&P, Vol. XI: 663, 672 & 698.

23 L&P, Vol. XI: 712.

24 Elton, *Reform and Reformation*, p.261.

25 M. Bush, *The Pilgrimage of Grace: A Study of the Rebel Armies of October 1536*, Manchester, 1996, p.407.

26 Hoyle, *The Pilgrimage of Grace and the Politics of the 1530s*, Oxford, 2001, p.9; Shagan, *Popular Politics and the English Reformation*, p.89.

27 Elton, *Reform and Reformation*, p.264; Elton, 'Politics & the Pilgrimage of Grace', p.43; A.G. Dickens in 'The Pilgrimage of Grace' in his *Reformation Studies*, London, 1982, p.58.

28 Dickens, 'Secular & Religious Motivation', p.81; Hoyle, *The Pilgrimage of Grace and the Politics of the 1530s*, p.453; Peter Marshall, *Religious Identities in Henry VIII's England*, Aldershot, 2006, p.10; Shagan, *Popular Politics and the English Reformation*, p.127; J.J. Scarisbrick, *Henry VIII*, Yale, 1997, p.341.

29 Bush, *The Pilgrimage of Grace: A Study of the Rebel Armies of 1536*, pp. 415–16; Scott Harrison, *The Pilgrimage of Grace in the Lake Counties, 1536–37*, London, 1981, p.87; Hoyle, *The Pilgrimage of Grace and the Politics of the 1530s*, p.423.

30 Elton, 'Politics and the Pilgrimage of Grace', p.33.

31 Elton, *Reform and Reformation*, p.252; 'Politics and the Pilgrimage of Grace', pp. 40, 41, 45, 47 & 52.

32 Elton, *Reform and Reformation*, p.259.

33 Elton, 'Politics and the Pilgrimage of Grace', p.31.

34 Dickens, 'Secular & Religious Motivation', p.64.

35 C.S.L. Davies, 'The Pilgrimage of Grace Reconsidered', *Past and Present*, No. 41 (Dec 1968), p.76.

36 Andy Wood, *The 1549 Rebellions and the Making of Modern England*, Cambridge, 2007, pp.4 & 12.

37 Andy Wood, *Riot, Rebellion and Popular Politics in Early Modern England*, Basingstoke, 2002, pp.49 & 54.

38 Fletcher and MacCulloch, *Tudor Rebellions*, 2004, p.15.

39 Haigh, *The English Reformation Revised*, p.24.

40 Michael Bush, *The Pilgrimage of Grace: A Study of the Rebel Armies of October 1536*, p.409.

41 Madeleine Hope Dodds and Ruth Dodds, *The Pilgrimage of Grace 1536–37, and the Exeter Conspiracy*, Cambridge, 1915.

42 W. Gordon Zeeveld, *Foundations of Tudor Policy*, London, 1969, p.200.

43 Rachel Reid, *The King's Council in the North*, London, 1921, p.1.

44 A.J. Pollard, *North-Eastern England during the Wars of the Roses*, Oxford, 1990, p.316.

45 Zeeveld, *Foundations of Tudor Policy*, p.171.

46 S.G. Ellis, 'Civilizing Northumberland: Representations of Englishness in the Tudor State', *Journal of Historical Sociology*, Vol. XII (1999), pp.103–27. This assessment is reiterated by Steve Gunn, David Grummitt & Hans Cools in *War, State and Society in England and the Netherlands, 1447–1559*, Oxford, 2007, p.318. The North was a more militarised region than the South and the extreme borders were 'thoroughly attuned to war'.

47 Pollard, *North-Eastern England during the Wars of the Roses*, p.397.

48 Scarisbrick, *Henry VIII*, 1997, pp.351.

49 Richard Rex, *Henry VIII and the English Reformation*, p.46; Roger Bigelow Merriman, *Life and Letters of Thomas Cromwell*, Vol. I, Oxford, 1968, pp.182–83.

Chapter 1

1   *L&P*, Vol. X: 121.

2   Fletcher and MacCulloch, *Tudor Rebellions*, p.45.

3   W.J. Sheils, *The English Reformation 1530–1570*, Harlow, 1989.

4   G.R. Elton, *Policy and Police: The Enforcement of the Reformation in the Age of Thomas Cromwell*, Cambridge, 1972.

5   Bush, Michael, *The Pilgrims' Complaint: A Study of Popular Thought in the Early Tudor North* (Farnham: Ashgate, 2009), p.47.

6   The Statues of the Realm (Stat. Realm), Volume III, A. Luder (ed.), London, (1810–28), pp.663–66; *L&P*, Vol. XI: 1087, 8 June.

7   *L&P*, Vol. X: 11 (quotation).

8   *L&P*, Vol. X: 34.

9   British Library, Cotton, Vespasian, C/XIV/2, f.47; *L&P*, Vol. X: 246.

10 *Calendar of Letters, Despatches and State Papers Relating to the Negotiations Between England and Spain, Preserved in the Archives of Simancas and Elsewhere* (*CSP Sp.*), Pascual De Gayangos (ed.), Ontario, 1536–38: p.601.

11 *L&P*, Vol. X: 308; TNA, SP1/103, f.139 (*L&P*, Vol. X: 693); *L&P*, Vol. X: 1036.

12 *L&P*, Vol. XI: 270.

13 Bray, *Documents of the English Reformation*, p.175.

14 Eamon Duffy, *The Stripping of the Altars: Traditional Religion in England c. 1400–c. 1580*, London, 1992 pp.338 & 347.

15 Bush, *The Pilgrimage of Grace: A Study of the Rebel Armies of 1536*, p.424.

16 Elton, *Policy and Police*, Chapter 3, pp.83–170.

17 TNA, SP1/96, ff.210–13 (*L&P*, Vol. XI: 408).

18 Elton, *Policy and Police*, 1972, p.112.

19 TNA, SP1/102, f.45 (*L&P*, Vol. X: 318); *L&P*, Vol. X: 1140; *L&P*, Vol. XI: 354.

20 *L&P*, Vol. XI: 1239.

21 *L&P*, Vol. XI: 514.

22 G.R. Elton, *Reformation Europe 1517–1559*, 2nd edition (Oxford, 1999) pp.79, 109 & 112.

23 Scarisbrick, *Henry VIII*. Although Charles had attempted to prevent the divorce of Henry and Katherine by putting pressure on Pope Clement VII and encouraging delaying tactics, he had not become militarily involved. Indeed, in April 1536, just a

few months after Katherine's death, he appeared to entertain rapprochement with Henry and this was reinforced by the execution of Anne Boleyn the following month (see p.335).

24 Ibid., pp.334, 335 & 282.

25 *L&P*, X: 141; Scarisbrick, *Henry VIII*, p.335.

26 BL, Cotton, Caligula, B/III, f.195.

27 *L&P*, Vol. X: 494.

28 *L&P*, Vol. X: 575 & 619.

29 *L&P*, Vol. X: 666.

30 *L&P*, X: 698, 699, 752 & 950 (*The Ten Articles, the First Definition of the Faith*, produced by Henry as Supreme Head, was published this year).

31 *L&P*, Vol. X: 908. See also Dodds, *The Pilgrimage of Grace*, p.339.

32 Ronald H. Fritze, *Historical Dictionary of Tudor England, 1485–1603*, London, 1991, p.62.

33 *L&P*, Vol. XI: 376.

34 TNA, SP1/106, f.134 (*L&P*, Vol. XI: 405).

35 TNA, SP1/106, f.183 (*L&P*, Vol. XI: 470).

36 David Loades, *Power in Tudor England*, Basingstoke, 1997, pp.4, 11, 24 & 45.

37 Hoyle, *The Pilgrimage of Grace and the Politics of the 1530s*, p.39; Gunn, Grummitt & Cools, *War, State, and Society in England and the Netherlands*, p.317.

38 Loades. *Power in Tudor England*, pp.123–4.

39 Ibid., p.32.

40 Ibid., p.30.

41 Ibid., p.31.

42 Steven G. Ellis, *Tudor Frontiers and Noble Power: The Making of the British State*, Oxford, 1995, pp.15, 20, 40, 41, 47 & 48.

Chapter 2

1 Fletcher & MacCulloch, *Tudor Rebellions*, pp.26 & 28.

2 R. Hoyle, *The Pilgrimage of Grace and the Politics of the 1530s*, p.206.

3 TNA, SP1/110, f.6 (*L&P*, Vol. X: 909).

4 Bush, *The Pilgrimage of Grace: A Study of the Rebel Armies of October 1536*, p.436.

5 BL, Cotton, Vespasian, F/XIII, f.213; TNA SP1/106, f.248 (*L&P*, Vol. XI: 531 & 533).

6 Fletcher & MacCulloch, *Tudor Rebellions*, p.26; Bush, *The Pilgrimage of Grace: A Study of the Rebel Armies of October 1536*, p.425.

7 *L&P*, Vol. XI: 585.

8 Davies, 'The Pilgrimage of Grace Reconsidered', No 41, p.70.

9 TNA, SP1/106, f.248 (*L&P*, Vol. XI: 533); SP1/106, f.250 (*L&P*, Vol. XI: 534).

10 TNA, SP1/106, f.301 (*L&P*, Vol. XI: 569); SP1/107, f.76 (*L&P*, Vol. XI: 598) (spelling modernised.)

11 BL, Cotton, Vespasian, F/XIII, f.213 (*L&P*, Vol. XI: 531).

12 TNA, SP1/106, f.260 (*L&P*, Vol. XI: 547); SP1/106, f.268 (*L&P*, Vol. XI: 552).

13 Dickens, 'Secular and Religious Motivation', p.75.

14 *L&P*, Vol. XI: 563.

15 TNA, SP1/107 (*L&P*, Vol. XI: 611) (spelling modernised.)

16 *L&P*, Vol. XI: 567.

17 *CSP Sp.*, Vol. 5.2, Henry VIII, 1536–1538: 104; *CSP Sp.*, Vol. 5.2: 105; *L&P*, Vol. XI: 597.

18 TNA, SP1/107, f.116 (*L&P*, Vol. XI: 622).

19 TNA, SP1/107, f.136 (*L&P*, Vol. XI: 645); SP1/107, f.144 (*L&P*, Vol. XI: 655).

20 *L&P*, Vol. XI: 698 (quotation).

21 TNA, SP1/108, f.43 (*L&P*, Vol. XI: 704).

22 TNA, SP1/108, f.50 (*L&P*, Vol. XI: 705(i)). As Fletcher and MacCulloch have stated, these five articles had been drawn up at Lincoln on 9 October and now survive only in the archives of York. See *Tudor Rebellions*, pp.142–43. Hoyle has stated that the document was addressed to 'lords, knights, masters, kinsmen and friends', and casts doubt about whether or not they were presented to the mayor. See *The Pilgrimage of Grace and the Politics of the 1530s*, pp. 203–4.

23 *L&P*, Vol. XI: 705(ii). This version taken from Hoyle, *The Pilgrimage of Grace and the Politics of the 1530s*, pp.456–57.

24 *L&P*, Vol. XI: 729.

25 TNA, SP1/108, f.140 (*L&P*, Vol. XI: 759); SP1/108, f.169 (*L&P*, Vol. XI: 774).

26 *L&P*, Vol. XI: 704(iv) (my italics). This version is taken from Fletcher & MacCulloch, *Tudor Rebellions*, pp.143–44. Also in Hoyle, *The Pilgrimage of Grace and the Politics of the 1530s*, pp.457–58. Original document in the Lancashire Record Office, 'Derby Correspondence', DDF/1 (unfoliated). Fletcher and MacCulloch date the oath as being 17 October, whilst Hoyle gives it a date of 24 October. Given the fact that Shrewsbury, Rutland and Huntingdon were aware of it on 18 October, the earlier date appears more accurate. In any event, the fact that the rebels were so eager to receive it at this point is what is of real significance.

27 TNA, SP1/108, f.180 (*L&P*, Vol. XI: 784); SP1/108, f.183 (*L&P*, Vol. XI: 785); SP1/108, f.184 (*L&P*, Vol. XI: 786).

28 Ibid. See Mary Bateson, 'The Pilgrimage of Grace', *English Historical Review*, Vol. 5, No 18 (April 1890), pp.330–45. See also Fletcher & MacCulloch, *Tudor Rebellions*, pp.144–45.

29 TNA, SP1/108 (*L&P*, Vol. XI: 826) (spelling modernised).

30 Ibid.

31 Shagan, *Popular Politics and the English Reformation*, p.127; pp.120–21.

32 Shagan, *Popular Politics and the English Reformation*, p.119; Davies, 'The Pilgrimage of Grace Reconsidered', p.63; Shagan, *Popular Politics and the English Reformation*, p.99; Davies, 'The Pilgrimage of Grace Reconsidered', p.65.

33 TNA, SP1/110, ff.141–48 (*L&P*, Vol. XI: 970).

34 *L&P*, Vol. XI: 848.

35 Fletcher & MacCulloch, *Tudor Rebellions*, p.32.

36 Elton, 'Politics & the Pilgrimage of Grace', pp.32 & 36.

37 *L&P*, Vol. XI: 569, 956, 957, 1175.

38 TNA, SP1/106, f.301 (*L&P*, Vol. XI: 569 & 780).

39 TNA, SP1/108, f.118 (*L&P*, Vol. XI: 748) (spelling modernised); SP1/109, f.251, f.257; SP1/110 f.1 (*L&P*, Vol. XI: 906, 907, 908). See also, Gunn, Grummitt & Cools, *War, State and Society in England and the Netherlands*, 2007, p.319. This assessment is yet another at odds with Elton's claim with regard to the size of the movement.

40 TNA, SP1/110, f.6 (*L&P*, Vol. XI: 909).

41 Bush, *The Pilgrimage of Grace: A Study of the Rebel Armies of 1536*, p.433.

42 TNA, SP1/110, f.8 (*L&P*, Vol. XI: 910).

43 TNA, SP1/110, ff. 100–14 (*L&P*, Vol. XI: 956). See, for instance, *L&P*, Vol. XI: 957, 1064.

44 *L&P*, Vol. XI: 995.

45   TNA, SP1/111, f.9 (*L&P*, Vol. XI: 1007).

46   TNA, SP1/111, f.59 (*L&P*, Vol. XI: 1045).

47   TNA, SP1/111 f.9 (*L&P* Vol. XI: 1007).

48   TNA, SP1/110, f.137 (*L&P*, Vol. XI: 969).

49   *L&P*, Vol. XI: 1069; TNA, SP1/111, f.117 (*L&P*, Vol. XI: 1079).

50   TNA, SP1/111, f.122 (*L&P*, Vol. XI: 1086) (spelling modernised); SP1/111, ff.133–34 (*L&P*, Vol. XI: 1096); SP1/112, f.2 (*L&P*, Vol. XI: 1167) (spelling modernised).

51   Elton, 'Politics & the Pilgrimage of Grace', p.37; TNA, SP1/106, ff.234–41 (*L&P*, Vol. XI: 522).

52   Hoyle, *The Pilgrimage of Grace and the Politics of the 1530s*, p.273.

53   See TNA, SP1/108, f.33, SP1/108, f.106 (*L&P*, Vol. XI: 692, 729, 739).

54   TNA, SP1/108, f.29 (*L&P*, Vol. XI: 689).

55   TNA, SP1/107, f.154, SP1/107, f.156, SP1/108, f.3 (*L&P*, Vol. XI: 663, 665, 672).

56   Elton, 'Politics & the Pilgrimage of Grace', p.37; Dodds, *The Pilgrimage of Grace 1536–37*, p.19.

57   Bush, *The Pilgrimage of Grace: A Study of the Rebel Armies of 1536*, p.425.

58   Elton, 'Politics & the Pilgrimage of Grace', p.39.

59   Davies, 'The Pilgrimage of Grace Reconsidered', p.41.

60   Scarisbrick, *Henry VIII*, p.342; Dodds, *The Pilgrimage of Grace*, p.337.

61   Scarisbrick, *Henry VIII*, p.347.

62   *L&P*, Vol. XI: 714 (quotation).

63   Fletcher & MacCulloch, *Tudor Rebellions*, 2004, p.35.

64   BL, Add MS 38133 (*L&P*, Vol. XI: 1128).

65   *L&P*, Vol. XI: 1128 (quotation).

66   *L&P*, Vol. XI: 1143, 1159.

67   *L&P*, Vol. XI: 1173, 1183.

68   Elton, *Reform and Reformation*, p.252; 'Politics & the Pilgrimage of Grace', pp. 40, 41, 45, 47 & 52.

69   *L&P*, Vol. XI: 1175 (quotation).

70   TNA, SP1/112, ff.151–57 (*L&P*, Vol. XI: 1271). Bush, *The Pilgrimage of Grace: A Study of the Rebel Armies of October 1536*, 1996, p.409. The concept of the body politic was the accepted political analogy in Tudor England and 'conceived of social structure through the prism of the human body'. See Jonathan Gil Harris, *Foreign Bodies and the Body Politic: Discourses of Social Pathology in Early Modern England*, Cambridge, 1998, p.1. This theme is recurrent and will be discussed in subsequent chapters.

71   *L&P*, Vol. XI: 1228.

72   Bush, *The Pilgrimage of Grace: A Study of the Rebel Armies of 1536*, pp.10 & 12.

73   *L&P*, Vol. XI: 1236.

74   TNA, SP1/112, f18 (*L&P* Vol. XI: 1246).

75   Scarisbrick, *Henry VIII*, pp.110–11, 113, 115–17.

76   Germain Marc'hadour, 'Fisher and More: a note', in *Humanism, Reform and the Reformation: The Career of Bishop John Fisher*, Brendan Bradshaw & Eamon Duffy (eds), Cambridge, 1989, p.105.

77   Brendan Bradshaw, 'Bishop John Fisher, 1469–1535: the man and his work' in *Humanism, Reform and Reformation*, p.9.

78   Scarisbrick, *Henry VIII*, p.401.

79   Marshall, *The Reformation: A Very Short Introduction*, p.4.

80   Elton, *Reformation Europe*, p.101.

81   G.W. Bernard, 'The Making of Religious Policy, 1533–46: Henry VIII and the Search

for the Middle Way', *The Historical Journal*, Vol. 41, No 2 (June 1998), pp.321–49.

82 David Sandler Berkowitz, *Humanist Scholarship and Public Order: Two Tracts against the Pilgrimage of Grace by Sir Richard Morison*, London, 1984, p.168.

83 Elton, *Reformation Europe*, p.42; Bray, *Documents of the English Reformation*, pp.162–74.

84 Daniel Eppley, *Defending Royal Supremacy and Discerning God's Will in Tudor England*, Aldershot, 2007, pp.19–21.

85 Henry Chadwick, 'Royal Ecclesiastical Supremacy', in Bradshaw & Duffy (eds), *Humanism, Reform and Reformation*, p.178.

86 Eppley, *Defending Royal Supremacy*, pp.19–21.

87 Bray, *Documents of the English Reformation*, p.179.

88 Eppley, *Defending Royal Supremacy*, p.7.

89 TNA, SP1/108, f.45 (*L&P*, Vol. XI: 705).

90 Merriman, *Life and Letters of Thomas Cromwell*, Vol. I, p.182.

91 See Jacqueline Rose, 'Kingship and Counsel in Early Modern England', *The Historical Journal*, Vol. 54 (March 2011) pp.47–71, and Gunn, Grummitt and Cools, *War, State and Society in England and the Netherlands*, p.244.

92 Dickens, 'Secular and Religious Motivation', pp.76–77.

93 Eppley, *Defending Royal Supremacy*, p.7; Gary W. Jenkins, *John Jewel and the English National Church: The Dilemmas of an Erastian Reformer*, Aldershot, 2006, p.17; Elton, *Policy and Police*, p.187.

94 Chadwick, 'Royal Ecclesiastical Supremacy', in Bradshaw & Duffy (eds), *Humanism, Reform and Reformation*, p.169; Marshall, 'Is the Pope Catholic?' in Ethan Shagan (ed.), *Henry VIII and the Semantics of Schism*, 2005, p.25.

95 Lucy Wooding, *Henry VIII*, Oxford, 2009, pp.201–2.

96 Rex, *Henry VIII and the English Reformation*, pp.49–50; Merriman, *The Life and Letters of Thomas Cromwell*, Vol. I.

97 *L&P*, Vol. XI: 42.

98 Wooding, *Henry VIII*, 2009, p.213.

99 Bateson, Mary, 'The Pilgrimage of Grace', *The English Historical Review*, Vol. 5, No 18 (April 1890), pp.330–45; Fletcher & MacCulloch, *Tudor Rebellions*, p.150.

100 Scarisbrick, *Henry VIII*, p.3.

101 See Eric Ives, *The Life and Death of Anne Boleyn: 'The Most Happy'*, Oxford, 2004, pp.153–54; Garret Mattingly, *Catherine of Aragon*, London, 1950, pp.89 & 284; Philip Hughes, *The Reformation in England: The King's Proceedings*, 2nd edition, London, 1952, p.277.

102 Wooding, *Henry VIII*, p.200; Scarisbrick, *Henry VIII*, p.352.

103 Fletcher & MacCulloch, *Tudor Rebellions*, 2004, p.46.

104 Bush, *The Pilgrimage of Grace: A Study of the Rebel Armies of 1536*, p.436.

105 See, for instance, Bush & Bownes, *The Defeat of the Pilgrimage of Grace*, p.19.

Chapter 3

1 *L&P*, Vol. XI: 1064, 1228.

2 *L&P*, Vol. XI: 1235, 1236.

3 TNA, SP1/112, ff.151–57 (*L&P*, Vol. XI: 1271); SP1/114, ff.18–19 (*L&P*, Vol. XII.I: 20).

4 See Bush & Bownes, *The Defeat of the Pilgrimage of Grace*, pp.12 & 25. TNA, SP1/110, ff.100–14 (*L&P*, Vol. XI: 956, 957, 1064); SP1/111, f.59 (*L&P*, Vol. XI: 1045).

5 *L&P*, Vol. XII.I: 201.

6 TNA, SP1/112, f.197 (*L&P*, Vol. XI: 1306).

7   *L&P*, Vol. XII.I: 6. 'The manner of the taking of Robert Aske in Lincolnshire, and the use of the same Robert unto his passage from York.'

8   Ibid.

9   TNA, SP1/120, f.134 (*L&P*, Vol. XII.I: 1224).

10 TNA, SP1/114, ff.49–51 (*L&P*, Vol. XII.I: 43).

11 TNA, SP1/114, ff. 51–52 (*L&P*, Vol. XII.I: 44) (spelling modernised).

12 *L&P*, Vol. XII.I: 46.

13 TNA, SP1/114, ff.52–53 (*L&P*, Vol. XII.I: 45).

14 TNA, SP1/114, ff.64–66 (*L&P*, Vol. XII.I: 64); SP1/114, ff.69–72 (*L&P*, Vol. XII.I: 67); SP1/114, ff.72–73 (*L&P*, Vol. XII.I: 68).

15 TNA, SP1/114, ff.75–77 (*L&P*, Vol. XII.I: 71); SP1/114, f.77 (*L&P*, Vol. XII.I: 72).

16 TNA, SP1/114, ff.127–28 (*L&P*, Vol. XII.I: 102); Hoyle, *The Pilgrimage of Grace and the Politics of The 1530s*, pp.382–3.

17 TNA, SP1/103, f.83 (*L&P*, Vol. X: 742); SP1/101, f.33 (*L&P*, Vol. X: 49).

18 TNA, SP1/115, ff.209–16 (*L&P*, Vol. XII.I: 369).

19 TNA, SP1/119, f.73 (*L&P*, Vol. XII.I: 1087).

20 TNA, SP1/115, ff.65–67 (*L&P*, Vol. XII.I: 234); SP1/11, f.73 (*L&P*, Vol. XII.I: 1087); Shagan, *Popular Politics and the English Reformation*, p.120.

21 Hoyle, *The Pilgrimage of Grace and the Politics of the 1530s*, p.378; TNA, SP1/114, ff.17–21 (*L&P*, Vol. XII.I: 202); SP1/114, ff.169, 171 (*L&P*, Vol. XII.I: 140, 141); SP1/115, ff.209–16 (*L&P*, Vol. XII.I: 370); Hoyle, *The Pilgrimage of Grace*, pp.380 & 383.

22 TNA, SP1/114, ff.178–79 (*L&P*, Vol. XII.I: 145).

23 TNA, SP1/114, ff.179–81 (*L&P*, Vol. XII.I: 146).

24 *L&P*, Vol. XII.I: 147.

25 TNA, SP1/114, ff.164–66, ff.166–67 (*L&P*, Vol. XII.I: 136, 137).

26 TNA, SP1/114, ff.167–68 (*L&P*, Vol. XII.I: 138).

27 *L&P*, Vol. XII.I: 315.

28 *L&P*, Vol. XII.I: 201; TNA, SP1/115, ff.51–57 (*L&P*, Vol. XII.I: 227).

29 TNA, SP1/115, ff.130–32 (*L&P*, Vol. XII.I: 292, 293).

30 TNA, SP1/115, ff.173–76 (*L&P*, Vol. XII.I: 318) (my italics).

31 TNA, SP1/115, f.240 (*L&P*, Vol. XII.I: 381); SP1/116, ff.20–24 (*L&P*, Vol. XII.I: 416).

32 TNA, SP1/116, ff.20–24 (*L&P*, Vol. XII.I: 416).

33 *L&P*, Vol. XII.I: 426 (quotation).

34 TNA, SP1/116, f.83 (*L&P*, Vol. XII.I: 468); SP1/116, f.85 (*L&P*, Vol. XII.I: 469) (spelling modernised); SP1/116, ff.108–12 (*L&P*, Vol. XII.I: 498) (spelling modernised).

35 TNA, SP1/117, ff.189–201 (*L&P*, Vol. XII.I: 786, 787, 788).

36 BL, Cotton, Cleo, E/IV, f.297 (*L&P*, Vol. XII.I: 832).

37 TNA, SP1/118, ff.96–98 (*L&P*, Vol. XII.I: 881).

38 TNA, SP1/118, ff.96–98 (*L&P*, Vol. XII.I: 1157).

39 *L&P*, Vol. XII.I: 923; *L&P*, Vol. XII.I: 1189 (quotation).

40 TNA, SP1/115 ff.190–91 (*L&P XII.I:* 336).

41 TNA, SP1/115, f.49; ff 51–57, ff.57–61 (*L&P*, Vol. XII.I: 226, 227, 228); SP1/115, ff.206–208 (*L&P*, Vol. XII.I: 362); *L&P*, Vol. XII.I: 401.

42 TNA, SP1/115, ff.209–16 (*L&P*, Vol. XII.I: 369).

43 TNA, SP1/116, ff.92–99 (*L&P*, Vol. XII.I: 479).

44 *L&P*, Vol. XIV.I: 13, 37. See Gunn, Grummitt & Cools, *War, State and Society in England and the Netherlands*, p.277, and Peter Lake & Michael Questier, 'Agency, Appropriation and Rhetoric under the Gallows: Puritans, Romanists and the State in Early Modern England', *Past & Present*, No 153 (1996), pp.64–107, p.71; see also

Scarisbrick, *Henry VIII*, p.354. The king was called 'a tyrant more cruel than Nero' and 'a beast and worse than a beast', *L&P*, Vol. XIII.II: 986.

45 *L&P*, Vol. XII.I: 498.
46 *L&P*, Vol. XII.I: 558.
47 *L&P*, Vol. XII.I: 576.
48 Scarisbrick, *Henry VIII*, p.352.
49 *L&P*, Vol. XII.I: 581.
50 TNA, SP1/116, ff.210–12 (*L&P*, Vol. XII.I: 590).
51 TNA, SP1/116, f.214 (*L&P*, Vol. XII.I: 593).
52 TNA, SP1/116, ff.232–34 (*L&P*, Vol. XII.I: 609); *L&P*, Vol. XII.I: 616 (quotation) (my italics).
53 TNA, SP1/116, f.253 (*L&P*, XII.I: 632).
54 TNA, SP1/117, ff.14–18 (*L&P*, Vol. XII.I: 666).
55 TNA, SP1/117, ff.75–83 (*L&P*, Vol. XII.I: 698).
56 Lake & Questier, 'Agency, Appropriation and Rhetoric', p.69.
57 *L&P*, Vol. XII.I: 734.
58 Lake & Questier, 'Agency, Appropriation and Rhetoric', pp.65 & 71. In later treason trials, the ritual violence even extended to cutting off the traitor's privy members to demonstrate that 'his issue is disinherited with the corruption of blood', p.70.
59 TNA, SP1/117, ff.183–84 (*L&P*, Vol. XII.I: 783).
60 *L&P*, Vol. XII.I: 846.
61 *L&P*, Vol. XII.I: 184.
62 TNA, SP1/115, ff.2–4 (*L&P*, Vol. XII.I: 192).
63 TNA, SP1/115, ff.28–29 (*L&P*, Vol. XII.I: 208, 209).
64 TNA, SP1/118, ff.14–20 (*L&P*, Vol. XII.I: 847); SP1/115, ff.28–29 (*L&P*, Vol. XII.I: 209).
65 *L&P*, Vol. XII.I: 848.
66 Ibid.
67 Ibid.
68 TNA, SP1/118, ff.20–43 (*L&P*, Vol. XII.I: 849) (spelling modernised).
69 Ibid.
70 TNA, SP1/118, ff.59–70 (*L&P*, Vol. XII.I: 863).
71 TNA, SP1/118, ff.125–27 (*L&P*, Vol. XII.I: 900).
72 TNA, SP1/118, f.123 (*L&P*, Vol. XII.I: 899) (spelling modernised).
73 *L&P*, Vol. XII.I: 901.
74 Ibid. Marshall has also described Aske as 'the most dangerous of Henry's internal opponents' in Shagan (ed.), *Catholics and the 'Protestant Nation'*, p.28.
75 *L&P*, Vol. XII.I: 901.
76 TNA, SP1/118, f.152 (*L&P*, Vol. XII.I: 918).
77 *L&P*, Vol. XII.I: 945.
78 TNA, SP1/118, f.213 (*L&P*, Vol. XII.I: 965).
79 TNA, SP1/118, f.258 (*L&P*, Vol. XII.I: 1012).
80 TNA, SP1/118, f.265 (*L&P*, Vol. XII.I: 1014, 1013).
81 TNA, SP1/118, f.275 (*L&P*, Vol. XII.I: 1020); *L&P*, Vol. XII.II: 1014.
82 Ibid.
83 TNA, SP1/118, f.277 (*L&P*, Vol. XII.I: 1021).
84 TNA, SP1/119, f.53 (*L&P*, Vol. XII.I: 1064).
85 TNA, SP1/119, f.57 (*L&P*, Vol. XII.I: 1080).
86 TNA, SP1/119, f.73 (*L&P*, Vol. XII.I: 1087) (spelling modernised).
87 *L&P*, Vol. XII.I: 1087 (quotation).

88 Ibid.
89 BL, Cotton, Caligula, B/I, f.341 (*L&P*, Vol. XII.I: 1156).
90 TNA, SP1/120, f.62 (*L&P*, Vol. XII.I: 1187).
91 *L&P*, Vol. XII.I: 1207.
92 Ibid.
93 TNA, SP1/120, f.132 (*L&P*, Vol. XII.I: 1223).
94 TNA, SP1/120, f.136 (*L&P*, Vol. XII.I: 1225).
95 TNA, SP1/120, ff.138, 148 (*L&P*, Vol. XII.I: 1227, 1239).
96 *L&P*, Vol. XII.I: 1243.
97 TNA, SP1/120, f.158 (*L&P*, Vol. XII.I: 1252) (spelling modernised).
98 TNA, SP1/121, f.157 (*L&P*, Vol. XII.II: 133) (spelling modernised).
99 *L&P*, Vol. XII.II: 156 (spelling modernised).
100 Ibid., 228 (spelling modernised).
101 TNA, SP1/115, f.49 (*L&P*, Vol. XII.I: 226).
102 Elton, *Policy and Police*, pp.389 & 403.
103 Hoyle, *The Pilgrimage of Grace and the Politics of the 1530s*, p.409.
104 TNA, SP1/134, ff.86–88 (*L&P*, Vol. XIII.I: 1311).
105 *L&P*, Vol. XIII.I: 1313.
106 TNA, SP1/135, f.19 (*L&P*, Vol. XIII.II: 20).
107 TNA, SP1/135, f.129 (*L&P*, Vol. XIII.II: 142).
108 TNA, SP1/135, ff.140–42 (*L&P*, Vol. XIII.II: 156).
109 *L&P*, Vol. XII.I: 46.

Chapter 4

1   TNA, SP1/120, f.200 (*L&P*, Vol. XII.I:1285) (spelling modernised).
2   G.R. Elton, *Policy and Police*.
3   Rex, *Henry VIII and the English Reformation*, p.181.
4   D.M. Loades, *Politics and the Nation 1450–1660 – Obedience, Resistance and Public Order*, 4th edition, London, 1992, pp.194–95.
5   Sharon Kettering, *Patrons, Brokers and Clients in Seventeenth-century France*, Oxford, 1986, p.9.
6   TNA, SP1/108, f.233 (*L&P*, Vol. XI: 827); SP1/111, f.139–41 (*L&P*, Vol. XI: 1105); SP1/111 f.177 (*L&P*, Vol. XI: 1120).
7   TNA, SP1/III, f.141–44 (*L&P*, Vol. XI: 1106).
8   TNA, SP1/116, f.2 (*L&P*, Vol. XII.I: 401); SP1/116, f.4 (*L&P*, Vol. XII.I: 402).
9   TNA, SP 1/116, f.13 (*L&P*, Vol. XII.I: 410).
10 Sarah L. Bastow, *The Catholic Gentry of Yorkshire, 1536–1642: Resistance and Accommodation*, New York, 2007, pp.18, 22, 23 & 25.
11 *L&P*, Vol. XII.I: 905; TNA, SP1/122, f.155 (*L&P*, Vol. XII.II:187).
12 S.T. Bindoff, *History of Parliament: 1509–1558*, 'Sir John Hussey', London, 1982, p.424.
13 *L&P*, Vol. XII: 1087.
14 J. Pollen (ed.), 'Unpublished Documents Relating to the English Martyrs, 1584–1603', *Catholic Record Society*, Vol. 5 (1908), p.30.
15 Christine Newman, 'Robert Bowes and the Pilgrimage of Grace', *North Eastern History*, No 7 (1997), p.27.
16 *Testamenta Eboracensia: A Selection of Wills from the Registry at York*, Vol. V, pp.306–19; TNA, Prob/11/41.
17 TNA, SP1/120, ff.138 & 148 (*L&P*, Vol. XII.I: 1227, 1239).
18 William Flower and Charles Best Norcliffe, *The Visitation of Yorkshire in the Years 1563 and 1564*, London, 1881, pp.314 & 153.

19 TNA SP1/114, ff.160–62 and 164–66 (*L&P*,Vol. XII.I: 134, 136); SP1/114, f.198 (*L&P*, Vol. XII.I: 160); SP1/114, ff.212–19 (*L&P*,Vol. XII.I: 174).

20 *L&P*,Vol. XII.I: 201;TNA, SP1/115, ff.57–61 (*L&P*,Vol. XII.I: 228).

21 *L&P*,Vol. XII.I: 734;TNA, SP1/117, ff.127–32 (*L&P*,Vol. XII.I: 731).

22 *L&P*,Vol. XII.I: 1207 (spelling modernised).

23 TNA, SP1/120, f.118 (*L&P*,Vol. XII.I: 1218).

24 TNA, SP1/121, f.51 (*L&P*,Vol. XII.II: 30); SP1/121, f.61 (*L&P*,Vol. XII.II: 43); *L&P*, Vol. XII.II: 100; SP1/121, f.133 (*L&P*,Vol. XII.II:102).

25 BL, Cotton, Caligula, B/III, f.246; TNA, SP1/122, f.239 (*L&P*,Vol. XII.II: 249, 250); SP1/123, f.102 (*L&P*,Vol. XII.II: 345); SP1/125, f.176 (*L&P*,Vol. XII.II: 914); *L&P*, Vol. XII.II: 918.

26 Reid, *The King's Council in the North, Part I–II*, pp.147–49 and pp.153, 154,157 & 159.

27 TNA, SP1/127, f.51 (*L&P*,Vol. XII.II: 1212).

28 TNA, SP1/130, f.22 (*L&P*,Vol. XIII.I: 487, 705).

29 *L&P*,Vol. XIII.I: 591, 597.

30 *L&P*,Vol. XIII.I: 1309 (21) (spelling modernised); *L&P*,Vol. XIII.I: 1309, nos (22), (2); *L&P*,Vol. XIII.I: 1509 (19); *L&P*,Vol. XIII.II: 734 (27);TNA, SP1/140, f.61 (*L&P*,Vol. XIII.II: 1010).

31 *L&P*,Vol. XIV.II: 239; *L&P*,Vol. XV: 831 (33). (Term twenty-one years: rent £18 14s 9d.)

32 J. Hodgson, *A History of Northumberland* (1820–58), Part 2,Vol 2, pp.171–248; *L&P*, Vol. XVI: 1274; *L&P*,Vol. XVII: 283 (13); *L&P*,Vol. XX.I: 465 (81).

33 TNA, SP1/127, f.127 (*L&P*,Vol. XXI.I: 694).

34 *L&P*,Vol. XXI.I: 1165; 1383 (16) (51) (91).

35 Chancery Court of York, Abp Reg 29, f.159.

36 TNA, C142/74/52.

37 *L&P*,Vol. XI: 921.

38 Newman, 'Robert Bowes and the Pilgrimage of Grace', p.23.

39 Ibid., pp.13, 16 & 17.

40 Ibid., p.19.

41 However, Norman Jones has shed more light on this situation. Jones maintains that when Knox proposed marriage to Marjory Bowes, her father resisted the idea. Marjory and her mother abandoned the rest of the family (who appear to have rejected the new doctrine) to follow Knox to Geneva. See Jones, 'Living the Reformations: Generational Experience and Political Perception in Early Modern England', *Huntington Library Quarterly*,Vol. 60, No 3, (1997), pp.273–88, p.277.

42 Newman, *Robert Bowes and the Pilgrimage of Grace*, p.24, p.11.

43 *L&P*,Vol. XII.I: 259.

44 TNA, SP1/117, ff.189–201 (*L&P*,Vol. XII.I: 786).

45 BL, Cotton,Titus, B/I, f.447 (*L&P*,Vol. XII.I: 1106); *L&P*, Vol. XII.I: 1207; *L&P*, Vol. XII.II: 100;TNA, SP1/121, f.133 (*L&P*,Vol. XII.II: 102).

46 TNA, SP1/123, f.102 (*L&P*,Vol. XII.II: 345); SP1/124, f.115 (*L&P*,Vol. XII.II: 589); SP1/125, f.176 (*L&P*,Vol. XII.II: 914); *L&P*,Vol. XII.II: 1150 (11).

47 TNA, SP1/131, f.40 (*L&P*,Vol. XIII.I: 705); SP1/140, f.61 (*L&P*,Vol. XIII.II: 1010); SP1/144, f.145 (*L&P*,Vol. XIV.I: 566); Bindoff, 'Sir Robert Bowes', *History of Parliament*, p.472; *L&P*,Vol. XIX.I: 278 (45).

48 *L&P*,Vol. XX.I: 465 (53); BL, Add MS 32646.

49 TNA, SP1/202, f.183 (*L&P*,Vol. XX.I: 1042, 1085); *L&P*,Vol. XX.II: 1035; SP1/218, f.76 (*L&P*,Vol. XXI.I: 804); *L&P*,Vol. XXI.II: 771 (26).

50 Hodgson, *A History of Northumberland* (1820–58), Part 3,Vol. 2, pp.171–248; Steven G. Ellis, 'Civilizing Northumberland: Representations of Englishness in the Tudor

State', *Twenty Years of the Journal of Historical Sociology*, Vol. 1, *Essays on the British State*, Oxford, 2008, p.208.

51 BL, Sloane, 2442, ff.138 & 140; Add MS 35844, f.213.

52 BL, Add MS 38136, f.27.

53 J.G. Nichols (ed.), *The Chronicle of Queen Jane, and of Two Years of Queen Mary*, Camden Society Old Series, No 48 (1850), p.100; Bindoff, *History of Parliament*, p.472; Newman, *Robert Bowes and the Pilgrimage of Grace*, p.6; James Raine, *Wills and Inventories from the Archdeaconry of Richmond*, Surtees Society, 1853, p.117; Christine M. Newman, 'The Bowes of Streatlam, Co. Durham: A Study of the Politics and Religion of a Sixteenth-century Northern Gentry Family', DPhil diss., University of York, 1991.

54 Raine, *Wills and Inventories*, p.117.

55 Raine, *Wills and Inventories*, p.145; TNA, C142/102/46 – this also included two manors in Yorkshire.

56 Newman, *Robert Bowes and the Pilgrimage of Grace*, p.28.

57 BL Add 32646, 'Transactions Between England and Scotland, 1532–1590'.

58 Dodds, *The Pilgrimage of Grace*, pp.219 & 235; *L&P*, Vol. XII.I: 1014.

59 TNA, SP1/118, f.275 (*L&P*, Vol. XII.I: 1020).

60 Reid, *The King's Council in the North*, part I–II, pp.103–104.

61 TNA, C142/59/11.

62 BL, Cotton, Titus, B/I, f.447 (*L&P*, Vol. XII.I: 1106).

63 TNA, SP1/121, f.175 (*L&P*, Vol. XII.II: 152) (spelling modernised); SP1/123, f.102 (*L&P*, Vol. XII.II: 345); R.B. Smith, *Land and Politics in the England of Henry VIII: The West Riding of Yorkshire, 1530–46*, Oxford, 1970, p.246; TNA, SP1/125, f.176 (*L&P*, Vol. XII.II: 914, 1150 (16)).

64 TNA, SP1/115, ff.247–59 (*L&P*, Vol. XII.I: 392).

65 Ibid.

66 Ibid.

67 Ibid.

68 Ibid.

69 Smith, *Land and Politics*, pp.172–73.

70 *L&P*, Vol. XII.I: 392.

71 Bindoff, 'William Stapleton', *History of Parliament*, p.375.

72 J. Clay (ed.), *North Country Wills*, Surtees Society, 1908, p.194.

73 Dodds, *The Pilgrimage of Grace*, p.237.

74 TNA, SP1/115, ff.2–4 (*L&P*, Vol. XII.I: 192) (spelling modernised).

75 TNA, SP1/123, f.134 (*L&P*, Vol. XII.II: 365); SP1/126, f.49 (*L&P*, Vol. XII.II: 1016).

76 J.T. Cliffe, *The Yorkshire Gentry: From the Reformation to the Civil War*, London, 1969, p.385.

77 Ibid.

78 Reid, *The King's Council in the North*, pp.104 & 138.

79 *L&P*, Vol. XI: 841.

80 Dodds, *The Pilgrimage of Grace*, pp.186, 308–09.

81 *L&P*, Vol. XII.I: 392.

82 *L&P*, Vol. XII.I: 901.

83 *L&P*, Vol. XII.I: 171.

84 *L&P*, Vol. XII.I: 1207 (1).

85 *L&P*, Vol. XVIII.II: 107 (67); J.T. Cliffe, 'Sir William Babthorpe (*c.* 1490–1555)', 'Babthorpe Family (*per. c.* 1501–1635)', *Oxford Dictionary of National Biography* (*ODNB*), Oxford University Press, 2004; online edition, January 2008 [http://www.

oxforddnb.com/view/article/71868, accessed 13 March 2013].

86 TNA, SP. Dom. Elizabeth Addenda, SP 15/vii/58.

87 Cliffe, *The Yorkshire Gentry*.

88 *L&P*, Vol. XI: 729; *L&P*, Vol. XI: 928; *L&P*, Vol. XII.I: 6; *L&P*, Vol. XII.I: 1207 (3).

89 J.T. Cliffe, 'Sir Christopher Danby (1503–1571)', 'Danby family (*per.* 1493–1667)', *ODNB*, Oxford University Press, 2004; online edition, May 2011 [www.oxforddnb. com/view/article/71867, accessed 13 March 2013].

90 Ibid.

91 Zeeveld, *Foundations of Tudor Policy*, pp.210–11.

92 *L&P*, Vol. XVIII.I: 226 (66).

93 Steven G. Ellis, 'Henry VIII, Rebellion and the Rule of Law' in *The Historical Journal*, Vol. 24, No 3 (September 1981), pp.513–31. See pp.515 & 529.

94 Newman, *Robert Bowes and the Pilgrimage of Grace*, p.27. See also Rosemary Horrox, *Richard III: A Study in Service*, Cambridge, 1989, pp.1 & 8; Gunn, Grummitt & Cools, *War, State and Society in England and the Netherlands*, p.191 and also Rose, 'Kingship and Counsel', p.132. The enforcement of laws and governance depended upon the co-operation of local elites.

95 Shagan, *Popular Politics and the English Reformation*, p.124.

96 Cliffe, *The Yorkshire Gentry*, p.169. Cliffe has conceded that the prevalence of outward conformity at this time makes it difficult to estimate the strength of the Catholic gentry 'with any degree of precision', but has attempted to do so using archiepiscopal visitation books, the Archbishop of York's lists of recusants compiled in 1577 and the records of the Northern High Commission. He has stated that 368 out of 567 Yorkshire gentry families were Catholic at the time.

97 Ibid., p.171.

Chapter 5

1 Kettering, *Patrons, Brokers and Clients*, p.6. However, Rosemary Horrox undertook a detailed study of English late medieval patronage in 1991 in her *Richard III: A Study in Service*. Kevin Sharpe described patronage as the principal currency in the exchange between sovereigns, subordinates and subjects in 'Representations and Negotiations: Texts, Images and Authority in Early Modern England', *The Historical Journal*, Vol. 42, No 3 (September 1999), pp.853–81. More recently, Jacqueline Rose has discussed patronage as a feature of personal rule in 'Kingship and Counsel in Early Modern England', p.47.

2 Kettering, *Patrons, Broker and Clients*, pp.3–4.

3 Gunn, Grummitt & Cools, *War, State and Society in England and the Netherlands*, p.200.

4 Horrox, *Richard III: A Study in Service*, pp.1, 3, 5 & 8; Kettering, *Patrons, Brokers and Clients*, pp.5, 8, 13 & 18.

5 Scarisbrick, *Henry VIII*, p.44.

6 Kettering, *Patrons, Brokers and Clients*, p.5.

7 D.M. Loades, *Politics and the Nation, 1450–1660*, p.195.

8 TNA, SP1/111, f.57 (*L&P*, Vol. XI: 1043); SP1/113, ff.202–3 (*L&P*, Vol. XI: 1496) (spelling modernised); *L&P*, Vol. XI: 1178.

9 *L&P*, Vol. XIII.II: 571, 254 & 853.

10 BL, Cotton, Cleo, E/IV, f.260 (*L&P*, Vol. XIII.II: 854) (spelling modernised).

11 *L&P*, Vol. XIII: II: 1179 (spelling modernised); Horrox, *Richard III: A Study in Service*, p.3.

12 TNA, SP6/6, ff.84–88; SP 1/110, ff.182–83 (*L&P*, Vol. XI: 987 & 988).

13   TNA, SP1/113, ff.181–82 (*L&P*, Vol. XI: 1481); Zeeveld, *Foundations of Tudor Policy*, p.179; TNA, SP1/127, f.158 (*L&P*, Vol. XII.II: 1330); Kettering, *Patrons, Brokers and Clients*, pp.10 & 25.

14   *L&P*, Vol. XV: 613 (3) & 831 (64); *L&P*, Vol. XVI: 678 (5), (24) & (25); *L&P*, Vol. XIX.I: 444 (10).

15   *L&P*, Vol. XX.II: 266 (6) & (32), 910 (67); *L&P*, Vol. XXI.II: 640. See also Horrox, *Richard III: A Study in Service*, p.12.

16   TNA, SP1/115, ff.95, 104, 105, 111, 113–16; *L&P*, Vol. XII.I: 261, 263–69.

17   Joseph Block, 'Thomas Cromwell's Patronage of Preaching', *The Sixteenth Century Journal*, Vol. 8, No 1 (April 1977), pp.37–50.

18   TNA, SP1/117, ff. 36–37 (*L&P*, Vol. XII.I: 678); SP1/121, f.57 (*L&P*, Vol. XII.II: 36); SP1/116, ff.175–78 (*L&P*, Vol. XII.I: 543).

19   TNA, SP1/116, ff.92–99 (*L&P*, Vol. XII.I: 479).

20   TNA, SP1/116, ff.210–12 (*L&P*, Vol. XII.I: 590) (spelling modernised); SP1/116, ff.271–75 (*L&P*, Vol. XII.I: 639) (spelling modernised); SP1/117, ff.32–36 (*L&P*, Vol. XII.I: 677); SP1/117, ff.101–03 (*L&P*, Vol. XII.I: 713).

21   TNA, SP1/116, ff.255–56 (*L&P*, Vol. XII.I: 633); SP1/116, ff.276–77 (*L&P*, Vol. XII.I: 641) (spelling modernised); SP1/118, ff.131–33 (*L&P*, Vol. XII.I: 905); *L&P*, Vol. XII.I: 973; SP1/118, f.237 (*L&P*, Vol. XII.I: 992) (spelling modernised); SP1/119, f.17 (*L&P*, Vol. XII.I: 1024).

22   TNA, SP1/119, ff.124, 126 & 128 (*L&P*, Vol. XII.I: 1112, 1113, 1114); SP1/120, f.112 (*L&P*, Vol. XII.I: 1215); SP1/120, f.114 (*L&P*, Vol. XII.I: 1216).

23   TNA, SP1/120, f.244 (*L&P*, Vol. XII.I: 1317).

24   TNA, SP1/121, f.164 (*L&P*, Vol. XII.II: 141); SP1/124, f.92 (*L&P*, Vol. XII.II: 567) (spelling modernised); SP1/125, f.182 (*L&P*, Vol. XII.II: 925).

25   TNA, SP1/122, f.207 (*L&P*, Vol. XII.II: 209).

26   TNA, SP1/125, f.213 (*L&P*, Vol. XII.II: 954); *L&P*, Vol. XII.II: 1008 (9).

27   TNA, SP1/122, f.213 (*L&P*, Vol. XII.II: 226); SP1/124, f.113 (*L&P*, Vol. XII.II: 588).

28   Smith, *Land and Politics*, p.246.

29   *L&P*, Vol. XII.II: 100; TNA, SP1/121, f.133 (*L&P*, Vol. XII.II: 102); SP1/125, f.176 (*L&P*, Vol. XII.II: 914); *L&P*, Vol. XII.II: 1060.

30   *L&P*, Vol. XIII.I: 591, 597; TNA, SP1/131, f.40 (*L&P*, Vol. XIII.I: 705); SP1/131, f.139 (*L&P*, Vol. XIII.I: 825).

31   *L&P*, Vol. XIII.I: 1519 (19), (38), (39), (40), (65).

32   TNA, SP1/140, f.61 (*L&P*, Vol. XIII.II: 1010); SP1/144, ff.53 & 68 (*L&P*, Vol. XIV.I: 455, 481); SP1/144, f.145 (*L&P*, Vol. XIV.I: 566); *L&P*, Vol. XII.I: 116, 622, 623; *L&P*, Vol. XII.II: 910 (76).

33   Dodds, *The Pilgrimage of Grace*, p.345; Smith, *Land and Politics*, p.194.

34   TNA, SP1/114, f.160–62 (*L&P*, Vol. XII.I: 134).

35   *L&P*, Vol. XII.I: 197 (spelling modernised).

36   TNA, SP1/118, f.216 (*L&P*, Vol. XII.I: 967); SP1/119, f.146 (*L&P*, Vol. XII.I: 1129).

37   C.H. Williams, *English Historical Documents*, Volume V: 1485–1558, London, 1967, p.108.

38   TNA, SP1/121, f.128 (*L&P*, Vol. XII.II: 97).

39   *L&P*, Vol. XII.II: 1060, 1008 (27).

40   *L&P*, Vol. XIII.I: 1115 (13).

41   *L&P*, Vol. XIV.I: 191 (43).

42   Smith, *Land and Politics*, p.245.

43   *L&P*, Vol. XIV.II: 572 (3); *L&P*, Vol. XVI: 379 (1), 1488 (5); *L&P*, Vol. XVII: 714 (18).

44   *L&P*, Vol. XVIII.I: 623 (5), (54), (100), 802 (1); *L&P*, Vol. XIX.I: 80 (23); *L&P*, Vol. XX.II: 266 (20); *L&P*, Vol. XXI.I: 1538.

45 Flower & Norcliffe (ed.), *The Visitation of Yorkshire: in the Years 1563 and 1564*, p.93.

46 Bastow, *The Catholic Gentry of Yorkshire, 1536–1642*, pp.18, 22, 23 & 25.

47 TNA, SP1/123, f.195 (*L&P*, Vol. XII.II: 432).

48 *L&P*, Vol. XIII.I: 1115 (1); TNA, SP1/126, f.173 (*L&P*, Vol. XII.II: 1151).

49 *L&P*, Vol. XIV.II: 264 (27); *L&P*, Vol. XVII: 714 (9); *L&P*, Vol. XVIII.I: 802 (10); *L&P*, Vol. XX.I: 690 (32).

50 Flower & Best, *The Visitation of Yorkshire in the Years 1563 and 1564*, p.92.

51 Dodds, *The Pilgrimage of Grace*, p.345

52 Bindoff, 'Sir William Parr', *History of Parliament*, p.61.

53 TNA, SP1/116, ff.210–12 (*L&P*, Vol. XII.I: 590); SP1/116, f.212 (*L&P*, Vol. XII.I: 591).

54 TNA, SP1/116, f.231 (*L&P*, Vol. XII.I: 608); SP1/116, ff.271–75 (*L&P*, Vol. XII.I: 639).

55 TNA, SP1/117, ff.32–36 (*L&P*, Vol. XII.I: 677).

56 *L&P*, Vol. XII.I: 795 (14).

57 TNA, SP1/120, f.106 (*L&P*, Vol. XII.I: 1213).

58 TNA, SP1/120, f.138 (*L&P*, Vol. XII.I: 1227).

59 TNA, SP1/120, f.218 (*L&P*, Vol. XII.I: 1298).

60 TNA, SP1/124, f.9 (*L&P*, Vol. XII.II: 489).

61 TNA, SP7/1, f.18 (*L&P*, Vol. XII.II: 657).

62 TNA, SP1/126, f.139 (*L&P*, Vol. XII.II: 1102).

63 TNA, SP1/128, f.55 (*L&P*, Vol. XIII.I: 65).

64 *L&P*, Vol. XIII.I: 887 (17), 1519 (13), 1520 (34).

65 Bindoff, *History of Parliament*, p.61.

66 *L&P*, Vol. XIV: II: 239.

67 TNA, SP1/144, f.51; (*L&P*, Vol. XIV.I: 453).

68 *L&P*, Vol. XVIII.II: 516.

69 *L&P*, Vol. XIX.I: 141 (75).

70 Bindoff, *History of Parliament*, p.61.

71 *L&P*, Vol. XXI.II: 476 (10).

72 TNA PRO, PROB 11/32, sig. 6. See Gunn, Grummitt & Cools, *War, State and Society in England and the Netherlands*, p.177, for discussion of power and patronage.

73 *L&P*, Vol. XI: 760 (2), 1155 (4).

74 TNA, SP1/114, f.68 (*L&P*, Vol. XII.I: 66); SP1/115, ff.65–67 (*L&P*, Vol. XII.I: 234).

75 TNA, SP1/116 f.4 (*L&P*, Vol. XII.I: 402).

76 *L&P*, Vol. XII.I: 558 (quotation – spelling modernised).

77 BL, Cotton, Titus, B/I f.447; (*L&P*, Vol. XII.I: 1106).

78 TNA, SP1/120, f.212 (*L&P*, Vol. XII.I: 1296); SP1/121, f.133 (*L&P*, Vol. XII.II: 102).

79 TNA, SP1/126, f.173 (*L&P*, Vol. XII.II: 1151).

80 TNA, SP1/127, f.51 (*L&P*, Vol. XII.II: 1212).

81 *L&P*, Vol. XIII.I: 887 (10).

82 Reid, *The King's Council in the North*, Part I–II, p.490; *L&P*, Vol. XII.II: 100.

83 Reid, *The King's Council in the North*, Part I–II, p.163.

84 BL, Cotton, Caligula, B/III, f.246; TNA, SP1/122, f.239 (*L&P*, Vol. XII.II: 249, 250); SP1/125, f.176 (*L&P*, Vol. XII.II: 914); *L&P*, Vol. XII.II: 1150 (11); *L&P*, Vol. XVII: 71 (39).

85 *L&P*, Vol. XIX.I: 223.

86 *L&P*, Vol. XX.I: 125 (3).

87 *L&P*, Vol. XX.I: 311.

88 *L&P*, Vol. XX.I: 846 (7).

89 J. Clay (ed.), *Testamenta Eboracensia: A Selection of Wills from the Registry at York*, Vol. VI, Surtees Society, 1902, p.183.

90 Ibid., p.185.

91   *L&P*, Vol. XII.II: 911.
92   Ibid.
93   TNA, SP1/137, f.89; SP1/17, f.236 (*L&P*, Vol. XIII.II: 528, 649).
94   *L&P*, Vol. XIII.I: 1519 (13).
95   *L&P*, Vol. XIV.II: 780 (12) & (13); *L&P*, Vol. XVII: 714 (15) & (17); *L&P*, Vol. XVIII.I: 982 (94b) & (100b).
96   *L&P*, Vol. XIX.II: 800 (16); *L&P*, Vol. XXI.I: 1538 (193b); *L&P*, Vol. XXI.II: 476 (25).
97   Bindoff, *History of Parliament*, pp.501–2.
98   *L&P*, Vol. XII.I: 615 (*L&P*, Vol. XII.II: 100, 102 (5), 250 (2), 914, 917, 918, 1016 & 1076).
99   TNA, SP1/127, ff.51 & 78 (*L&P*, Vol. XII.II: 1212, 1231).
100 TNA, SP1/127, f.37 (*L&P*, Vol. XII.II: 1192).
101 TNA, SP1/133, f.210 (*L&P*, Vol. XIII.I: 1269); *L&P*, Vol. XIV.II: 663.
102 *L&P*, Vol. XV: 515; TNA, SP1/160, f.8 (*L&P*, Vol. XV: 648).
103 *L&P*, Vol. XX.I: 1081 (21).
104 TNA, SP1/114, ff.173–74 (*L&P*, Vol. XII.I: 142) (spelling modernised).
105 TNA, SP1/115, f.126 (*L&P*, Vol. XII.I: 279) (spelling modernised).
106 TNA, SP1/119, f.126 (*L&P*, Vol. XII.I: 1113). The creation of knights with royal permission was a particularly important means for noblemen to bind followers. See Gunn, Grummitt & Cools, *War, State and Society in England and the Netherlands*, p.200.
107 *L&P*, Vol. XIII.I: 1519 (19); *L&P*, Vol. XV: 1032; *L&P*, Vol. IV: 100.
108 *L&P*, Vol. XVII: 1258 (62).
109 Clay, *Testamenta Eboracensia*, p.152.
110 *L&P*, Vol. XI: 580, 623.
111 *L&P*, Vol. XIV.II: 572 (3); *L&P*, Vol. XVI: 503 (22), 678 (47), 878 (42).
112 *L&P*, Vol. XVII: 71 (5), 163 & 220 (46); Fritze, *Historical Dictionary of Tudor England*, p.161.
113 TNA, SPI/174, f.96 (*L&P*, Vol. XVII: 1048, 1064).
114 *L&P*, Vol. XVIII.II: 107 (12).
115 *L&P*, Vol. XIX.I: 610 (8) (*L&P*, Vol. XX.I: 1081 (5)).
116 D.M. Loades, *Mary Tudor: A Life*, Oxford, 1989, p.195. TNA, LR 2/118; TNA, E.154/2/39.
117 Fletcher & MacCulloch, *Tudor Rebellions*, p.102.
118 Ibid., p.111.
119 'Bl. Thomas Percy', *The Catholic Encyclopedia*, Vol. 14 (New York: Robert Appleton Company, 1912) [accessed 21 March 2013, www.newadvent.org/cathen/14697a.htm].
120 Dodds, *The Pilgrimage of Grace*, p.345.
121 Smith, *Land and Politics*, p.173.
122 Clay, *Testamenta Eboracensia*, p.161.
123 TNA, SP1/131, f.116 (*L&P*, Vol. XIII.I: 790).
124 TNA, SP1/143, f.141 (*L&P*, Vol. XIV.I: 344).
125 Fletcher & MacCulloch, *Tudor Rebellions*, pp.107 & 111.
126 Dodds, *The Pilgrimage of Grace*, p.214; Smith, *Land and Politics*, pp.170 & 175.
127 *L&P*, Vol. XI: 634.
128 Dodds, *The Pilgrimage of Grace*, pp. 214–15.
129 TNA, SP1/108, f.176 (*L&P*, Vol. XI: 783).
130 TNA, SP1/109, f.224 (*L&P*, Vol. XI: 894).
131 L&P, Vol. XVII: 1258 (116).
132 TNA, SP1/111, f.47 (*L&P*, Vol. XI: 1038).
133 *L&P*, Vol. XIV.I: 551 & 651 (43).
134 *L&P*, Vol. XIV.II: 572 (3); *L&P*, Vol. XV: 1027 (22).

135 *L&P*, Vol. XVI.I:305 (67); *L&P*, Vol. XVI: 678 (6, 7), 878, 947 (11), 1056 (25).
136 *L&P*, Vol. XVI.I: 1088.
137 TNA, SP1/171, f.180 (*L&P*, Vol. XVII: 540); *L&P*, Vol. XVII: 714 (19); *L&P*, Vol. XVII: 881 (16).
138 *L&P*, Vol. XVIII.I: 474 (14).
139 *L&P*, Vol. XIV.I: 1056 (29).
140 *L&P*, Vol. XI: 537.
141 *L&P*, Vol. XI: 675.
142 TNA, SP1/110, f.91 (*L&P*, Vol. XI: 949).
143 TNA, SP1/114, ff.206–7.
144 TNA, SP1/115, f.49 (*L&P*, Vol. XII.I: 226).
145 *L&P*, Vol. XI: 687, 748, 749, 957, 1062.
146 *L&P*, Vol. XII.II: 1008 (9).
147 TNA, Chancery Close Rolls, C 54/412.
148 Lambeth Palace, London, *Talbot Papers*, MS A, f.61.
149 *L&P*, Vol. XII.I: 698 (3).
150 TNA, SP1/114, ff.75–77 (*L&P*, Vol. XII.I: 71, 72).
151 *L&P*, Vol. XIII.I: 1309 (2).
152 *L&P*, Vol. XVII: 283 (11). Clay, *Testamenta Eboracensia*, p.152.
153 Rex, *Henry VIII and the English Reformation*, p.69.
154 TNA, SP7.
155 Horrox, *Richard III: A Study in Service*, p.13; Kettering, *Patrons, Brokers and Clients*, p.22.

Chapter 6

1 Richard Morison, 'A Lamentation in Which is Showed What Ruin and Destruction Cometh of Seditious Rebellion' (1536), *Humanist Scholarship and Public Order: Two Tracts against the Pilgrimage of Grace by Sir Richard Morison*, David Sandler Berkowitz (ed.), London, Associated University Press, 1984, p.95.
2 BL, Cotton, Cleo, E/IV, f.138 (*L&P*, Vol. X: 92).
3 BL, Cotton, Cleo, E/V, f.301 (*L&P*, Vol. X: 172).
4 BL, Cotton, Cleo, E/IV, f.286 (*L&P*, Vol. X: 716).
5 Steven G. Ellis, 'England in the Tudor State', *The Historical Journal*, Vol. 26, No 1 (1983), p.203.
6 *L&P*, Vol. X: 725.
7 TNA, SP1/105, f.118 (*L&P*, Vol. XI: 156).
8 Harris, *Foreign Bodies and the Body Politic*, pp.30 & 36.
9 Thomas F. Mayer, *Thomas Starkey and the Commonweal: Humanist Politics and Religion in the Reign of Henry VIII*, Cambridge, 1989, pp.2 & 9.
10 BL, Cotton, Cleo, E/VI, f.379 (*L&P*, Vol. XI: 402).
11 TNA, SP1/106, f.51 (*L&P*, Vol. XI: 369).
12 *L&P*, Vol. XI: 656 (spelling modernised).
13 TNA, SP1/110, ff.100–14 (*L&P*, Vol. XI: 956).
14 *L&P*, Vol. XI: 888.
15 TNA, SP1/108, f.231 (*L&P*, Vol. XI: 826) (my italics).
16 TNA, SP1/109, ff.224–26 (*L&P*, Vol. XI: 894).
17 *L&P*, Vol. XI: 957 (spelling modernised).
18 TNA, SP1/111, f.144 (*L&P*, Vol. XI: 1110) (spelling modernised).
19 TNA, SP1/112, ff.71–87 (*L&P*, Vol. XI: 1227).
20 *L&P*, Vol. XI: 1236.

21　TNA, SP1/112, f.94 (*L&P*, Vol. XI: 1232).

22　*L&P*, Vol. XI: 1353.

23　Ibid., 1354.

24　Ibid., 1363.

25　Harris, *Foreign Bodies and the Body Politic*, p.3.

26　Block, 'Thomas Cromwell's Patronage of Preaching', pp.37 & 41.

27　TNA, SP1/99, f.213. Quoted in Richard Rex, 'The Crisis of Obedience: God's Word and Henry's Reformation', *The Historical Journal*, Vol. 39, No 4 (December 1996), p.885.

28　*L&P*, Vol. XII.I: 125.

29　BL, Cotton, Cleo, E/VI, f.377 (*L&P*, Vol. XII.I: 105).

30　Block, 'Thomas Cromwell's Patronage of Preaching', p.40.

31　Berkowitz, *Humanist Scholarship and Public Order*, p.21.

32　Ibid., pp.30–31.

33　Ibid., p.85.

34　Ibid., pp.86–88.

35　Harris, *Foreign Bodies and the Body Politic*, p.2.

36　Berkowitz, *Humanist Scholarship and Public Order*, pp.89–92.

37　Shagan, *Catholics and the 'Protestant Nation'*, p.17.

38　Berkowitz, *Humanist Scholarship and Public Order*, p.93, 95 & 97.

39　R.W. Hoyle, 'Petitioning as Popular Politics in Early Sixteenth-century England', *Historical Research*, Vol. 75, No 190 (November 2002), p.367.

40　*L&P*, Vol. XI: 780 (2) (spelling modernised).

41　Berkowitz, *Humanist Scholarship and Public Order*, pp.98–99.

42　Ibid., p.100.

43　Ibid., pp.46–47.

44　Ibid., pp.116–17.

45　Ibid.

46　Fletcher & MacCulloch, *Tudor Rebellions*, 5th edition, p.3.

47　Berkowitz, *Humanist Scholarship and Public Order*, p.119.

48　Ibid., p.117.

49　Ibid., pp.128–29.

50　This principle was accepted in the Holy Roman Empire as part of the Religious Peace of Augsburg in 1555. Essentially it meant that the prince dictated the religion of his subjects.

51　As Harris has observed, an external threat was frequently complicit in domestic conflict – see Harris, *Foreign Bodies and the Body Politic*, p.13.

52　Berkowitz, *Humanist Scholarship and Public Order*, p.130.

53　Ibid., p.131.

54　Ibid., pp.137–38.

55　Ibid., p.142.

56　Ibid., pp.144–46.

57　Ibid., p.131.

58　BL, Cotton, Calig, B/I, f.56 (*L&P*, Vol. XII.I: 1313).

59　TNA, SP1/116, ff.251 (*L&P*, Vol. XII.I: 630).

60　TNA, SP1/118, ff.96–98 (*L&P*, Vol. XII.I: 881).

61　TNA, SP1/119, f.146 (*L&P*, Vol. XII.I: 1129).

62　*L&P*, Vol. XII.II: 848.

63　Ibid., 1181.

64 TNA, SP1/127, f.58 (*L&P*, Vol. XII.II: 1216).
65 *L&P*, Vol. XIII.I: 378. Ellis, 'England in the Tudor State', pp.201–12.
66 TNA, SP6/3, ff.1–4 (*L&P*, Vol. XIII.II: 281) (spelling modernised).
67 Bray, *Documents of the English Reformation*; (*L&P*, Vol. XIII: 281).
68 TNA, SP1/140, ff.209–16 (*L&P*, Vol. XIII.II: 1171) (spelling modernised).
69 *L&P*, Vol. XIII.II: 1279.
70 *L&P*, Vol. XIII.II: 1164 (spelling modernised).
71 *L&P*, Vol. XIV.I: 401.
72 Ibid., 406.
73 Ibid., 628.
74 Bernard, 'The Making of Religious Policy,' p.330; Rex, 'The Crisis of Obedience', p.864.
75 Bindoff, 'Edward Hall', *History of Parliament*, p.279; Williams, *English Historical Documents V: 1485–1558*, p.141.
76 *Hall's Chronicle*, London, 1809, p.822.
77 Ibid. (My italics, spelling modernised.)
78 For Norfolk's description, see Chapter 2. Estimates of the numbers of Pilgrims varied between 30,000 and 50,000 – Eustace Chapuys used this assessment (see Chapter 2). On 23 October 1536, the Bishop of Faenza put a figure of 40,000 on the rebel forces and Sir Brian Hastings corroborated this approximation.
79 *Hall's Chronicle*, p.823 (spelling modernised).
80 Ibid., p.823 (spelling modernised).
81 Scarisbrick, *Henry VIII*, p.408.
82 *Hall's Chronicle*, p.823 (spelling modernised).
83 Ibid.
84 Ibid.
85 Prior to the Pontefract meeting between 2 and 4 December, the king thought that the rebels would be 'stiff' with regard to the issues of a free pardon and a northern parliament.
86 *Hall's Chronicle*, p.823 (spelling modernised).
87 Ibid.
88 For instance, the Yorkist victory at the Battle of Barnet on Easter Sunday, 14 April 1471, was attributed to the sudden descent of a mist. See A.J. Pollard, *The Wars of the Roses*, London, 1988, p.32, and Anthony Goodman (ed.), *The Wars of the Roses*, London, 1991, p.172.
89 *Hall's Chronicle*, p.823.
90 See Hoyle, 'Thomas Master's Narrative of the Pilgrimage of Grace', pp.53–79.
91 Hoyle, 'Thomas Master's Narrative', p.55.
92 Ibid., p.71.
93 Ibid.
94 Ibid., pp.71–72.
95 Ibid., p.75.
96 Ibid.
97 Ibid., p.76. As Hoyle has pointed out, this letter of 3 December (*L&P*, Vol. XII.I: 1022) makes no mention with regard to the sacraments and Purgatory. My italics – Master's emphasis on the 'military' dimension to the Pilgrimage and its illegality.
98 Ibid., pp.77–79.
99 Jones, 'Living the Reformations', p.197.

Chapter 7

1   Scarisbrick, *Henry VIII*, p.338.
2   M.A.R. Graves, *Henry VIII: A Study in Kingship*, London, 2003, p.45.
3   Fletcher & MacCulloch, *Tudor Rebellions*, 2004, p.14.
4   TNA, SP1/108, f.212 (*L&P*, Vol. XI: 807).
5   *L&P*, Vol. XI: 860.
6   *L&P*, Vol. XI: 920.
7   TNA, SP1/107, f.144 (*L&P*, Vol. XI: 655); *L&P* XI: 841.
8   *L&P*, Vol. XI: 1231; Gunn, Grummitt & Cools, *War, State and Society in England and the Netherlands*, p.320.
9   *L&P*, Vol. XI: 1393.
10   Ibid., 1425.
11   Ibid., 1245.
12   TNA, SP1/112, f.178 (*L&P*, Vol. XI: 1292) (spelling modernised).
13   *L&P*, Vol. XI: 1319.
14   Gunn, Grummitt & Cools, *War, State and Society in England and the Netherlands*, p.244.
15   BL, Cotton, Cleo, E/IV f.157 (*L&P*, Vol. X: 594).
16   TNA, SP1/112, ff.114–16 (*L&P*, Vol. XI: 1244).
17   TNA, SP1/112, f.116 (*L&P*, Vol. XI: 1245).
18   TNA, SP1/112, f.18 (*L&P*, Vol. XI: 1246).
19   TNA SP1/114, ff.201–3 (*L&P*, Vol. XII: 163).
20   TNA, SP1/118, f.277 (*L&P*, Vol. XII.I: 1021).
21   TNA, SP1/119, f.1 (*L&P*, Vol. XII.I: 1022).
22   TNA, SP1/117, ff.5–7 (*L&P*, Vol. XII.I: 652); SP1/117, ff.42–65 (*L&P*, Vol. XII.I: 687); SP1/117, ff.175–77 (*L&P*, Vol. XII.I: 778).
23   TNA, SP1/115, f.244 (*L&P*, Vol. XII.I: 384); SP1/116, f.30 (*L&P*, Vol. XII.I: 424) (spelling modernised).
24   *L&P*, Vol. XII.I: 976 (quotation).
25   TNA, SP1/130, ff.140–42 (*L&P*, Vol. XIII.I: 604).
26   Quoted in Elton, *Policy and Police*, pp.129–30, who discusses this event in more detail.
27   TNA, SP1/133, f.233 (*L&P*, Vol. XIII.I: 1282).
28   TNA, SP1/134, f.30 (*L&P*, Vol. XIII.I: 1346).
29   *L&P*, Vol. XIII.I: 1428.
30   *L&P*, Vol. XIII.II: 561.
31   Hoyle, *The Pilgrimage of Grace and the Politics of the 1530s*, p.43.
32   *L&P*, Vol. X: 576.
33   TNA, SP1/107, f.83 (*L&P*, Vol. XI: 603).
34   *L&P*, Vol. XI: 1012, 1160; *CSP Sp.*, *1536*, p.124 (*L&P*, Vol. XI: 1204). David Starkey and Susan Doran, *Henry VIII: Man and Monarch*, London, 2009, p.165.
35   *L&P*, Vol. XI: 1250.
36   *CSP Sp.*, 1536, p.306 (quotation).
37   *L&P*, Vol. XII.I: 463.
38   *L&P*, Vol. XII.I: 368 (quotation).
39   Ibid.
40   Elton, *Reform and Reformation*, pp.252 & 267. Elton attributed the Pilgrimage to a disappointed Aragonese court faction and maintained that the conspiracy did not go as planned. See also Introduction.
41   *L&P*, Vol. XII.I: 665.
42   *L&P*, Vol. XII.I: 779 (quotation).

43　*L&P*, Vol. XII.I: 1189.

44　Ibid., 696.

45　Ibid., 1242. Scarisbrick, *Henry VIII*, p.347.

46　*L&P*, Vol. XII.I: 988 (quotation, spelling modernised).

47　Ibid.

48　*L&P*, Vol. XII.II: 310 (quotation, spelling modernised).

49　*L&P*, Vol. XII.I: 696.

50　S.G. Ellis, 'The Kildare Rebellion and the Early Henrician Reformation', *The Historical Journal*, Vol. 19, No 4, 1976, pp. 815, 822 & 825.

51　TNA, SP1/128, ff.66–69 (*L&P*, Vol. XIII.I: 77).

52　*L&P*, Vol. XIV.I: 36.

53　*L&P*, Vol. XIII.II: 1087. See also, Arthur F. Marotti, *Religious Ideology and Cultural Fantasy: Catholic and Anti-Catholic Discourses in Early Modern England*, Notre Dame, 2005, p.16.

54　*L&P*, Vol. XII.I: 987.

55　*L&P*, Vol. XIV.I: 37.

56　*CSP Sp.*, 1539, Vol. 1, Part 1, No 37 (*L&P*, Vol. XIV.I: 98) (quotation).

57　Scarisbrick, *Henry VIII*, pp.362–63. See also Wim Blockmans, *Emperor Charles V: 1500–1558*, London, 2002, pp.108–9. Blockmans argues that although Charles emphasised his position as protector of all Christendom, political interests forced him to override dynastic and religious scruples.

58　A.G. Dickens, 'Robert Parkyn's Narrative of the Reformation' in *The English Historical Review*, Vol. 62, No 242 (1947), p.58.

59　Ibid.

60　Ibid., pp.64–65. My italics for emphasis.

61　Ibid., p.63.

62　Wooding, *Henry VIII*, pp.171 & 227.

63　Rose, 'Kingship and Counsel in Early Modern England', p.67.

64　Ronald Hutton, 'The Local Impact of the Tudor Reformations' in *The Impact of the English Reformation: 1500–1640*, Peter Marshall (ed.), London, 1997, p.143. Only 1/13 of 198 sets used for the years between 1535 and 1570 related to the third of England north of the Trent. The four northernmost counties have yielded only one set each.

65　Diana Newton, 'The Impact of Reformation on North-East England: A Preliminary Survey', *Northern History*, Vol. XLV (2008), p.38.

66　Sheils, *The English Reformation*, p.75; Rex, *Henry VIII and the English Reformation*, p.162.

67　Clay, *Testamenta Eboracensia*, pp.1–309.

68　Clay, *Testamenta Eboracensia*, p.152.

69　Ibid., p.166.

70　Ibid., p.183.

71　Ibid., p.185.

72　Ibid., pp.200–2.

73　*Exchequer Court of York*, Vol. 13, f.70; TNA C142/73/58.

74　Clay, *Testamenta Eboracensia*, p.152.

75　Ibid., p.66.

76　Clay, *North Country Wills*, pp.138–246.

77　Ibid., pp. 144, 162 &163.

78　Ibid., pp. 232 & 245.

79　James Raine (ed.), *Wills and Inventories of the Northern Counties of England from the Registry at Durham*, Vol. II, Surtees Society, 1835.

80   Ibid., p.112.

81   Ibid., p.115.

82   Ibid., p.118.

83   Ibid., p.171.

84   J.C. Hodgson (ed.), *Wills and Inventories from the Registry of Durham*, Part III, Surtees Society, 1906.

85   Ibid., pp.8, 12 & 16.

86   Rex, *Henry VIII and the English Reformation*, p.159.

87   Sheils, *The English Reformation*, p.77.

88   Andrew Clark, *Lincoln Diocese Documents: 1450–1544*, London, 1914, p.221.

89   Christopher J. Sansom, 'The Wakefield Conspiracy of 1541 and Henry VIII's Progress to the North Reconsidered', *Northern History*, Vol. XLV (2008), pp.217 & 220.

90   Bastow, *The Catholic Gentry*, pp.31–32.

91   Diana Newton, 'The Impact of Reformation on North-East England' in *Northern History*, p.39.

92   Bastow, *The Catholic Gentry of Yorkshire, 1536–1642*, pp.34 & 40.

93   Clay, *Testamenta Eboracensia*. See Clifford, p.127. Lord Latimer also made a very traditional will – see Clay, *Testamenta Eboracensia*, p.159. Latimer, as previously mentioned, was at the Pilgrim's Council at Pontefract between 2 and 4 December 1536 but appears to have extricated himself from any further intrigues.

94   John E. Neale, *Queen Elizabeth*, London, 1945, p.203.

Conclusion

1   Fletcher & MacCulloch, *Tudor Rebellions*, 2004, p.47.

2   Heal, *The Reformation in Britain and Ireland*, p.30.

3   Ibid.

4   Williams, *English Historical Documents 1485–1558*, p.379–98.

5   Ibid., p.334–35.

6   'Thomas Lever's Social Theory Illustrated from his Sermons', in Williams, *English Historical Documents 1485–1558*, pp.356, 358–59.

7   Haigh, *The English Reformation Revised*, pp.19–33. See pp.20–22.

8   Ibid., p.27.

9   The necessity of religious conformity versus respect for individual conscience is discussed in Shagan, *Catholics and the 'Protestant Nation'*, p.17, Bastow, *The Catholic Gentry of Yorkshire, 1536–1642* and Marshall, '(Re)defining the English Reformation', p.585.

10   Norman Jones, *The English Reformation*, Oxford, 2002, pp.73 & 94.

11   *L&P*, Vol. XII.I: 200.

12   Perez, Zagorin, *Rebels and Rulers, 1500–1660, Volume I, Society, States & Early Modern Revolution*, Cambridge, 1982, p.18.

13   E. Dormer, *Gray of Reading: A Sixteenth-century Controversialist and Ballad Writer*, Reading, 1923, p.77.

14   *L&P*, Vol. XII.I: 131.

15   *L&P*, Vol. XIII.II: 852.

16   Andy Wood, 'Poore Men Woll Speke One Daye', in Tim Harris (ed.), *The Politics of the Excluded: c. 1500–1850*, Basingstoke, 2001, p.78.

17   Fletcher & MacCulloch, *Tudor Rebellions*, p.6 (cite Stone, 1965).

18   Horrox, *Richard III: A Study in Service*, p.21, has drawn attention to the fact that in late medieval England it could be argued that the relationship between the nobility

and the Crown and that of the gentry and the Crown was different. The gentry were inherently more responsive to the king's wishes. How much more so now that they had the incentive of a richer pool of patronage?

19 Sir Thomas More, 'Utopia', p.138, cited in Zeeveld, p.212.

20 Steven G. Ellis, 'Rebellion and the Rule of Law', p.519.

21 Horrox, *Richard III: A Study in Service*, p.22.

22 Bastow, *The Catholic Gentry of Yorkshire, 1536–1642*, p.84.

23 Michael Hicks, 'Talbot, Gilbert, 7th Earl of Shrewsbury (1552–1616)', in *Oxford Dictionary of National Biography*, Oxford University Press, 2004; online edition, May 2008 [www.oxforddnb.com/view/article/26930]; E.B. Stuart, 'Talbot, John, 16th Earl of Shrewsbury and 16th Earl of Waterford (1791–1852)', Rev. G. Martin Murphy, *Oxford Dictionary of National Biography*, Oxford University Press, 2004, online edition, January 2009 [www.oxforddnb.com/view/article/38048].

24 The 'papist' label was a useful propaganda tool. See Marshall, 'Is the Pope Catholic?' in Shagan (ed.), *Catholics and the 'Protestant Nation'*, p.35.

25 Andy Wood, 'Poore Men Woll Speke One Daye', p.72.

26 *L&P*, Vol. XVI: 466.

27 Wood, 'Poore Men Woll Speke One Daye', pp.222–23.

28 Ibid., pp.226, 217, 236–37.

29 Wooding, *Henry VIII*, p.227.

30 *L&P*, Vol. XI: 780.

31 Eric Ives, 'Henry VIII: the Political Perspective', in Diarmaid MacCulloch (ed.), *The Reign of Henry VIII: Politics, Policy and Piety*, Basingstoke, 1995, p.31.

32 Rex, *Henry VIII and the English Reformation*, p.171.

33 *Hall's Chronicle*, pp. 838–39.

34 Bush and Bownes, *The Defeat of the Pilgrimage of Grace*.

35 Fritze, *Historical Dictionary of Tudor England*, p.70. Henry Tudor's army at Bosworth in August 1485 numbered 5,800 men.

36 Cliffe, *The Yorkshire Gentry*, p.171.

37 Bastow, *The Catholic Gentry of Yorkshire, 1536–1642*, p.47.

38 Wabuda, 'The Reformation Revised: The English Reformation Beyond Revisionism', p.3.

39 Scarisbrick, *Henry VIII*, p.327. Originally quoted in Foxe, pp.viii & 110.

List of Abbreviations

BL	British Library, London.
Cotton Calig.	Cotton, 'Caligula'.
Cotton Cleo.	Cotton, 'Cleopatra'.
Cotton Vesp.	Cotton, 'Vespasian'.
CSP, Sp.	*Calendar of Letters, Despatches and State Papers Relating to the Negotiations Between England and Spain, Preserved in the Archives of Simancas and Elsewhere*, edited by Pascual De Gayangos, Tanner Ritchie, Ontario.
HJ	*The Historical Journal.*
JBS	*The Journal of British Studies.*
L&P	*Letters & Papers, Foreign and Domestic of the Reign of Henry VIII*, Vols X–XXI, arranged & catalogued by Gairdner & Brodie, H.M. Stationery Office, London, 1905.
PP	*Past and Present.*
TNA	The National Archives, Kew.
TNA, SP 1	State Papers, Foreign and Domestic, Henry VIII: General.
TNA, SP 6	State Papers, Foreign and Domestic, Henry VIII: Theological Tracts.
TNA, SP 7	State Papers, Foreign and Domestic, Henry VIII: Wriothesley Papers, 1536–1540.
TNA, SP 15	State Papers Domestic, Edward VI–James I: Addenda.
Stat. Realm	*The Statues of the Realm*, Volume III, A. Luder (ed.), London, 1810–28.

Bibliography

Manuscripts

British Library
BL, Cotton, Caligula, B/I.
BL, Cotton, Cleopatra, E/IV.
BL, Cleopatra, E/V.
BL, Cotton, Cleopatra, E/VI.
BL, Cotton, Titus, B/I.
BL, Sloane, 2442.
BL, Cotton, Vespasian.
Manuscripts Add. – 32646, 38133 & 38544.

The University of York – Borthwick Institute for Archives
Chancery Court of York.
Archbishop's Registers: Abp Reg. 29, f.159.
Exchequer Court of York, Vol. 13, f.70.

The National Archives
Chancery Close Rolls.
Inquisitions Post Mortem, C142.
TNA, SP1: State Papers, Foreign and Domestic, Henry VIII: General (246 volumes).
TNA, SP 6: State Papers, Foreign and Domestic, Henry VIII: Theological Tracts.
TNA, SP 7: State Papers, Foreign and Domestic, Henry VIII: Wriothesley Papers, 1536–1540.
TNA, SP 15: State Papers Domestic, Edward VI–James I: Addenda (44 volumes).

Lambeth Palace, London
Talbot Papers – MSS 3192 & 3193.

Printed Primary Sources

Calendar of the Close Rolls – Preserved in the Public Record Office: Henry VII, Volume II, 1500–1509 (London: Her Majesty's Stationery Office, 1963).
Calendar of the Inquisitions Post Mortem, Preserved in the Public Record Office: Henry VII, Volumes I, II & III (London: HMSO, Eyre & Spottiswoode, 1898).
Calendar of Letters, Despatches and State Papers Relating to the Negotiations Between England and Spain, Preserved in the Archives of Simancas and Elsewhere, edited by Pascual De Gayangos (Ontario: Tanner Ritchie).
Calendar of the Patent Rolls: Henry VII, Volume II, 1494–1509, Preserved in the Public Record Office (London: 1916).

Depositions and other Ecclesiastical Proceedings from the Courts of Durham – Extending from 1311 to the Reign of Elizabeth (London: Surtees Society, 1845).

Hall's Chronicle. Containing the History of England, during the reign of Henry the Fourth and the succeeding monarchs, to the end of the reign of King Henry the Eighth, in which are particularly described the manners and customs of those periods. Carefully collated with the editions of 1548 and 1550, H. Ellis & J. Johnson (eds), (London: 1809).

'Letters of the Cliffords, Lords Clifford and Earls of Cumberland, *c.* 1500–*c.* 1565' in *Camden Miscellany*, Vol. 31, Camden Fourth Series, 44 (1992), pp.1–189, R.W. Hoyle (ed.).

North Country Wills, 1383 to 1558, J.W. Clay (ed.), Publications of the Surtees Society, Vol. CXVI, 1908.

The Plumpton Letters and Papers, Camden Fifth Series, Vol. 8, Joan Kirby (ed.) (Cambridge University Press, 1996).

The Statutes of the Realm, Volume III, A. Luder (ed.), (London: 1810–28).

Testamenta Eboracensia: A Selection of Wills from the Registry at York, Vol. V, J. Raine (ed.), (Surtees Society, 1884).

Testamenta Eboracensia: A Selection of Wills from the Registry at York, Vol. VI, J. Clay (ed.), (Surtees Society, 1902).

Tudor Royal Proclamations: The Early Tudors (1485–1553), Vol. 1, Paul L. Hughes & James F. Larkin (eds), (New Haven: Yale University Press, 1964).

The Visitation of Yorkshire in the Years 1563 and 1564, William Flower & C.B. Norcliffe (ed.), (London: 1881).

Wills and Inventories of the Northern Counties of England from the Registry at Durham, Vol. II, James Raine (ed.), (Surtees Society, 1835).

Wills and Inventories from the Registry of the Archdeaconry of Richmond, extending over portions of the counties of York, Westmorland, Cumberland and Lancaster, by James Raine (ed.), Surtees Society, Vol. 26 (London: 1853).

Wills and Inventories from the Registry of Durham, Part III, J.C. Hodgson (ed.), (Durham: Surtees Society, 1906).

Secondary Sources

Appleby, John C., & Paul Dalton (eds), *Government, Religion and Society in Northern England, 1000–1700* (Bodmin: Sutton Publishing, 1998).

Bastow, Sarah L., *The Catholic Gentry of Yorkshire, 1536–1642: Resistance and Accommodation* (New York: Edwin Mellen Press, 2007).

Bateson, Mary, 'The Pilgrimage of Grace', *The English Historical Review,* Vol. 5, No 18 (April 1890), pp.330–345.

Berkowitz, David Sandler, *Humanist Scholarship and Public Order: Two Tracts against the Pilgrimage of Grace by Sir Richard Morison* (London: Associated University Press, 1984).

Bernard, G.W. (ed.), *The Tudor Nobility* (Manchester University Press, 1992).

Bernard, G.W., 'The Making of Religious Policy, 1533–46: Henry VIII and the Search for the Middle Way', *The Historical Journal,* Vol. 41, No 2 (June 1998), pp.321–49.

Bernard, G.W., *Power and Politics in Tudor England* (Aldershot: Ashgate, 2000).

Bindoff, S.T., *History of Parliament, The Commons 1509–1558* (London: Secker & Warburg, 1982).

Block, Joseph, 'Thomas Cromwell's Patronage of Preaching', *The Sixteenth Century Journal,* Vol. 8, No 1 (April 1977), pp.37–50.

Blockmans, Wim, *Emperor Charles V: 1500–1558* (London: Hodder, 2002).

Bossy, John, *The English Catholic Community, 1570–1850* (London: Darton, Longman & Todd, 1975).

Bradshaw, Brendan, & Eamon Duffy (eds), *Humanism, Reform and the Reformation: The Career of Bishop John Fisher* (Cambridge University Press, 1989).

Bray, Gerald (ed.), *Documents of the English Reformation*, Library of Ecclesiastical History (Cambridge: James Clarke & Co., 1994).

Brigden, Susan, *New Worlds, Lost Worlds – The Rule of the Tudors 1485–1603* (London: Penguin, 2000).

Bush, M., *The Pilgrimage of Grace: A Study of the Rebel Armies of October 1536* (Manchester University Press, 1996).

Bush, Michael & David Bownes, *The Defeat of the Pilgrimage of Grace* (University of Hull Press, 1999).

Bush, Michael, *The Pilgrims' Complaint: A Study of Popular Thought in the Early Tudor North* (Farnham: Ashgate, 2009).

Catholic Encyclopedia [www.catholic.org/encyclopedia].

Clark, Andrew, *Lincoln Diocese Documents: 1450–1544* (London: Early English Text Society, 1914).

Cliffe, J.T., *The Yorkshire Gentry: From the Reformation to the Civil War* (London: The Athlone Press, 1969).

Cross, Claire, *The Puritan Earl: the Life of Henry Hastings, Third Earl of Huntingdon 1536–1595* (London: Macmillan, 1966).

Cross, Claire, *Church and People: England 1450–1660* (Glasgow: Fontana, 1976).

Cross, Claire, *York Clergy Ordinations, 1520–1559*, Borthwick List and Index 32 (University of York, 2002).

Davies, C.S.L., 'The Pilgrimage of Grace Reconsidered', *Past and Present*, No 41 (December 1968) pp.54–76.

Davies, C.S.L., *Peace, Print & Protestantism 1450–1558* (London: Paladin, 1986).

Dickens, A.G., 'Sedition and Conspiracy in Yorkshire During the Later Years of Henry VIII', *Yorkshire Archaeological Journal*, Vol. 34 (1939), pp.379–98.

Dickens, A.G., *The English Reformation* (London: Collins, 1972).

Dickens, A.G., *Lollards and Protestants in the Diocese of York, 1509–1558*, 2nd edition (London: Hambledon Press, 1982).

Dickens, A.G., 'Robert Parkyn's Narrative of the Reformation', LXII (CCVLII), *The English Historical Review*, l 62, 242 (January 1947), pp.58–83.

Dickens, A.G., 'Secular & Religious Motivation in the Pilgrimage of Grace', *Reformation Studies* (London: Hambledon Press, 1982) pp.57–82.

Dickens, A.G., & D. Carr, *The Reformation in England: To the Accession of Elizabeth I* (London: Arnold, 1967).

Dodds, Madeleine Hope, & Ruth Dodds, *The Pilgrimage of Grace 1536–37, and the Exeter Conspiracy 1538* (Cambridge University Press, 1915).

Dodds, Madeleine Hope & Ruth Dodds, 'Political Prophecies in the Reign of Henry VIII', *Modern Language Review*, Vol. 11 (1916), pp.276–84.

Dormer, E., *Gray of Reading: A Sixteenth-century Controversialist and Ballad Writer* (Reading: Bradley & Sons, 1923)

Duffy, Eamon, *The Stripping of the Altars: Traditional Religion in England c. 1400–c. 1580* (London: Yale University Press, 1992).

Duffy, Eamon, *Marking the Hours: English People and their Prayers 1240–1570* (London: Yale University Press, 2006).

Duffy, Eamon, 'The English Reformation after Revisionism', *Renaissance Quarterly*, Vol. 59 No. 3 (2006), pp.720–31.

Duffy, Eamon, *Fires of Faith: Catholic England under Mary Tudor* (London: Yale University Press, 2009).

Ellis, S.G., 'Civilizing Northumberland: Representations of Englishness in the Tudor State', *Journal of Historical Sociology*, Vol. XII (1999), pp.103–27.

Ellis, S.G., 'The Kildare Rebellion and the Early Henrician Reformation', *The Historical Journal*, Vol. 19, No 4 (December 1976), pp.807–30.

Ellis, S.G., 'Henry VIII, Rebellion and the Rule of Law', *The Historical Journal*, Vol. 24, No 3 (September 1981), pp.513–31.

Ellis, S.G., 'England in the Tudor State', *The Historical Journal*, Vol. 26, No 1 (1983), pp.201–12.

Ellis, S.G., 'The Pale and the Far North: Government and Society in Two Early Tudor Borderlands', The O'Donnell Lecture, 1986.

Ellis, S.G., *Tudor Frontiers and Noble Power: The Making of the British State* (Oxford: Clarendon Press, 1995).

Ellis, Steven G., with Christopher Maginn, *The Making of the British Isles: The State of Britain and Ireland, 1450–1660* (Harlow: Longman, 2007).

Ellis, Steven G., & Raingard Esser et al. (eds), *Frontiers, Regions and Identities in Europe* (Pisa University Press, 2009).

Elton, G.R., *Policy and Police: The Enforcement of the Reformation in the Age of Thomas Cromwell* (Cambridge University Press, 1972).

Elton, G.R., *Reform and Reformation: England 1509–1558* (London: Arnold, 1977).

Elton, G.R., 'Politics & the Pilgrimage of Grace' in *After the Reformation*, edited by B.C. Malament (Manchester University Press, 1980).

Elton, G.R., *Reformation Europe 1517–1559*, 2nd edition (Oxford: Blackwell, 1999).

Eppley, Daniel, *Defending Royal Supremacy and Discerning God's Will in Tudor England* (Aldershot: Ashgate, 2007).

Everitt, A., 'Social Mobility in Early Modern England', *Past and Present*, Vol. 33 (1996), pp.56–73.

Fletcher, Anthony & Diarmaid MacCulloch, *Tudor Rebellions*, 5th edition (Harlow: Longman, 2004).

Fletcher, Anthony & John Stevenson (eds), *Order and Disorder in Early Modern England* (Cambridge University Press, 1985).

Fritze, Ronald H. (ed.), *Historical Dictionary of Tudor England, 1485–1603* (London: Greenwood Press, 1991).

Goodman, Anthony (ed.), *The Wars of the Roses* (London: Routledge, 1991).

Graves, M.A.R., *Henry VIII: A Study in Kingship* (London: Longman, 2003).

Gunn, S.J., *Charles Brandon, Duke of Suffolk c. 1484–1545* (Oxford: Blackwell, 1988).

Gunn, S.J., 'Peers, Commons and Gentry in the Lincolnshire Revolt of 1536', *Past and Present*, 123 (1989), pp.52–79.

Gunn, Steve, David Grummitt & Hans Cools, *War, State, and Society in England and the Netherlands: 1477–1559* (Oxford University Press, 2007).

Guy, John, *Tudor England* (Oxford University Press, 1988).

Haigh, Christopher, *The Last Days of the Lancashire Monasteries and the Pilgrimage of Grace* (Manchester University Press, 1969).

Haigh, Christopher, 'The Continuity of Catholicism in the English Reformation', *Past and Present*, Vol. 93, No. 1 (1981), pp.37–69.

Haigh, Christopher, *The English Reformation Revised* (Cambridge University Press, 1987).

Harris, Jonathan Gil, *Foreign Bodies and the Body Politic: Discourses of Social Pathology in Early Modern England* (Cambridge University Press, 1998).

Harris, Tim (ed.), *The Politics of the Excluded, c. 1500–1850* (Basingstoke: Palgrave, 2001).

Harrison, Scott, *The Pilgrimage of Grace in the Lake Counties, 1536–37* (London: Royal Historical Society, 1981).

Heal, Felicity, *Reformation in Britain and Ireland* (Oxford University Press, 2003).

Hoak, Dale, 'Politics, Religion and the English Reformation, 1533–1547: Some Problems and Issues', *History Compass*, Vol. 3, 139 (2005) pp.1–7.

Hodgson, John, *A History of Northumberland – in Three Parts*, Part II, Vol. II (Surtees Society, 1832).

Horrox, Rosemary, *Richard III: A Study in Service* (Cambridge University Press, 1989).

Hoyle, R.H., 'Thomas Master's Narrative of the Pilgrimage of Grace', *Northern History*, Vol. 21 (1985), pp.53–79.

Hoyle, R.H., *The Pilgrimage of Grace and the Politics of the 1530s* (Oxford University Press, 2001).

Hoyle R.H., 'Petitioning as Popular Politics in Early Sixteenth-century England', *Historical Research*, Vol. 75, No 190 (November 2002), pp.365–89.

Hoyle, R.H., 'The Fortunes of the Tempest Family of Bracewell and Bowling in the Sixteenth Century', *Yorkshire Archaeological Journal*, Vol. 74 (2002), pp.169–89.

Hughes, Paul L., & James F. Larkin, *Tudor Royal Proclamations – Vol I, The Early Tudors (1485–1553)* (New Haven and London: Yale University Press, 1964).

Hughes, Philip, *The Reformation in England: The King's Proceedings*, 2nd edition (London: Hollis & Carter, 1952).

Ives, Eric, *The Life and Death of Anne Boleyn: 'The Most Happy'* (Oxford: Blackwell, 2004).

James, M.E., 'Obedience and Dissent in Henrician England, The Lincolnshire Rebellion 1536', *Past and Present*, No. 48 (August 1970), pp.3–78.

James, Mervyn, *Family, Lineage and Civil Society: A Study of Society, Politics and Mentality in the Durham Region, 1500–1640* (Oxford: Clarendon Press, 1974).

Jansen, Sharon L., *Political Protest and Prophecy under Henry VIII* (Suffolk: The Boydell Press, 1991).

Jenkins, G.W., *John Jewel and the English National Church: The Dilemmas of an Erastian Reformer* (Aldershot: Ashgate, 2006).

Jones, Norman, 'Living the Reformations: Generational Experience and Political Perception in Early Modern England', *Huntington Library Quarterly*, Vol. 60, No 3, The Remapping of English Political History, 1500–1640 (1997), pp.273–288.

Jones, Norman, *The English Reformation* (Oxford: Blackwell, 2002).

Kesselring, K.J., 'Deference and Dissent in Tudor England: Reflections on Sixteenth-Century Protest', *History Compass*, Vol. 3, No 163 (2005) pp.1–16.

Kettering, Sharon, *Patrons, Brokers and Clients in Seventeenth-century France* (Oxford University Press, 1986).

Kirby, Joan W., *The Plumpton Letters and Papers*, Camden Fifth Series, Vol. 8 (Cambridge University Press, 1996).

Kitching, C.J., 'The Chantries of The East Riding of Yorkshire At the Dissolution in 1548', *Yorkshire Archaeological Journal*, 44 (1972) pp.178–94.

Kuhn, Thomas, *Second Thoughts on Paradigms* (Chicago University Press, 1974).

Lake, Peter, & Michael Questier, 'Agency, Appropriation and Rhetoric under the Gallows: Puritans, Romanists and the State in Early Modern England', *Past & Present*, Vol. 153, No. 1 (1996), pp.64–107.

Lamburn, David, *The Laity and the Church: Religious Developments in Beverley in the First Half of the Sixteenth Century*, Borthwick Paper No 97 (University of York, 2000).

Lander, Jesse, *Inventing Polemic: Religion, Print and Literary Culture in Early Modern England* (Cambridge University Press, 2006).

Loades, David, *John Dudley: Duke of Northumberland, 1504–1553* (Oxford: Clarendon Press, 1996).

Loades, D.M., *Mary Tudor: A Life* (Oxford, 1989), p.195.

Loades, D.M., *Politics and the Nation 1450–1660 – Obedience, Resistance and Public Order*, 4th edition (London: Fontana History of England, 1992).

Loades, D.M., *Power in Tudor England* (Basingstoke: Macmillan, 1997).

Lipscomb, Suzannah, *1536: The Year that Changed Henry VIII* (Oxford: Lion Hudson, 2009).

MacCulloch, Diarmaid (ed.), *The Reign of Henry VIII: Politics, Policy and Piety* (Basingstoke: Macmillan, 1995).

Marotti, Arthur F., *Religious Ideology and Cultural Fantasy: Catholic and Anti-Catholic Discourses in Early Modern England* (University of Notre Dame Press, 2005).

Marshall, Peter, *The Face of the Pastoral Ministry in the East Riding, 1525–1595*, Borthwick Paper No 88 (University of York, 1995).

Marshall, Peter, *The Impact of the English Reformation: 1500–1640* (London: Arnold, 1997).

Marshall, Peter, *Religious Identities in Henry VIII's England* (Ashgate: Aldershot, 2006).

Marshall, Peter, *The Reformation: A Very Short Introduction* (Oxford University Press, 2009).

Marshall, Peter, '(Re)defining the English Reformation', *The Journal of British Studies*, Vol. 48 (2009), pp.564–86.

Mattingly, Garret, *Catherine of Aragon* (London: Butler & Tanner, 1950).

Mayer, Thomas F., *Thomas Starkey and the Commonweal: Humanist Politics and Religion in the Reign of Henry VIII* (Cambridge University Press, 1989).

Merriman, Roger Bigelow, *Life and Letters of Thomas Cromwell, Volume I* (Oxford: Clarendon Press, 1968).

Merriman, Roger Bigelow, *Life and Letters of Thomas Cromwell, Volume II, Letters from 1536* (Oxford: Clarendon Press, 1968).

Neale, John E., *Queen Elizabeth* (London, 1945), p.203.

Newman, Christine M., 'Robert Bowes and the Pilgrimage of Grace', *North Eastern History*, No 7 (1997).

Newman, Christine M., 'The Bowes of Streatlam, Co. Durham: A Study of the Politics and Religion of a Sixteenth-century Northern Gentry Family', DPhil diss., (University of York. 1991).

Newton, Diana, 'The Impact of Reformation on North-East England: A Preliminary Survey', *Northern History*, Vol. XLV, No 1 (March 2008), pp.35–49.

Nichols, J.G. (ed.), *The Chronicle of Queen Jane, and of Two Years of Queen Mary*, Camden Society Old Series, 48 (1850).

O'Day, R., 'The Law of Patronage in Early Modern England', *Journal of Ecclesiastical History*, Vol. 26 (1975), pp.247–60.

O'Grady, Paul, *Henry VIII and the Conforming Catholics* (Collegeville, Minn.: Liturgical Press, 1990).

Pollard, A.J., *The Wars of the Roses*, British History in Perspective (London: Macmillan, 1988).

Pollard, A.J., *North-Eastern England during the Wars of the Roses: Lay Society, War and Politics, 1450–1500* (Oxford: Clarendon Press, 1990).

Pollen, J., (ed.), *Unpublished Documents Relating to the English Martyrs, 1584–1603*, Catholic Record Society, Vol. 5 (1908).

Raine, James, *Wills and Inventories from the Archdeaconry of Richmond* (Publications of the Surtees Society, 1853).

Redworth, G., *In Defence of the Church Catholic: the Life of Stephen Gardiner* (Oxford: Wiley-Blackwell, 1990).

Reid, R.R., *The King's Council in the North*, Parts I–II and III–IV (London: Longmans Green, 1921).

Rex, Richard, *Henry VIII and the English Reformation* (Basingstoke: Palgrave Macmillan, 1993).

Rex, Richard, 'The Crisis of Obedience: God's Word and Henry's Reformation', *The Historical Journal*, Vol. 39, No 4 (December 1996), pp.863–94.

Rose, Jacqueline, 'Kingship and Counsel in Early Modern England', *The Historical Journal*, Vol. 54 (March 2011) pp.47–71.

Ryrie, Alec, *The Gospel and Henry VIII: Evangelicals in the Early English Reformation* (Cambridge University Press, 2003).

Sansom, Christopher J., 'The Wakefield Conspiracy of 1541 and Henry VIII's Progress to the North Reconsidered', *Northern History*, Vol. XLV, No 2 (September 2008), pp.217–38.

Scarisbrick, J.J., *The Reformation and the English People* (Oxford: Blackwell, 1984).

Scarisbrick, J.J., *Henry VIII* (Yale University Press, new edition, 1997).

Shagan, Ethan (ed.), *Henry VIII and the Semantics of Schism* (2005), p.25.

Shagan, Ethan, *Popular Politics and the English Reformation* (Cambridge University Press, 2003).

Shagan, Ethan (ed.), *Catholics and the 'Protestant Nation': Religious Politics and Identity in Early Modern England* (Manchester University Press, 2005).

Sharpe, Kevin, 'Representations and Negotiations: Texts, Images and Authority in Early Modern England', *The Historical Journal*, Vol. 42, No 3 (September 1999), pp.853–81.

Sheils, W.J., *The English Reformation, 1530–1570*, Seminar Studies in History (London: Longman, 1989).

Slack, Paul (ed.), *Rebellion, Popular Protest and the Social Order in Early Modern England* (Cambridge University Press, 2008).

Smith, R.B., *Land and Politics in the England of Henry VIII: The West Riding of Yorkshire: 1530–46* (Oxford: Clarendon Press, 1970).

Starkey, David, *The Reign of Henry VIII: Personalities and Politics* (London: Vintage Books, 1985).

Starkey, David & Susan Doran, *Henry VIII: Man and Monarch* (London, 2009), p.165.

Thomas, Keith, *Religion and the Decline of Magic: Studies in Popular Beliefs in Sixteenth and Seventeenth-century England* (London: Penguin, 1981).

Thornton, Tim, *Prophecy, Politics and the People in Early Modern England* (Woodbridge: Boydell Press, 2006).

Tittler, Robert & Norman Jones (eds), *A Companion to Tudor Britain* (Oxford: Blackwell, 2004).

Todd, Margo, *Reformation to Revolution: Politics and Religion in Early Modern England* (London: Routledge, 1995).

Victoria County History of York, 'The Sixteenth Century: Religious Life', A History of the County of York East Riding, Vol. 6: The Borough and Liberties of Beverley (1989), pp.76–80.

Wabuda, Susan, 'The Reformation Revised: The English Reformation Beyond Revisionism', *History Compass*, Vol. 1, No 11 (2003) pp.1–5.

Walker, Greg, *Writing under Tyranny: English Literature and the Henrician Reformation* (Oxford University Press, 2007).

Walsham, Alexandra, *Providence in Early Modern England* (Oxford University Press, 1999).

Walsham, Alexandra, *Charitable Hatred – Tolerance and Intolerance in England, 1500–1700* (Manchester University Press, 2006).

Webb, C.C., *Churchwardens' Accounts of St Michael, Spurriergate, York, 1518–1548*, Vols I & II, Borthwick Texts and Calendars 20 (University of York, 1997).

Williams, C.H. (ed.), *English Historical Documents 1485–1558*, Vol. V (London, 1967).

Wood, Andy, *Riot, Rebellion and Popular Politics in Early Modern England* (Basingstoke: Palgrave, 2002).

Wood, Andy, *The 1549 Rebellions and the Making of Modern England* (Cambridge University Press, 2007).

Wooding, Lucy, *From Humanists to Heretics: English Catholic Theology and Ideology c. 1530–1570* (Oxford University Press, 1994).

Wooding, Lucy, *Rethinking Catholicism in Reformation England* (Oxford University Press, 2000).

Wooding, Lucy, *Henry VIII* (Oxford: Routledge Historical Biographies, 2009).

Yorkshire Archaeological and Topographical Association, *Feet of Fines of the Tudor Period*, Part I, Record Series, Vol. II, 1887.

Zagorin, Perez, *Rebels & Rulers 1500–1660, Volume I, Society, States & Early Modern Revolution* (Cambridge University Press, 1982).

Zeeveld, W. Gordon, *Foundations of Tudor Policy* (London: Methuen, 1969).

Acknowledgements

This work is based upon my doctoral thesis and I would like, firstly, to express my sincere gratitude to the National University of Ireland, Galway, and in particular the College of Arts, for endowing me with a fellowship. I would like to thank my supervisor, Professor Steven Ellis, for his encouragement, guidance and support and Dr Alison Forrestal for her constructive criticism and advice.

I would like to acknowledge the assistance given to me by the staff of the National Archives, Kew, the British Library, London, and the Borthwick Institute for Archives at the University of York, in particular, Victoria Hoyle. In addition, I am grateful for the help of the Special Collections staff in National University of Ireland, Galway.

I wish to convey my gratitude to Mark Beynon, commissioning editor at The History Press, for helping the work to see the light of day and for all his assistance, patience and understanding. I would also like to thank my editor, Naomi Reynolds, for her guidance, attention and support.

A number of people have sustained me throughout this project and special thanks go to Louise Rooney, Mairead Murphy and Katherine O'Driscoll. I would also like to express my sincere appreciation to Carmel McGuinn and Rona McLaughlin who were steadfast in their support during difficult times.

I would like to express my love and thanks to Brendan, Mairead, Ciara, Patrick and Sean Loughlin. I also wish to acknowledge the friendship, loyalty and encouragement of Liza O'Malley.

I wish to recognise the contribution of my grandparents in igniting my curiosity and fostering my love of learning – Edward and Una Loughlin and Martin and Bridget Duffy. Finally, my enduring and heartfelt love and appreciation to my parents, John and Kathleen Loughlin, without whom none of this would have been possible.

In nomine Patris et Filii et Spiritus Sancti.

Index